Exile
Within

Exile Within

The Schooling of Japanese Americans 1942–1945

Thomas James

Harvard University Press
Cambridge, Massachusetts
London, England   1987

Library of Congress Cataloging in Publication Data

James, Thomas, 1948–
    Exile within.

    Bibliography: p.
    Includes index.
    1. Japanese Americans—Evacuation and relocation, 1942–1945.
2. Japanese Americans—Education—History—20th century.
I. Title.
D769.8.A6J345   1987   370' 89956'073   86-25792
ISBN 0-674-27526-8 (alk. paper)

Designed by Gwen Frankfeldt

for Regina

Acknowledgments

DEBTS—emotional, intellectual, financial—accumulate rapidly in historical research. I would especially like to thank David Tyack for the many ways he has supported me in my work over the past six years. Barton Bernstein, Shirley Brice Heath, and Henry M. Levin offered constructive criticism at every stage along the way. The suggestions of Elisabeth Hansot, Mary Ellen James, J. Douglas Willms, and a historian who reviewed the book for Harvard University Press helped me to clarify the aims of the book. I am also grateful to Harumi Befu, Albert Camarillo, Roger Daniels, and Carl Degler for making suggestions on earlier essays and drafts. Much as these friends and colleagues were helpful to me, the responsibility for wrong-headedness and errors is entirely my own.

Richard Drinnon, Peter Sano, Peter Suzuki, and Sylvia Yanagisako kindly shared unpublished manuscripts with me. Thomas Bodine was a generous source of information and good will. Peter Brown, Nicholas Burbules, James Catterall, Ann Grillo, Richard Grillo, Ann Haas, John A. Herzig, Aiko Herzig-Yoshinaga, Robert Lowe, Betty McAfee, Valerie Matsumoto, Arturo Pacheco, Craig Richards, and Elizabeth Simpson all were helpful in sundry ways that made it possible for me to complete the project. Readers will surmise from the evidence I have used that I am deeply indebted to archivists and

Acknowledgments

librarians at several institutions, including the Bancroft Library, University of California, Berkeley; the Hoover Institution, Stanford University; the Huntington Library, San Marino, California; the Japanese American Research Project Collection, University of California, Los Angeles; and the Mills College Archives, Oakland, California. I would particularly like to mention the assistance provided by Mary Walton Livingston and Aloha P. South at the National Archives. Stanford University and Wesleyan University furnished research and travel grants that allowed me to read in distant archives and present my findings to scholarly conferences. Some material in this book was published as articles in *History of Education Quarterly* 25 (1985), copyright 1985 by the History of Education Society, and *Pacific Historical Review* 56 (1987), copyright 1986 by The Regents of the University of California. For quotations from poems I am grateful for permission given by Ruth Tanaka Gray, the American Folklore Society, *Amerasia Journal* (Asian American Studies Center, University of California, Los Angeles), and the Yardbird Publishing Company.

The list of thanks is only just begun, but I want most of all to acknowledge the strength and care of Regina Cortina, Mark Moulton, and my parents. The late Mrs. Ichihashi, who employed me as a gardener when I was growing up in California, supplied me with the initial impressions and questions that led to the writing of this book.

Contents

Prologue: Thirty Thousand Children of War   1

1   Between Past and Future Homes   10

2   The First Year Inside   43

3   Loyalty and Its Lessons   80

4   Educating "Projectiles of Democracy"   112

5   "The Children Don't Do It That Way"   140

Epilogue: Remembering the Past   165

Notes   173

Index   207

Photographs

Girl waiting for bus, California, April 1942. (Clem Albers; courtesy of the National Archives, Washington, D.C.) *2*

Schoolgirl on swing, Heart Mountain, Wyoming, November 24, 1943. (Hikaru Iwasaki; courtesy of the Bancroft Library, University of California, Berkeley.) *6*

Grandfather carrying grandson, Manzanar, Owens Valley, California, July 2, 1942. (Dorothea Lange; courtesy of the National Archives, Washington, D.C.) *16*

Military police, Santa Anita Assembly Center, California, April 6, 1942. (Clem Albers; courtesy of the Bancroft Library, University of California, Berkeley.) *24*

Volunteer teacher, Manzanar, Owens Valley, California, July 1, 1942. (Dorothea Lange; courtesy of the National Archives, Washington, D.C.) *26*

Two children, Heart Mountain, Wyoming, September 18, 1942. (Tom Parker; courtesy of the Bancroft Library, University of California, Berkeley.) *48*

Nursery school children, Tule Lake, California, November 9, 1942. (Francis Stewart; courtesy of the Mills College Archives, Mills College, Oakland, California.) *54*

Third grade class, Rohwer, Arkansas, November 22, 1942. (Tom Parker; courtesy of the Bancroft Library, University of California, Berkeley.) *58*

Children landscaping in front of barracks, Amache, Colorado, April 24, 1943. (Joe McClelland; courtesy of the Bancroft Library, University of California, Berkeley.) *66*

Two high school graduates, Tule Lake, California, summer 1943. (John D. Cook; courtesy of the National Archives, Washington, D.C.) *78*

High school students, Rohwer, Arkansas, November 17, 1943. (Tom Parker; courtesy of the National Archives, Washington, D.C.) *88*

Dancing in the high school gymnasium, Heart Mountain, Wyoming, November 24, 1943. (Hikaru Iwasaki; courtesy of the Bancroft Library, University of California, Berkeley.) *90*

Boy on train to Tule Lake Segregation Center, California, August 9, 1943. (Photographer unknown; courtesy of the Bancroft Library, University of California, Berkeley.) *102*

Girl studying, Tule Lake, California, November 19, 1945. (Jack Iwata; courtesy of the National Archives, Washington, D.C.) *150*

Family packing, Topaz, Utah, January 3, 1945. (Charles E. Mace; courtesy of the Bancroft Library, University of California, Berkeley.) *162*

Exile
Within

PROLOGUE

Thirty Thousand Children of War

At first glance, *Memoirs 1944* is a yearbook like any other. "The staff of Hunt High School," writes the principal, "has set itself the ultimate goal of developing in its pupils the ideals, habits, and personal traits which will best enable them to adhere to the American democratic tradition." The vice-principal urges students to "conquer our common enemies in the hope that totalitarian ideologies will forever be banished from the earth." The tone of the yearbook is uplifting, as befits the genre. The drawings and photographs suggest a rustic locale, exactly the ambiance one might expect in a place like Hunt, somewhere in Idaho. Judging by the stilted language of the text, a casual reader would be inclined to think that these are normal adolescents and the words on the page are platitudes that educators and students anywhere would have said on formal occasions during the war. "Facing the future, we feel a twinge of hesitancy," confesses the class of 1944 in its message, "but not for long, for we are eager to test the strength of our knowledge . . . The need for courage and sacrifice is great in these trying times, and we modern pioneers must be ready, willing, and able to accept the responsibility for bettering this world."[1]

Memoirs 1944 is not, however, a normal yearbook, and Hunt was not an all-American town in Idaho. Every student on the pages of

*Expelled from her home
by Executive Order 9066,
this girl waits for the bus
that will take her and
her family to the camps,
California, April 1942.*

the yearbook has a Japanese face; the teachers, except for a few assistants, are all Caucasian. Hunt, better known as the Minidoka Relocation Center, was a mile-square camp built by the government of the United States, surrounded by barbed wire fence and guard towers, enclosing barracks that held more than 9,000 Japanese Americans. In ten camps like Minidoka, more than 110,000 Japanese Americans, two-thirds of them citizens of the United States, were incarcerated during World War II, after having been evacuated from their homes in western states during the spring of 1942. Roughly 30,000 pupils went to schools much like Hunt High School from 1942 to 1945.[2]

Their experiences were part of a larger pattern, the forced migration of a racial minority from the West Coast to the interior of the United States. Executive Order 9066, signed by President Franklin D. Roosevelt on February 19, 1942, authorized the U.S. Army to exclude populations from designated zones when deemed necessary for security reasons. Applied to people of Japanese descent living in the West, this policy excluded them from large parts of the states where most Japanese Americans lived. The initial order led subsequently to Executive Order 9102, signed on March 18, 1942, which set up the War Relocation Authority (WRA), a federal civilian agency whose purpose was to relocate and supervise the excluded population once it had been brought together into assembly and reception centers by the army. These orders were accompanied by other policies, both military and civilian, authorizing the detention of evacuated Japanese Americans within guarded "relocation centers" built by the government and operated by the WRA. The great majority of Japanese Americans lived in these camps during World War II, and there the children attended public schools.[3]

What did it mean for thirty thousand young citizens of the United States to attend public schools in the midst of what the American Civil Liberties Union has called "the greatest deprivation of civil rights by government in this country since slavery"? What did educators think they were doing there? What sort of education took place? A quarter of the incarcerated population, the schoolchildren were swept along, like children of war everywhere, by currents much stronger than they could comprehend. In the most famous photographs of the event, their faces reveal only an uncomprehending innocence, tinged with sadness. Though subject to events greater than themselves, the children also had a history of their own during the years of exile. Their wartime experience and the institutions that coalesced to produce it left a tangle of social meanings that has not been explored with nearly the care it deserves. Because they were schoolchildren and citizens, theirs was, in large part, an educational history, a story of teaching and learning, of family, school, and society—indeed, of education and democracy, as the high school yearbook declares in its opening pages.[4]

This book suggests a new way of remembering the history of Japanese Americans during World War II. The camps were, among other things, educational institutions. Though hardly normal ones, they were intensely purposeful and will long be remembered for the teaching and learning they fostered. Within these temporary institutions, the transmission of culture through formal schooling became a consuming occupation of both the government and the evacuated population. Much has been written about the nation's "worst wartime mistake," as Eugene Rostow called the evacuation, but relatively little is known about the life of the young people who spent their most impressionable years in the camps. In the growing literature on the camps no one has explored the implications of their experience for understanding the incarceration of Japanese Americans.[5]

"Since I have come to the camp, I no longer feel I am part of the world," wrote one student in a composition during the 1942–43 school year. "I feel like I am a dangerous enemy spy being held in prison." This recognition contradicted many of the school experiences of the children before the war, when they had Caucasian friends and often heard teachers emphasizing citizenship and democracy. In another composition a ninth grader worried about the impact of camp events on the morale of her peers. "As incidents show, the ordinary life here in camp is not doing the larger percentage of youths any good."[6]

Parents, too, expressed their dismay at the prospects for their children. "There are times when a person is in a trance," wrote one father to the administration of Tule Lake Relocation Center in the fall of 1942. He explained that he was "very painfully hurt" by what was happening to the vast numbers of children in the camp. As a block manager in the barracks community, he gave voice to the silent despair of many other parents:

School has started. What a school! Yes, I can appreciate the efforts made by the WRA, but—I oftentimes wonder. Do you know the real existing conditions? How, I wonder, how are we going to make real Americans out of these innocent young children. Teaching them the principles of Democracy, "I pledge allegiance to the flag. One nation, indivisible, with liberty and justice to all" while—they are penned up. Barbed wire fences, guard towers all around playing their search lights on us at night, guards with tommy guns, pistols, and weapons standing over us. I open my arms and cry out in despair—God! Oh, what is this? We who were born here, reared here, educated here, we are bewildered . . . my children ask me: "Daddy, why can't we go home? Why do we have to stay here? . . ." What can I tell them—tell them because we are Americans but of Japanese ancestry. No, heavens, no! Then what are we to tell them? Their replies would be: I didn't learn anything like that in school, where one type of Americans should be put into a camp.[7]

What lessons were this man's children learning in their classrooms? "The understanding of catastrophes, like the death of a father," wrote Anna Freud and Dorothy Burlingham in *War and Children,* "has little to do with reasoning." Freud and Burlingham worked with evacuated children outside of London during World War II, but their concerns are relevant to the experience of Japanese American children in the United States. They recognized that education was a way of channeling the impulses of children away from the "aim of doing harm" and toward the problems of the world around them. The growth of emotions in children was endangered during a war, not because children would turn away from inhuman acts, frightened by what they saw; on the contrary, the more likely prospect was that children would leap into inhumanity "with primitive excitement," their fantasy stimulated all the more because they could see that adults, too, were abandoning the constraints of civilization on a grand scale. "Our educational success in the war," concluded Freud and Burlingham, "will largely depend on whether we can succeed in creating, or conserving for the children, their proper emotional relationship with the outside world."[8]

The camps in the United States were not the same as the billeting of English children in rural homes and nurseries during the German blitzkrieg, but the perception about their emotional growth is the essential point for children of war in both instances. Bombing, violent death, and loss of loved ones had exposed the English children to aggressive impulses being unleashed without social constraints. Japanese American children saw something less ferocious but equally disturbing. Their loyal and hard-working parents had been rounded up by soldiers; their families had been incarcerated under humiliating conditions, deprived of property and livelihood, then subjected

Schoolgirl on a playground swing at Heart Mountain, the camp in Wyoming, November 24, 1943.

to public authorities claiming to be helping them, required to profess their loyalty to those authorities, and finally dispersed back into American society to begin again. If English children might have become destructive without genuine care to lead them back into normal paths of development, one danger here was that Japanese American children might have embraced such uses of authority as legitimate. Not only the authorities but also their subjects might have adjusted themselves to the contrived normalcy of the learning environment. The children might have learned to refashion their consciences so that they could participate in social institutions that would make similar demands of other people in the future. Authoritarian institutions can and do teach obedience to authority, just as violence begets violence in the rearing of children.

During the 1942–43 school year Japanese American children spent most of their daytime hours doing roughly what they had done a year before: going to school. But they did so in a strange, new community—segregated, excluded, concentrated, controlled. The crux of the issue for understanding the history of these children of war is the organization of social meanings and aspirations that was shaped and tempered by greatly expanded public authority in the camps. An educational history, broadly construed, can offer new insight into this aspect of the camps. For if the history of these children was one of exile, it was also a story of public schools and civic learning as these terms were defined in society at large, but intensified to such a degree that the fusion of opportunity and oppression, the interplay of identity and renunciation, became tragically acute.

Several strands of experience make up the history of the schoolchildren and are therefore discussed in this book. The first chapter interprets the educational background of Japanese American families and their children before the war, then describes their efforts to create schools on their own initiative while in temporary assembly centers during the summer of 1942, before they were transported to more permanent relocation centers by the following autumn. The chapter also traces the development of policies for administering the relocation centers, including school programs for the children. Subsequent chapters cover the school life of students and teachers, the issue of loyalty testing and its educational implications, the experience of those who were allowed to leave the camps to go to college, the resistance and countercultures that flourished behind barbed wire, and the use of public education to stimulate resettlement into normal communities. Unlike prior accounts, which describe the evacuation and major events of camp life, this book explores how the perennial conflicts encountered by Japanese Americans as a minority group in public schools took on heightened meaning in the camps, and how students and teachers responded. The documentary evidence is rich for such an inquiry, bringing to light the problems of authority and culture that arose in the camp schools, problems that reached far beyond the war years into the past and the future for Japanese American children.

A recurring theme in the daily life of schooling was the insistence by educators that the program could be used to explore the nature of democracy and to prepare students as citizens. For educators, the connection between democracy and education was an article of faith—but exactly how did they go about keeping that faith? The evidence proves to be more complex than one might expect, and it is not overwhelmingly on the side of Orwellian doublespeak. Many teachers invited social criticism as well as bland civicism; many students, traumatized by the evacuation, needed time to purge their emotions and remonstrate against their circumstances before they were able to continue with the standard material of the curriculum. In light of the receptive attitude of many teachers, and the pained but expressive participation of many students, this book offers evidence to describe connections between democracy and education as articulated by the students themselves. Any serious interpretation of how the schoolchildren learned to be citizens in public schools must come to grips with the political dilemma underlying their predicament in the camps: how in good faith to prepare for future life in a democratic society while suffering an undemocratic imposition of authority and deprivation of rights.

A year before the war began, the median age of the children of Japanese immigrants had been about sixteen, or high school age. By the end of the war it was approaching twenty-one, when most young people are well on their way to work and adult life. Schooled in the camps, Japanese Americans entered a booming postwar economy. They emerged as one of the better educated groups in American society and took advantage of an expanding white-collar sector for the next several decades, quite often finding niches in occupations that had been beyond their reach before Pearl Harbor. Behind the success story lurks a pair of questions that comparative figures on education and income do not answer: What happened to the schoolchildren in the camps, and what does this mean for understanding the history of our society?[9]

To understand the import of these questions, one must press beyond the analysis of educational levels, material success, and ethnic persistence. One must attempt to recapture the presence of the camps as something taught and learned, something more than an assemblage of facts and circumstances. For the children, the camps fused oppression and opportunity into a historic moment that defies simplification into categories of racism or war hysteria or just plain evil. In its complexity the incarceration of Japanese Americans offers a window on the contradictory life of politics and education in the United States. Some of the recurring tensions of this society—between authority and consent, majority and minority cultures, public purpose and private dignity—were fully present in the camps, and they were not eradicated by dispersing the victims and regretting the error. The experience of the camps remains a touchstone for understanding American society and resolving to improve its educational institutions of all kinds.

1

Between Past and Future Homes

WHEN they came to the United States, Japanese immigrants brought with them a strong commitment to schooling. Because of the expansion of public education in Japan during the Meiji Era (1868–1912), they had gained enough experience with formal education to recognize its value. In later life, many of the Issei, or first generation immigrants, recalled their childhood in Japan with images reminiscent of one-room rural schools in the United States: rising early, walking long distances, following a strict regimen of studies laden with moral precepts, then dropping out after a few years to work in the family business. The immigrants who came before the Gentlemen's Agreement of 1908, a diplomatic accord that excluded laborers, were mostly from poor rural prefectures in Japan and were motivated primarily by a desire for economic advancement. Intent on finding jobs, they had also heard the "golden story," in the words of an Issei historian, about educational opportunity in the United States. When the Dillingham Commission reported to Congress in 1911 on the recent waves of immigrants to the United States, it was struck by "the ambition and eagerness of members of this race to learn Western civilization." No immigrant group except Jews, concluded the commission, had shown such "great desire to learn the English language."[1]

As a group, the Japanese were unusually literate. By 1910, reported the U.S. census for that year, the rate of illiteracy among Japanese immigrants ten years of age or older was only 9.2 percent. This compared well with the 15.8 percent rate of illiteracy for Chinese, 12.7 percent for all foreign-born whites, and 7.7 percent for the entire population of the United States. With so large a base of literacy to build upon, Japanese immigrants fashioned their social lives within a tight configuration of community institutions: voluntary associations based on a family's place of origin in Japan, Buddhist and Christian organizations, cooperative arrangements for maintaining economic solidarity, and the Japanese language press. The immigrant communities also supported local Japanese associations that were linked to regional governing bodies and from there to the Japanese consulate and the government of Japan, which hoped to sit among the first rank of world powers and did not relish the notion of its emigrants living abjectly while the nation sought equality of status. These various community institutions actively encouraged efforts to improve the literacy of Japanese immigrants.[2]

Another source of commitment to schooling was the traditional organization of immigrant families. For the first generation, the family bore the distinctive characteristics of the home in Japan at the end of the nineteenth century: strong patriarchal control, limited rights of expression for women, expectations that children would conform and participate in the family economy. Although these general traits characterized many immigrant families from agrarian backgrounds, some features of child rearing in Japanese families corresponded to the demands of formal schooling in exceptional ways. Forrest LaViolette argued that the wives showed an "exaggerated devotion to their children as a means of emotional compensation" for the rigid domination and social distance of the husband. The children were made "ultra-sensitive to the demands of family loyalty and the minutest social proprieties" by means of ridicule, ostracism, denial of praise, close monitoring of behavior, and invidious comparisons with other people. Intense devotion to the children created emotional attachment and dependency during the years of schooling, while the constant threat of rejection and dishonor inculcated a strong desire among children to satisfy in advance the requirements of any social situation that might cause loss of face. Educational success, highly valued by the parents, became a matter of honor; failure to succeed and prove oneself worthy was a moral failure, not only for the individual but for the family, the local community, and the entire ethnic group.[3]

Family values grew in importance with the arrival of larger numbers of women, especially after the Gentlemen's Agreement of 1908 stopped the influx of male laborers from Japan. Most often coming as "picture brides" through a tradition of arranged marriages, the women brought a conserving influence to the pioneer immigrants, a demand for stable family life. As their numbers increased, the women bore children and attempted to instill the values they had learned in Japan. One of these was school attendance; but parents soon recognized that public schools in the United States impelled children outward from their family and community, into the English language, toward different traditions of social intercourse. Meanwhile, the children born on American soil grew in numbers, from 4,502 in 1910 to 29,672 in 1920 to 68,357 in 1930—in percentages, from about 6 to 27 to 49.2 percent of all Japanese Americans during those decades. As families expanded, parents sought a means of teaching Japanese culture to their American-born children, in part to be able to communicate with them in Japanese, the language of the home.[4]

Their main strategy for preserving Japanese culture in the younger generation was to create private language schools. Starting in Hawaii in 1896 and soon spreading to California and the Northwest, these schools began as appendages to Buddhist churches, providing a way of resisting the acculturating influences of Christian churches and the public school system. Christians soon followed suit with similar institutions, designed to maintain contact between children and the language and traditions of the parents. It was not long before these language schools became a standard feature of Japanese communities in western states. Japanese American children attended them after their public school classes and on Saturdays. According to one study of such schools in Southern California, the curricula consisted not only of "writing, dictation, reading, memorizing, translation from Japanese to the English language and translation from English into the Japanese language," but also such things as "honesty, truth, morality . . . singing, speaking, and history," all of which were evaluated separately on the report card. Through the language schools, parents hoped to instill ethical character and sense of duty as well as cognitive competence in their children.[5]

Thus, children of Japanese immigrants came to American education with an organized commitment to schooling. The immigrant community expressed its determination, through the Japanese Educational Association in 1913, "to bring up the child who shall live and die in America in the spirit of the instruction received in the public schools of America." In 1915 Kiyo S. Inui reported to the annual meeting of the National Education Association, where he was listed on the program as secretary of the Japan Society of America, that there were 3,008 students of Japanese descent in American elementary schools, 293 in high schools, and 14,142 Japanese American children altogether, most of them still under legal school age, of whom all but 1,497 were born in the United States. A resolution adopted by the Japanese Association of America in 1918 demonstrated the commitment of Japanese immigrants to public education for their children. The secretary of the association, Kiichi Kanzaki, wrote that "to lead them to American ideals, the parents were asked to pledge to send them to public schools not later than one year after their arrival in this country. This work was carefully supervised by the local affiliated Associations. If [the children were] of the school age, the attendance at the public schools was made compulsory through the same supervision." By the 1920s, as the second generation, the Nisei, began to reach school age in growing numbers, their educational aspirations were already developed, having been instilled by an interlocking network of cultural values. This network, based on literate communication and other forms of social control, extended from the family to community institutions to a foreign government anxious about its status among the great powers of the world.[6]

The children of Japanese immigrants impressed educators with their drive and diligence. One superintendent of schools wrote that "a child of six pursues his studies with the intensity of an American youth working his way through college; and the constant struggle of the public schools is not to compel the Japanese to attend, but to keep out youngsters below school-age who resort to all manner of subterfuge in order to gain entrance." When measured by intelligence testers working under Lewis M. Terman in the 1920s, the Nisei were found to be somewhat behind in "mental processes involving memory and abstract thinking based upon concepts represented by verbal symbols of the English language," but they were "at least equal and possibly superior to Americans in mental processes involving memory and thinking based upon concrete, visually presented situations of a nonverbal character," and they were found to be definitely superior to the rest of the population "in mental processes involving acuity of visual perception and recall, and tenacity of attention." A parallel analysis of teacher ratings by the same testers found Japanese American children to be less confident, less vain, and more "sensitive to approval" than other children in

American schools, and they were judged to be more stable emotion-
ally, more cheerful, more optimistic, and more appreciative of beauty
than other children. Using the newly developed Stanford Achievement Tests, the study found a "remarkable" showing of Japanese
American children aged eleven and twelve on the informational tests
in history and literature. "The results should tend to dispose definitely," concluded the study, "of the idea that Japanese children are
inclined to remain ignorant of American ideas when given the opportunity to acquire them."[7]

Judging only by the drive of Japanese American children to succeed in educational settings, one would not hesitate to predict a
smooth transition to citizenship and participation in the social and
economic life of the nation. But as Japanese immigrants worked to
make a place for themselves in American society, they were opposed
by organized interests and influential newspapers, and they were
perennial targets for the hostile rhetoric of western politicians. The
anti-Japanese movement, spearheaded by groups like the Native
Sons of the Golden West and the California Joint Immigration Commission, attacked even the achievements of immigrant communities
as signs of irreconcilable conflict: efficiency became unfair competition, adaptability the subversion of colonizers, school success proof
positive of arrogance and dark designs. "The melting pot does not
affect them as it does even the most refractory of the European
races," wrote V. S. McClatchey, the most eloquent of the California
exclusionists, in 1919. "They remain always Japanese. They maintain their racial purity more jealously than any other race which
comes to our shores. They preserve their ideals, their customs, their
language . . . It is a dangerous experiment to attempt to make good
American citizens out of such material." The question of equal access
to public schooling was especially galling to the exclusionists, since
it represented one of the most powerful channels carrying immigrants into normal citizenship and social life. "They send their children," complained Governor William D. Stephens of California, "to
our white schools, and in many of the country schools of our state
the spectacle is presented of having a few white children acquiring
their education in classrooms crowded with Japanese. The deep-
seated and often outspoken resentment of our white mothers at this
situation can only be appreciated by those people who have struggled
with similar problems."[8]

For the Issei, the older generation, racial exclusion was the law
in the United States. In 1894 a U.S. district court held that immi-

grants born in Japan could not become naturalized citizens of the United States because they were members of one of the races ineligible for citizenship. In 1922 the U.S. Supreme Court reaffirmed that a Japanese alien was not eligible for naturalized citizenship under the law. Yet the children were citizens; the Fourteenth Amendment to the U.S. Constitution conferred citizenship upon anyone born within the borders of the United States. The status of American-born children had remained secure, in spite of numerous attempts to restrict it, ever since the U.S. Supreme Court ruled in 1898 that an Asian born in the United States was a citizen even if the parents were aliens ineligible for citizenship. Blanket exclusion of the parents from citizenship and ready access to public education for young citizens existed side by side in Japanese American families with Issei parents and Nisei children.[9]

In California, where the majority of Japanese Americans lived, this contrast of inclusion and exclusion led to an embattled history over the educational rights of the group. If the parents could be excluded, it seemed only proper to many people that the children's right of citizenship should be abridged to exclude them from public institutions. Segregated schools were legal in California; the state supreme court had upheld their legality in 1874, and the U.S. Supreme Court had affirmed the doctrine of "separate but equal" in *Plessy* v. *Ferguson* (1896). The legislature in California passed a law allowing school districts to establish separate schools for "Chinese and Mongolians" in 1885. San Francisco built its Chinese school before the end of the year. A federal court later upheld the power of public officials to establish a separate school for Chinese students, whether citizens or not.[10]

When Japanese immigrants had begun to come to the United States in increasing numbers around the turn of the century, segregation of Asians into separate public schools had been the official policy in California, though it was not universally followed. In 1906 the school board in San Francisco passed a resolution to place Japanese and Korean pupils in the same institution with the Chinese, and to call it the Oriental School. The outcome of the international crisis that ensued was that diplomatic pressure by the Japanese government stopped the segregation of Japanese American children, thereby guaranteeing their access to the most universal of public institutions for entry into citizenship. Wary of Japan's growing power, President Theodore Roosevelt invited the whole school board of San Francisco to Washington and ended the crisis through negotiation.

*Wizened by decades of
endurance, a grandfather
carries his grandson on his
shoulders at Manzanar,
the camp in the Owens
Valley of California,
July 2, 1942.*

The Japanese government voluntarily restricted emigration, and the local school board agreed to admit Japanese children to public schools.[11]

As Japanese American children attended public schools alongside whites, their status remained a target of the exclusionists. After California passed alien land laws in 1913 and 1920, using the category of "alien ineligible to citizenship" to keep Japanese farmers from buying property, children, with their citizenship rights, became a means of retaining title to the family's economic base. As other western states passed alien land laws but found that many Japanese immigrants could own land through their older children, the exclusionists fought to withdraw citizenship rights from the Nisei. They pressed for an amendment to the U.S. Constitution if necessary, claiming that because the children held dual citizenship, they were colonizers and not genuine native-born citizens who could be considered loyal to the United States.

In the years leading up to Japanese exclusion in the federal Immigration Act of 1924, the anti-Japanese movement continued to demand more than exclusion of new immigrants. They decried the high birthrate of the Japanese already in the country, the existence of Japanese language schools, the competition, the alleged unassimilability. Alarmed by the vigor and efficiency of these immigrants, they planted fears of sabotage and subversion as well. "The longing to hack a path to greatness by the samurai sword lurks ever in the back of Japanese minds," warned Lothrop Stoddard in *The Rising Tide of Color against White World-Supremacy*. Public education only helped the children "to use their American citizenship for the glory of the Mikado and the benefit of the Japanese race," warned McClatchey, and anyone who did not understand this was abetting their plans for "peaceful penetration." Governor Stephens declared openly, "the people of California are determined to repress a developing Japanese community in our midst." In the end the anti-Japanese movement did achieve its goal of closing immigration to the Japanese, but it failed to abridge the citizenship of the younger generation. Although California's legislature passed a bill in 1921— one in a long line of such proposals over the years—calling for the segregation of Japanese Americans in separate schools, the children were already well ensconced in public schools, and only a few rural schools outside Sacramento enforced the law.[12]

The clamor for exclusion died after the Immigration Act of 1924. Newspapers turned to other issues; most of the exclusionist organizations disbanded; the public lost sight of Japanese Americans.

Politicians, by the early 1930s, had different problems on their minds. Under the pressure of Franklin D. Roosevelt and a transformed Democratic party, they enlarged the role of government to relieve the suffering of a vast underclass of unemployed, minority, and rural people who had been shaken loose from traditional institutions by rapid economic development and its sudden collapse. Through this decade of change, Japanese Americans lived quietly apart, relatively untouched by the social programs and public assistance of the era. Drawing strength from their traditions of mutual aid, while continuing to encounter discrimination in the larger world of employment and politics, most Japanese American families lived separately in their own enclaves. Their most sustained contact with the world of the white majority was during childhood, the years of public schooling.[13]

After the tumultuous decades of immigration and anti-Japanese agitation, Japanese Americans settled down to a localized life of family, community pursuits, and hard work to maintain the economic foothold they had established in American society. In 1930 the U.S. census counted 138,834 residents of Japanese descent in the United States, of whom 120,251 lived in the Pacific Coast states and 11,418 in the mountain states of the West. Of the total in 1930, more than 70 percent lived in California; of those, more than a third lived in Los Angeles County. Of all Japanese Americans counted that year, 68,357—or about half—were born in the United States and were therefore citizens. Roughly 30,000 of these were attending public school at the beginning of the decade, a figure that remained about the same a decade later, even though the total population declined somewhat over that time. By 1930 the average age of a Japanese American born in the United States and living in California was less than ten years; only about 12 percent were eighteen or more years of age.[14]

As the pioneer Issei began to pass away or return to Japan, the Nisei, the American-born second generation, became a larger percentage of the group's population. And as the younger generation reached higher levels of schooling, its members became increasingly aware of the line separating the two worlds of their childhood. In school they might have been friends with every sort of person, and they were honored equally for good work and strong character. At home, more often than not, they lived restricted lives, set apart from the surrounding world. For most Nisei, the larger society of which their schools were part became inaccessible to them by the time they reached late adolescence. The opportunities and friendships of whites suddenly grew distant, even though the educational attainments of the two groups were roughly equivalent by the 1930s for the younger generation. As some Nisei went on to college, they became more conscious of their racial isolation. Recognizing that people in western states often perceived them as more Japanese than American, they harbored a growing sense of foreboding as they saw the worsening condition of international tensions: Japan's seizure of Manchuria and China, its rejection of the League of Nations, its repudiation of the agreement to limit naval armaments, its attack on the USS *Panay,* the growth of military power in the United States, and the use of economic sanctions against Japan.

Some of the most articulate Nisei brushed off the foreboding and celebrated the wonders of U.S. citizenship. The public schools had Americanized them; their rights were ultimately secure. If they were loyal and worked hard, their country would stand by them. Schools, the English language, and American customs became the staples of Nisei social life. The Japanese American press recorded Nisei school achievements each year as dozens were honored as valedictorians, salutatorians, prize essayists, debate champions, and commencement speakers. The message was that problems confronting Japanese Americans could be overcome by the extraordinary efforts of loyal individuals.

Still, there was an undercurrent of discontent, the memory of past campaigns against the group, and always the presence of invisible limits, despite the success of the Nisei in their school world. The Nisei might study to become teachers, but they usually could not teach in the public schools. Preparing to be a nurse or a lawyer, they would find their entry into these professions blocked or severely constrained. They could master a trade, only to fall back into the ethnic community when they found unions and associations closed to them. Cut off from the vistas that had seemed open to them by virtue of their educational achievement, they often returned to work for their parents in the family business, in a profession serving only the ethnic community, or in an occupation requiring less education than they had received.

The 1930s was a decade of quiet travail for the Issei and frustrated hope for the Nisei, one generation still clinging to values brought over years ago from an older Japan, the other grasping at the promising vision of America offered to them in the classrooms and civic lessons of public schools. Together the generations shared differing degrees of exclusion from the world around them in the United States. Longing for a coherent culture to sustain immigrant communities, the Issei persisted in their desire to have their children learn the Japanese language, which they saw as a basis for close rapport within the family, including relatives abroad. The language could also help the Nisei to do business within the ethnic group and with people involved in trade with Japan. In addition to the language schools, which expanded in enrollment during the 1930s, many families sent one child to Japan for part of his or her education. These Kibei, or Nisei educated in Japan, helped to preserve Japanese traditions as their siblings embraced the middle-class culture of the United States. By World War II this group numbered more than 9,000 of the roughly 70,000 offspring of the Issei in the camps.[15]

Such initiatives served to protect the traditional identity of ethnic communities. A contrasting effort reflected the desire of the second generation to come to terms with the society their families had joined. The Japanese American Citizens League (JACL), which held its first annual meeting in 1930, developed and sponsored social activities throughout the 1930s. The JACL was one of the many community organizations serving the social needs of Japanese Americans, but it specialized in patriotic citizenship, the quest to be recognized as one-hundred percent Americans. Though relatively few Nisei participated in the early years of the organization, it represented the struggle to move from a successful education to normal citizenship and social life as equals in the United States. Beginning with its 1934 convention, as William Hosokawa reports in his organizational history, the JACL held a yearly speech contest for high school Nisei. The winning speech that first year was entitled "The Role of Citizenship in the Crisis of Democracy." The 1934 convention also considered a resolution to make all teachers in Japanese language schools take at least one year of Americanization classes before being allowed to teach. By emphasizing citizenship, the JACL was seeking to shift the culture of Japanese Americans away from the traditional authority of the older generation. As a result, the traditional institutions and attitudes of the immigrant community were sometimes derided, since these could be seen as obstacles to rapid integration into the dominant pattern of American society. According to one of its leaders, the style of the league was to help individuals win the battle against discrimination "in the American way—above board, in the open, through courts of law, by education,

by proving myself to be worthy of equal treatment and considera-
tion." [16]

Growing up amidst contrasting styles—communal cohesion on
one side, politicized assimilation on the other—the younger generation continued to perform well in school. The children received
encouragement from their parents' faith in education and the support of a resilient network of community institutions reinforcing
that faith. The Nisei were also lured onward by the desire for opportunity and equality of social status, the promised land of the
classroom and a democratic society. By the early 1930s, according
to California survey results analyzed by researchers at Stanford
University, the average level of education among males and females
of Japanese descent born in the United States and more than twenty
years old was 12.5 and 12.0 years of schooling. When questioned by
the Stanford survey team, the Nisei described vocational aspirations
commensurate with their education. Many wanted to be doctors,
dentists, pharmacists, and engineers. Many others hoped to enter
business and the skilled trades. Some expressed an interest in teaching, but did not mark it as a vocational preference because they
knew the field was closed to them. Once schooled, many Nisei wanted
to escape the farm, the stores in "Little Tokyo," and occupations
providing services for whites.[17]

In many ways the Nisei found themselves stranded between the
world of the white majority and the traditional community life of
the Issei. That the latter was often as distasteful to them as the
former was inhospitable became apparent in their unwillingness to
master the Japanese language. Whether Christian or Buddhist, most
Nisei observed only the forms of their language school education
after public school each day. "The mother-tongue of these children
is English," observed Professor Yamato Ichihashi of Stanford University, who wrote the most definitive history of the Japanese in
America and had named his own son after Woodrow Wilson. "It has
been impossible for these schools to do anything against the training
given the children in American public schools."[18]

Yet, it was equally impossible to erase the stigma that many
people attached to the race of these minority students, no matter
how well they performed. In 1935 the California legislature considered yet another bill to provide segregated schools for Japanese
Americans. Although the bill did not pass, it is significant that it
was given attention at all. With the threat of exclusion always near

at hand, Japanese Americans continued to believe in the value of their schooling. "I am especially grateful to America for my education," wrote the president of the Central Japanese Association of America in 1941, "as I have studied in American schools from elementary school to college. In school, I was accorded the same privileges with all the rest of the students. There in school, I found a real Democracy, lived and practiced by the students and faculty members alike; I saw the fundamental principles of America translated into action."[19]

A year later, the nation plunged into war, and the world of the Nisei turned topsy-turvy. "On Monday, December 8, 1941, we went to school with some anxiety," remembered a young Japanese American in a composition she wrote later at the Manzanar Relocation Center. On the previous day a surprise attack by Japanese planes and submarines had crippled the U.S. Pacific fleet at Pearl Harbor. All persons of Japanese descent, whether citizens or not, were in danger of being identified with the enemy because of their race and culture. Within six months the entire Japanese American population on the West Coast was forced to migrate from the designated military zone in Washington, Oregon, California, and Arizona.[20]

A few thousand were able to move east during the fleeting weeks when voluntary evacuation was possible. Then the Western Defense Command froze their movements by fiat and removed them, community by community, into makeshift assembly centers in fairgrounds, racetracks, and public facilities. Issei leaders and language school teachers had been rounded up by FBI agents and placed in separate detention centers immediately after Pearl Harbor. Communities lost their center and waited for the next move of the government. The young Nisei soon found that their fate was to be no different from that of their parents, the "enemy aliens" in government parlance. The JACL, representing a fraction of the Nisei but benefiting from effective organization and articulate leadership, sprang into action to affirm the policy of the government, while also trying to mitigate its severity. A strategy of accommodation did not deflect the blow: citizen and noncitizen went into the camps together.[21]

In California the former attorney general, Ulysses S. Webb, launched a court action to deprive the younger generation of its U.S. citizenship. Similar proposals for harsher treatment of Japanese Americans came up repeatedly in Congress as the nation mobilized for war on two fronts. Senator Tom Stewart of Tennessee, part of the southern bloc that had traditionally stood with western congressmen in their attempts to legislate against Asian immigrants, proposed a bill in June 1942 to incarcerate all persons of Japanese descent throughout the United States, even those living outside the military zones of the Western Defense Command, so that there would be none left at large in the country, whether citizen or not. Senator Murdock of Utah retorted in the discussion that led to withdrawing the bill before a vote: "If we can wink at the Constitution in the case of the citizen of Japanese descent, then the next step, of course, is to move out and begin putting in concentration camps citizens of German descent, and every other citizen of foreign descent in the United States who may have come or whose parents or ancestors may have come from some nation with which we are today at war." A publication of the American Friends Service Committee warned that this was "legislation of the Nuremburg variety" for Japanese instead of Jews.[22]

Not so, reasoned Representative Leland Ford in another debate as he urged the U.S. House of Representatives to pursue a policy of mass evacuation: "I believe that a patriotic native-born Japanese, if he wants to make his contribution, will submit himself to a concentration camp as his contribution, as against the native-born American, who lays his life down for his country. If these Japanese are patriotic and have the welfare of our country at heart, they should not object to that small sacrifice." Representative John E. Rankin of Mississippi, a state hardly prone to subversion by Asian immigrants on the West Coast, agreed with his colleagues from California on the necessity of evacuation: "Once a Jap, always a Jap. We cannot afford to trust any of them." Rankin also reminded lawmakers of the old racist maxim from his own region, "The leopard cannot change his spots," a view which the official report of the U.S. War Department on the evacuation later seconded by declaring that "racial affinities are not severed by migration. The Japanese race is an enemy race."[23]

Subjected to such logic during the national mobilization for war, the evacuated population moved from their homes into sixteen temporary assembly centers in Pacific Coast states from late March through June of 1942. They lost their livelihood; many lost their property. "Human vultures pounced on our misfortunes," recalled a farmer who had recently expanded his holdings and bought new equipment. Behind barbed wire, Japanese Americans became a concentrated multitude, a nameless mass of prisoners. "Since yesterday

*Military police manning
one of the watchtowers
at Santa Anita Assembly
Center in California,
April 6, 1942.*

we Japanese have ceased to be human beings," wrote Hatsuye Egami in his wartime diary after arriving to Tulare Assembly Center in California. "We are numbers. We are no longer Egamis, but the number 23324. A tag with that number is on every trunk, suitcase and bag. Tags, also, on our breasts." Outside the fence, the evacuated population had been diverse; inside they were the excluded Japanese. Outside they had lived as families; now they saw long lines for food, latrines without partitions, acres of inactive manpower, swarms of children running apart from their families during the day. The fence and military guard had come as a surprise—no one had told them that their "protective custody" would turn into incarceration. Around them now were the most visible instruments of state coercion: machine guns, rifles with bayonets, barbed wire, guard towers, search lights, military police. "The elders slump in their seats like weakened fish, imbibing sleep," wrote Egami in his diary. "But the children," he added incongruously, "are cheerful and playful. They noisily frolic about as if they are on a picnic."[24]

By the time they entered the assembly centers, the incarcerated younger generation numbered more than 70,000. They had fewer memories of coping with adversity than the 40,000 or so Issei behind barbed wire, many of whom could recall having spent parts of their early manhood in camps of another sort, when they had started their lives in the United States as migrant agricultural laborers, lumberjacks, seasonal cannery workers. These Issei were probably less shocked when in the spring of 1942 the sugar beet industry and other growers in the western states lobbied to have Japanese American workers released on furlough programs under guard to harvest crops because of a labor shortage during the war. Decades of adversity had taught many Issei not to expect the government to take their side or defend their interests; they braced themselves for the inevitable. "The attitude of the first generation toward their American-born offspring is that of mild contempt and even antagonism," complained a writer in *The Evacuee Speaks,* a newsletter published by Nisei in the Santa Anita Assembly Center. Many Issei scoffed at the worthless citizenship of their patriotic children. Charles Kikuchi, the indefatigable Nisei diarist in the Tanforan Assembly Center, worried that "the argument that we are in camp just like them and therefore not Americans is beginning to influence many Nisei."[25]

Despite rumblings of antagonism, the generations continued to agree about the value of education. Within two weeks in May 1942

*A volunteer teacher
instructing elementary
school children in
the educational program
initiated during late
spring and summer of
1942 by Japanese
Americans incarcerated
at Manzanar, Owens
Valley, California,
July 1, 1942.*

at the Portland Assembly Center, camp residents established a kindergarten and English classes. The latter comprised the study of current events and history as well as English grammar. In the Santa Anita Assembly Center the incarcerated population responded immediately to the degradation of camp life by organizing classes for children and adults, taught by Japanese Americans. They created a parent-teacher association to strengthen ties between organized instruction and the home. By the end of May the center had classes at all educational levels "in the lobbies of the grandstand in front of the pari-mutuel betting windows," noted one description, "a somewhat questionable environment for the education of the young." By early June in Santa Anita, 2,470 people were attending classes taught by 130 teachers, and there were 125 preschoolers in nursery school. Through sympathetic Caucasians on the outside some arrangements were made with school officials from home communities to identify the credits missed by Japanese American children at the end of the school year because of the evacuation. At graduation time in late June, the keynote speaker in the commencement ceremony inside the assembly center was the superintendent of schools from Los Angeles.[26]

A report on the self-initiated program in the Merced Assembly Center gives some idea of the remarkable organization of educational activities that was achieved within days after Japanese Americans arrived. Of 4,500 camp residents, about 1,000 were school-age children; 780 of these attended school within the assembly center during the summer of 1942. They were instructed by 20 teachers, all Japanese Americans, all of whom had at least two years of college—more than 10 had college degrees. The students were unruly but attendance was high, according to the director. The program was not compulsory; its aim was as much to organize and occupy the time of the children as it was to enlarge their cognitive skills, though the latter goal was also desired. Japanese American teachers struggled "to keep alive in the students the desire to learn," one report noted in describing the makeshift educational program.[27]

At the Tanforan Assembly Center the education of the young became a major endeavor as well. The organization of schools paralleled an attempt to set up self-government, which at first comprised both Issei and Nisei, then was limited to Nisei by government order. The schools taught democracy in the idealistic images of the educated Nisei, while camp residents tried to organize a community government and create a leadership. In August the army dissolved all self-government in the assembly centers. As the self-government wavered and then foundered on intergenerational struggle and army repression, the schools went on with their work. Henry Tani, supervisor of the high school at Tanforan, wrote a report describing how these community-spawned institutions operated. "The school had no official status," he emphasized. "It was temporary; its faculty had no experience; it sought no favors; it merely alleviated the problem of putting young people into constructive endeavor." The volunteer faculty of the high school was composed of Nisei college graduates from the San Francisco Bay area. "It is well to recall," Tani pointed out, "that teaching as a profession was never a welcome field for the Japanese college student. Hence it is not surprising that not one qualified and accredited teacher was among this group."[28]

Despite their lack of preparation as educators, these volunteers struggled to preserve and to transmit to others their hopes for the future. For a Fourth of July program in Fresno Assembly Center, "we decided to recite the Gettysburg Address as a verse choir," remembered one of the Nisei teachers years later. "We had an artist draw a big picture of Abraham Lincoln with an American flag behind him. Some people had tears in their eyes; some people shook their heads and said it was so ridiculous to have this kind of thing recited in camp. It didn't make sense, but it was our heart's cry."[29]

Initially, one hurdle facing these novice teachers was the difficulty of gaining respect from students accustomed to being taught by Caucasian teachers. "The situation placed a score of Nisei college graduates, some of them being the older brothers and sisters of the high school students, in charge of the six and seven hundred, teaching and guiding them in their thinking upon the academic and sometimes non-academic subjects at hand." But as the weeks passed, recalled Tani, "this lack of respect died away, and the just attitude of more obedience and attention to one more learned and experienced found its place. This is not to infer," he suggested, "that the Nisei are . . . a disrespectful group. It does bring to light the fact that the Nisei as a teacher was an unknown thing. It took Tanforan High School to prove to those youngsters that brand new textbooks, a football team, and a brass band are not the substance of a school."[30]

Yoshiko Uchida, one of these Nisei teachers, had just finished her undergraduate studies at the University of California when her family was evacuated from Berkeley. She received her diploma in the mail while living in a horse stall that had been converted into living quarters at the Tanforan racetrack, which was serving as an assembly center until more permanent facilities could be constructed in the interior of the country. As at Santa Anita—where streets between the barracks had been named after famous racehorses such as Man o' War, Whirlaway, and Seabiscuit—the environment entered the culture of the temporary camp in numerous ways. The camp newspaper, *Tanforan Totalizer,* drew its name from racetrack lingo for the pari-mutuel betting machines. Despite the associations of such imagery, the environment was no obstacle to spontaneous schooling, largely because of the dedication of these teachers and the enthusiastic response of parents and students.

"By the end of June," recalled Uchida, "40 percent of the residents of Tanforan were either teaching or going to school, and the education department's activities were extended to include classes in flower arrangement and first aid, and academic courses for adults as well." In her memoir of life in the camps, Uchida describes the experience of teaching in the elementary school. "I taught mostly by instinct. The children, however, were affectionate and devoted, and it didn't take them long to discover where I lived. Each morning I would find a covey of them clustered in front of my stall, and, like the Pied Piper, I would lead them to the school barrack. When school was over, many would wait until I was ready to leave and escort me back home."[31]

Her older sister, Keiko Uchida, who had a degree in early childhood education from Mills College, set up the first nursery school at Tanforan, then another in the camp at Topaz, Utah. Schoolmakers like Uchida and Grace Fujii, a fellow student from Mills College who later worked at the Walden School in New York and the Merrill-Palmer School in Detroit, brought with them a network of sympathetic Caucasians and a supply of materials from institutions of higher education on the West Coast. The main advisor of the Nisei who set up nursery schools at Tanforan and Topaz is illustrative of that network. Lovisa Wagoner, a professor of early childhood education and director of the Children's School at Mills College, was one of a growing number of academicians who were helping the federal and state governments to design preschool programs for young children. Wagoner and her students had consulted and done evaluations for the Farm Security Administration migrant camps, nursery schools operated by the Works Projects Administration, and urban preschool facilities under the Community Facilities Act of 1940. In their relations with the camps for Japanese Americans, they maintained the perspective that the nursery schools belonged to the people who used them and should empower the community to care for its own children.[32]

Started first in the assembly centers and then continued in the relocation centers, the community-initiated nursery schools served to countervail the degradation of camp life and helped to prepare children reared in Japanese-speaking homes to enter schools where only English was spoken. Children were taught new language skills through stories, poems, and finger-plays. The schools also helped to keep children healthy and to counter their "lack of emotional control," which was exacerbated by lack of sleep in crowded barracks. Parents were quick to recognize the value of these schools; at Manzanar about a thousand children between the ages of three and six were enrolled in the nursery schools during the first year.[33]

The cooperation between educated Nisei and sympathetic Caucasians took other forms besides the design of nursery schools. "The library grows in numbers of books and magazines," wrote another Nisei from Mills College as she watched the mobilization of learning resources taking place around her at Tanforan, "and it looks like a race between building shelves and accessioning books." Many of these books came from school districts that had enrolled the children before the war. For example, at Manzanar, which was located in the Owens Valley of eastern California, the tutoring program received a donation of a thousand textbooks at the beginning of the summer from the home districts of students in the Los Angeles area. Then a professor from Los Angeles City College arrived in a one-and-a-half-ton truck with two thousand books for the schoolchildren and their families, plus sports equipment, a phonograph, records, and magazines. He brought with him other faculty, students, and the principal of a junior high school where many of the children had been in school only a few weeks before.[34]

Another Caucasian sympathetic to the children of war, a teacher named Edith Waterman, frequently drove by the Santa Anita Racetrack. She was deeply moved by what she saw there. "At night, I viewed the thousands of barracks' lights and, to my amazement, from high towers, I saw the beacon search lights throwing their long, penetrating beams here and there over this entire territory now restricted." She was there when the army began transporting the Japanese Americans out of Santa Anita under armed guard to an inland relocation center. "Children stretched their heads and hands far out of the windows, some laughing, others crying—but all waved frantically until the long train bore them beyond me. Then and there, I resolved, would follow them and, to the best of my ability, help them bear their burdens." Edith Waterman went to work in the camps and became one of the teachers whom Japanese Americans remember with lasting gratitude from those dark times.[35]

Mine Okubo, a young artist who made drawings of life in Tanforan and Topaz, also worked in the schools. She expressed what was, to judge from the high attendance rates in voluntary schools, a widespread sentiment among Japanese Americans in the assembly centers: that the structured time and tasks of the schools were "an effective counterinfluence to the bad atmosphere of the camp." This sentiment became a commitment to action in the rapid development of a parental advisory council to negotiate for resources with the camp authorities. The council reviewed qualifications of teachers, coordinated the use of classroom space in the messhalls and beneath the grandstand, arranged for the distribution of books and supplies donated from the outside, staged assemblies, and approved a system for keeping track of report cards and school records, all in the hope that the children might be able to continue their education without losing ground because of the evacuation.[36]

The conviction of the elders came through not only directly in their efforts to maintain educational opportunities, but also indirectly in the writings of some of their children in these schools. "We must not let evacuation and relocation break our spirits," wrote one boy in his handwritten scrawl for a summer school composition. "We must not let ourselves sink lower in efficiency and in capacities because of mental inactivity . . . We must remember that we are going back to everyday American life again. It is important that we keep this in mind, and it is important that we act accordingly." Wrote another: "I must find ways and means of advancing my education so that when I eventually leave this camp life after the war I can be prepared for the future." An older Nisei writing to one of her former schoolteachers recognized the place of education for the children of war: "What all this will eventually do to them I don't know, but I do know that it is a truly discouraging situation which can be remedied only through an honest-to-goodness sympathetic effort on the part of those whom they are able to respect as elders and as teachers." The Caucasian to whom these words were addressed, Edythe Backus, was moved by the educational predicament of Japanese Americans; she came to the camps to teach shortly thereafter.[37]

"The school is a vast hubbub of voices—some low, some high

pitched," noted Kikuchi in his diary. "Above this din, the teachers try to compete and they have to speak very loudly in order to get themselves heard. Blackboards have been made from painted plywood. A sign painted 'Tanforan High School' sticks up from the mutuel windows and a girl stands behind it giving out information instead of selling mutuel racing tickets." Often the teachers were too inexperienced to control their classes; they had been students, but knew little about how to teach and had few of the appurtenances of a normal school around them. Still, the younger generation was schooling itself, organized by the older Nisei and by the remnants of Issei community leadership. "The Nisei as a whole rejoice that they no longer have to attend Japanese language schools," commented Kikuchi; the evacuation had made it inadvisable for parents to risk a confrontation over the maintenance of cultural differences. When the children of the junior high at Tanforan chose red and white for their school colors, an FBI agent appeared right away, declaring that "it was subversive because the colors are the same as the Japanese flag."[38]

Parental pressure, the educated Nisei, and sympathetic Caucasians had created momentum for sustaining formal education. The efforts of Japanese Americans to set up temporary programs for the children had attracted the help of many educators without the prodding of federal authority: former teachers, specialists in curriculum and preschool education, professors from universities, local administrators. The self-initiated schools took form in the chaotic weeks immediately after the mass evacuation had taken place. When officials of the War Relocation Authority (WRA) came to Manzanar in June "to select the site for school buildings," they found classrooms all around them, not in any school buildings, but emerging spontaneously from the incarcerated population's barracks. When the WRA later brought its first camp superintendent to Manzanar during the summer, according to an administrative report, "a summer program, already developed, was thrust on the Superintendent" when she reported for duty: fifty teachers, more than a thousand students, a school census, all twelve grades for the children, and a high school tutoring program led by credentialed Nisei teachers.[39]

These educational initiatives had little impact on the design of schools in the relocation centers where the evacuated Japanese Americans lived after the summer of 1942. In general, with the exception of nursery schools, the government went ahead creating policies as if the evacuated population had nothing to say about the education of its own children. The oversight arose, in part, from the two strains of federal authority over Japanese Americans in 1942. The first was military authority, set in motion by Executive Order 9066 and subsequent exclusion policies under the War Department's Western Defense Command. It had swept Japanese Americans from their home communities, concentrated them in assembly centers, and placed them under armed guard. A military agency, the Wartime Civil Control Administration (WCCA), managed the assembly centers, purposefully offering a minimum of social services, which was one reason for the appearance of self-initiated educational programs among Japanese Americans.

Soon after the military took control, a second kind of federal custody entered the picture under Executive Order 9102, which established the War Relocation Authority. The WRA was a liberal civilian agency modeled on New Deal social programs. In fact, it drew many of its top staff from such programs. While Japanese Americans lived under military authority in the assembly centers during the spring and summer of 1942, the WRA proceeded—independently of what was happening in the army-controlled assembly centers—with developing plans for social services in the relocation centers that would be opening through the summer and fall. At a couple of assembly points, Manzanar in California and Poston in Arizona, Japanese Americans were held in larger "reception centers" that later became relocation centers.[40]

In the relocation centers, the military controlled only the fence and gate, regulating all entry and exit, day and night, after the fences were built in 1942. The military also intervened occasionally within the camp when it was thought necessary for quelling unrest and maintaining order. Despite the visible presence of coercion, inside the fence the WRA instead of the WCCA managed the incarcerated population. A rhetoric of "human conservation" replaced that of "civilian control," and the humanitarian intent of WRA officials became one of the most salient forms of authority that Japanese Americans, especially the children, had to confront during the war years. Moreover, the politics of civilian agencies under the Roosevelt administration became an important variable for the well-being of Japanese Americans. Conflict and cooperation within the federal bureaucracy determined whether Japanese Americans would gain or lose crucial opportunities, such as the channels that existed for vocational training and job placement in war industries. Even when cooperation was assured in the executive branch of government, the WRA, an independent civilian agency created by executive order, lacked strong congressional backing. It sent changing signals to the camps as it tried to establish liberal policies that raised the ire of pressure groups and crusading congressmen. World War II was an era of resurgent congressional power, represented in part by campaigns to dismantle the policies of the past decade. The fate of Japanese Americans—including the education of children—became intertwined with the attack on all social programs and regulatory powers.[41]

The administrative hierarchy of the WRA, which determined the educational programs for the camps, came directly from other federal agencies. The most prominently represented were the Department of Agriculture in Washington and, in the WRA's powerful regional office on the West Coast, the Office of Indian Affairs in the Department of the Interior. The two directors of the WRA during the war, first Milton S. Eisenhower and then Dillon S. Myer, both came from the Department of Agriculture, and they brought a cadre of experienced staff with them. Beyond staffing continuities there were also administrative conveniences that helped the WRA to shape a program. Once the government decided to proceed with the total evacuation of Japanese Americans from the West Coast, it was able to acquire facilities in less than half a year—no mean feat during wartime. Built under the direction of the U.S. Army Corps of Engineers, the camps contained "theater of operations" barracks and messhalls that could be assembled quickly and had been used in the past for a variety of military and civilian purposes. A comparison of panoramic photographs in the National Archives reveals similarities between the camps for Japanese Americans and some of the more permanent camps established by the Civilian Conservation Corps (CCC), though the latter were built on a smaller scale for fewer residents. The camps for Japanese Americans, like those for the CCC, were controlled first by the Department of War, with civilian agencies providing social programs and services under a military regimen. Of course, the CCC camps were voluntary, whereas the camps for Japanese Americans were not.[42]

As early as April 1942, Milton Eisenhower conferred with western governors and their aides about the feasibility of setting up small work camps as in the 1930s. This strategy would have dispersed the evacuated population as widely as necessary to meet current labor needs, concentrating them in small numbers around existing communities with available employment instead of building new communities for the entire group. Under this plan, the children would have attended normal public schools. But state officials were vehemently opposed to the plan; they wanted concentration camps and called them exactly that. Their imagery was more severe than that of federal civilian officials trying to soften the impact of racial exclusion. Western governors, with the exception of Ralph Carr of Colorado, were in favor of armed guards accompanying work groups leaving camp, plus a guarantee that none of the evacuated population would remain in their states after the war. From this point onward, federal plans necessarily centered on concentration rather than dispersal, at least until a resettlement program could be implemented without stirring up public outcry and risking violence.[43]

Eisenhower recommended putting Japanese Americans to work on undeveloped land—hardly a surprising suggestion from a former employee of the Department of Agriculture. A plan subsequent to the one proposed by Eisenhower, developed under Dillon Myer in the summer of 1942, called for work programs drawing labor temporarily out of a planned community to which they would return, but which they would eventually leave for good when resettlement on the outside could be arranged. This community, as long as it existed, would be self-supporting. Ideally, it would contribute labor and goods to war production as well as engage in public works projects such as irrigation and land reclamation. It was thought that such an endeavor, even if temporary, could become a community in most senses of the word, except that its council, its schools, and its economy would be under the administrative control of the federal government.[44]

Running into opposition as they attempted to develop policies for the evacuated population, federal civilian officials felt varying degrees of ambivalence about their helping role. They had not created the camps, after all. But, reflecting the activist policy traditions of the 1930s, they hoped that efficient planning and community education could mitigate the dislocation that had taken place in the lives of Japanese Americans. Milton Eisenhower took the job of WRA director because he was asked personally by President Roosevelt to run the new agency, but he felt growing regret in his short tenure until he managed to transfer to the Office of War Information. Within the WRA before and after Eisenhower's departure in June 1942, conflict arose among staff members in the central office over whether there should be social policies at all in the camps, and whether it was even appropriate to seek the maximum possible benefit of social programs and community development. One view was that there should only be maintenance functions to keep people busy until something else could be worked out. Another view continued to emphasize small work camps, regional dispersal, and planned resettlement such as had been implemented with some success in the past for other groups. A minority view, which did not prevail in early policy discussions, was that nothing should be done if there were any chance of pursuing a less restrictive policy in the near future after public opinion had settled down. In spite of qualms, the idea of self-sufficient communities of some duration was widely publicized and became central to the administrative vision of the camps in the first few months of operation. The idea strongly appealed to some administrators even after a resettlement program was launched in 1943.[45]

Two of the camps, Poston and Gila in Arizona, were on lands under the jurisdiction of the Office of Indian Affairs. The Indian connection became an important one in the creation of educational policy for the camps. In the early months of policy formation, especially for education and other social services, WRA administrative activity was more extensive on the West Coast than in Washington, D.C. The obvious reasons were the location of the excluded population and the need for continuing negotiation with the Western Defense Command and its WCCA. In 1942 the San Francisco office had three times as many employees as the WRA office in Washington. A less obvious reason was that the large regional office in San Francisco was forging ahead with community policies while the Washington staff tried to negotiate wider dispersal of Japanese Americans into small work camps modeled on prior social programs. In early April, when Milton Eisenhower proposed such a plan of dispersal in Washington, the assistant director of the western regional office in San Francisco had already prepared a proposal for a community management division to develop and administer planned communities. Within days the office had prepared its first "regional instruction" on education, long before a national policy had been formulated.[46]

The greater interest in stable communities over transient camps within the western regional office grew out of the prior experience of its top leadership, which was closely linked to New Deal programs for American Indians and especially to the experiments in progressive education with Navajo children. The WRA's western regional director, E. R. Fryer, came from being superintendent of the Navajo

Indian Reservation in Arizona. He brought with him, as the first acting head of the WRA's Education Section, Lucy W. Adams, who had directed the school system at the Navajo Reservation in the late 1930s. Adams habitually reported progress on school planning to Willard Beatty, national director of education in the Office of Indian Affairs and a past president of the Progressive Education Association.[47]

From April to midsummer of 1942, the WRA's regional office in San Francisco developed policies that mimicked the community schools set up for Navajos during the 1930s. Those schools, still operating in the 1940s, had been designed to integrate schooling with a planned community life in which federal authorities attempted to instill the social competencies thought to be necessary for living in contemporary society. From the standpoint of the Indian Service staff in the WRA's regional office in San Francisco, the evacuated Japanese Americans were a familiar quantity: a dependent population under federal authority. Under the leadership of Lucy Adams, the regional office developed policies that called for community schools, a "core" program of progressive education plus state and college entrance requirements, compulsory attendance for ages six to eighteen, an option for half-time apprentice training or work experience for those over age sixteen, some vocational training for all students, instruction in English only; Japanese language schools were not permitted. Anticipating that Japanese American children would lose ground in their schooling because of the evacuation, the planners also hoped that WRA public schools could operate throughout the year and provide an education at least as good as what the children received in their home communities before the war.[48]

These policies evolved through successive meetings until they were codified in an administrative instruction issued by the Washington office in August, laying out the policy for the schools. The WRA proceeded to recruit public school teachers through its regional offices and contacts in existing federal programs, including the Office of Indian Affairs. In hiring teachers, the WRA bypassed and largely ignored the educational initiatives taking place in the assembly centers, even though some of the Nisei leaders sent letters and reports to communicate what they were doing and make recommendations on the educational needs of the children. In the school system being designed by WRA, Japanese Americans would fill hundreds of jobs as assistants and trainees under Caucasian supervision. [49]

Taking shape only after the evacuation had already occurred in the spring of 1942, the vision of planned communities affected official thinking in a way that would have a great impact on the children of war. It became a working assumption that these isolated camps could speed up the assimilation of Japanese Americans into the dominant pattern of American life, in much the same way that social programs in the 1930s had helped to relocate needy groups in the social order. Inevitably, an element of rehabilitation crept into the picture, an assumption, sometimes stated and otherwise left implicit, that Japanese Americans were in the camps partly because of a cultural pathology that must now be corrected. A congressional committee had presaged this tacit fixing of blame as early as March 1942 when it concluded that "resettlement must depend upon a determination to Americanize the Japanese-American community." Some months later, the superintendent of schools at the Minidoka Relocation Center argued that Japanese Americans before the war, including the citizens among them, "had little opportunity to practice the principles of democracy, but here . . . is a chance ready-made to live such experiences and thus be made aware of the advantages of our country."[50]

Those who directed the educational program believed that the schools in the camps could become even more important in the lives of children than the schools they had attended before the war, because all the features of community life would be close at hand: town councils, diverse occupations, health care, recreation, law enforcement, enterprises. "Help the child," urged the administrative manual, "to adjust himself to the broader environment of the total community at the center and compare it with the more desirable aspects of living in a normal American community." An education report from Poston went so far as to argue that the camp itself was "an educational institution in its entirety—in a much truer sense than is the case with any normal community even in abnormal times."[51]

Faced with the challenge of creating an entire school system over one summer, Adams and other WRA planners maintained contact with educators who could provide assistance in designing programs. For example, the educational planners sought and received help, during the summer of 1942, from a graduate seminar in curriculum taught by Paul R. Hanna, a professor of education at Stanford University who was an expert on planned change and community schools. After visiting Tule Lake Relocation Center in Northern California, the members of his seminar delivered to the WRA's western regional office a proposal arguing that the curriculum of the schools should be based upon processes of work and community life as experienced directly by the students and their families. The document later went to all the camps as recommended guidelines for setting up the curriculum of the schools and for orienting teachers. Its concepts were also central to the discussions of an educational planning conference, called by the director of the WRA's western regional office in July of 1942 and attended by the educational staff and consultants for all ten relocation centers.[52]

The Stanford proposal recommended a curriculum for meshing school and community life as closely as possible. This curriculum would be organized around an integrative theme, such as "adaptation of our socio-economic arrangements to the control and direction of technological development." School learning, then, would reflect the experiences available in the community, thus giving traditional book learning a social context and meaning. Yet, these were peculiar communities, not at all like the ones in which the graduate students and educational planners had grown up. The implications of this difference were enormous for the educational process being implemented in the camps. As one illustration, a chart on the scope and sequence of the curriculum, shown in the Stanford proposal and subsequently used for curriculum planning in the camps, placed the administrative structure of the camps on a horizontal axis and educational objectives for each grade level on a vertical axis. One would plan the curriculum, then, by connecting educational objectives with administrative functions within the camps. The "community" of these community schools was federal authority itself. Unwittingly, the structure of the curriculum had been designed to mirror not the normal world outside, but the bureaucratic divisions of responsibility that the government had set up for managing the incarceration.[53]

The WRA's educational planners were aware of the possibilities for social control under such conditions, but they were optimistic that it could be used for a good purpose. These compact communities under federal authority "presented a controlled situation whereby many educational ventures might be undertaken," wrote a curriculum supervisor in 1942. Describing the program in *Education for Victory,* the magazine published by the U.S. Office of Education during the war, an architect of school policy for the camps declared that these new schools "can become, in a measure often dreamed of by educators but seldom realized, an effective instrument of community planning and building." Educators writing in other journals at the time evoked the experimental value of communities that, though born of military necessity, could be turned to positive ends through the redeeming use of appropriate educational practices. A curriculum report from Minidoka in Idaho, summarizing the initial planning of the schools, pointed out that "there were no traditions, practices, or ties that would prevent the adoption of an extremely progressive type of curriculum or even a very radical one if so desired."[54]

The purpose of these schools, as defined by the WRA's *Community School Forum* in an article by Lucy Adams, was to guide students toward "behavior or generalized controls of conduct which, if developed, will lead to the realization of the democratic ideal." As in many normal schools, this process of learning would be enhanced, and could even become "democracy in action," through such things as student councils, clubs, and parent-teacher associations. Following a pattern that had met with approval in many public schools in California, students would gain perspective on their social development in a core class that combined English and Social Studies to teach common ideals of democratic citizenship. The traditional cognitive activities of schooling would be harnessed to the "dynamics of social action," again in the words of the *Community School Forum,* so that social life and the resources of the community could be used as "power tools" to improve traditional modes of learning. One administrator, conscious of the importance of such ideas in the evolution of educational theory during the previous decades, observed that the curriculum proposed for the camps reflected that of schools selected for the prestigious Eight-Year Study, sponsored by the Progressive Education Association, which had measured the success of progressive methods for college-bound students in American schools.[55]

Although the educational policy for the camps at least caricatured the thinking of respected educators in the United States, it must also be remembered that many educators, even those who helped in designing programs for Japanese Americans during the war, were deeply ambivalent about public, and especially federal, authority. The controlled setting of the camps magnified a set of issues that was troubling many leaders of American education. The war, while increasing efficiency and cooperation in public institutions, was also making educational planners aware of the perils of national mobilization and its attendant forms of social control. Discipline was perhaps better than ever in the schools, accentuated by the federally sponsored High School Victory Corps, but many educators feared that there was a danger of sacrificing tolerance, democratic values, and human dignity if paramilitary programs and propaganda were to transform the culture of the school. Similarly, the vocational aspect of schooling was never more apparent than in wartime. This emphasis, most educators would agree, was good for achieving the nation's strategic aims. But much of what education was all about could be lost in the rush to accelerate industrial production for the war. Then again, centralization and national leadership were necessary during wartime; yet, educators distrusted such tendencies. With these conflicts built into their helping role, the educational planners tried to offer a solution that, they believed, would maximize the opportunities of Japanese Americans as much as possible under the circumstances. It is clear from the evidence that they had little idea the camps would become such restricted communities when they helped to design a progressive strategy of community schools.[56]

Despite good intentions on the part of its creators, the proposed educational strategy held the danger of making the coercive environment of the camps the "community" that would socialize the children. The efficiency of relating school work to local community life, and the oppressive features of doing so, were nowhere more manifest than in the opportunities for vocational education. WRA policy specified that students above the age of sixteen could spend half their school time in various industrial, commercial, agricultural, and homemaking programs of vocational education. Until some arrangements with the National Youth Administration fell through, there were plans to link up the training in the camps with diverse federal channels for training and job placement. Only a few of the many promising connections, however, notably some war industries and Farm Security Administration camps for seasonal agricultural labor, led to large movements of Japanese American workers into jobs, and most of those jobs turned out to be temporary. Because of these exigencies, vocational education became tied more directly to life in the camps than to work opportunities on the outside. The camps themselves, wrote one educator, would become "the major textbook" for the discovery of vocational futures.[57]

Federal planners still hoped that the camps, far from being oppressive under such circumstances, could address the problems created by the evacuation of so many schoolchildren from normal school districts. Though segregated, these schools were to provide accelerated socialization for normal life. Though isolated geographically, they would function as channels to the main currents of American culture. And though temporary, they represented the conviction that a positive change could be made in the lives of Japanese Americans as a result of the misfortune that had befallen them.

2

The
First
Year
Inside

"SCHOOL is school, and you must go," wrote a girl in the seventh grade at Poston after classes had begun in the fall of 1942. One of every four Japanese Americans in the camps was a child who did precisely that during the 1942–43 school year. Besides being racially segregated, these camps and their public schools were far-flung: Manzanar and Tule Lake in eastern California, Minidoka in Idaho, Topaz in Utah, Heart Mountain in Wyoming, Amache in Colorado, Poston and Gila in Arizona, Jerome and Rohwer in Arkansas. The schoolchildren exiled to these barren sites inhabited tarpaper barracks with their families in remote deserts, prairies, and swamplands. They received instruction from about 600 Caucasian teachers, 50 certified Japanese American teachers, and 400 Japanese American assistant teachers. The ratio of students to teachers, often taken as one indicator of the quality of education, ran well above national norms for that year: 48 to 1 for elementary schools, 35 to 1 for secondary, while the combined ratio for all public schools in the nation was just over 28 students per teacher. Shortcomings notwithstanding, the WRA had succeeded in establishing public schools for the children of war. The officials charged with administering these schools believed that the programs could be effective and humane, that what happened in the classroom could compensate for the loss of normal community life.[1]

After their arrival, parents and students encountered a barren world far removed from the administrative vision. Teachers observed the hesitancy, ranging from amiable shyness to stage fright, as their pupils "looked around for the familiar blackboard and found none, for desks and found only rudely constructed tables and benches without backs, for books and saw a heterogeneous collection unrelated to their needs." The teacher at Minidoka who made this observation remarked that the children were no less bewildered than the teachers when they saw about them a sea of Japanese faces in segregated classrooms. "I never saw so many Japanese in all my life," remarked an eleventh grader in a school essay at Tule Lake. Before the war, these children had mingled with Caucasian classmates in the public schools; now, they were isolated from the world of normal communities. Three years later, writing just before graduating from high school, a student remembered, of those first days in camp, that an "incomprehensible air of tension hung over the confines of the entire center. Twenty thousand souls brooding. It was not pleasant."[2]

The teachers, too, were anxious. "The very first sensation was one of fright," wrote a teacher at Poston. The government truck that transported the educational staff around that camp was nicknamed by them "the hearse." It unnerved teachers when they arrived, not to the smoothly functioning planned community described by WRA officials, but to an unfinished camp of tarpaper barracks. They found there nothing resembling a school. Several classes were to take place simultaneously in a 20-by-120-foot room lacking partitions. In some instances, when too few or no classrooms were available, teachers assembled their students in messhalls, amidst the clatter of setting tables and cleaning up, until more facilities could be constructed. Many teachers did not report to work as school opened, leaving positions unfilled at the last moment. Many who came had never seen a Japanese face before, except in magazines or movies. "All the faces look alike," complained some of the teachers. Many had difficulty pronouncing and remembering the names of their students. Veterans of many years in the schools were sometimes unsure whether they could maintain control of the classroom in the new and unfamiliar environment of the camps. War propaganda against the enemy no doubt impelled some teachers to find disloyalty in the least unruliness, sedition in adolescent cheek. When the students filed into class, though, it was the initial silence that unsettled many teachers. That mass of Japanese faces on the first day struck not a few of them as "something out of another world."[3]

The majority of teachers probably had taken their jobs because they genuinely wanted to help during the national emergency. Altruism took on many shades of meaning, however, in places where few people had known Japanese Americans face to face. In the barren hinterlands where they were located, the camps were the largest and most immediate manifestation of the nation's war effort. For teachers who worked in these places, the call of duty was sweetened by relatively high wages compared to those offered in school districts in rural states. Many teachers were older women who had not taught for a few years after having stopped to raise their families. They decided that by working temporarily in the camps they could show their patriotism and make a contribution during a time of great need. Some teachers, including a few who had worked with Japanese Americans on the West Coast and in Hawaii, came to the camps at great sacrifice to themselves because they wanted to alleviate the injustice that they felt had been done to loyal citizens. Others were missionaries who had returned from faraway places at the onset of world war. A few were conscientious objectors whose pacifism brought them to the camps as an alternative form of service during wartime.

Whatever their motives, many teachers experienced inner conflicts when they started the school year in the camps. One teacher, never before confronted so blatantly with the color line in American society, said he had not realized until then that he was Caucasian. Another wondered what he would say to returning soldiers when they asked him what he had done for the cause while they had been fighting. "Or suppose my son asks me later, 'Where were you, Daddy, during the last war?' and I have to say, 'Sonny, I was out teaching the Japanese.'" On matters of race the teachers were neither saints nor villains, neither more nor less prone to prejudice than other Americans during the war. They were ordinary people who saw themselves as serving their country, while trying to give Japanese American pupils an education, just as they would children in any community.[4]

Parents, students, and teachers had one thing in common as school began in the fall of 1942. They were all anxious about what sort of education could take place under the circumstances. At Topaz, the camp that sat on a dry lake bed in the Utah desert, classes were barely under way when children observed the construction of a peripheral fence and guard towers as they played after school. Similar constraints appeared ubiquitously in the social environment: policies restricting entry and exit, curfews, bed checks at night, lights out at a certain hour, food rationing, clothing allowances, low fixed wages for menial labor. Nevertheless, classes began with many hopeful signs of forbearance and cooperation, no less than a pioneering spirit according to many accounts. Once the anticipatory fear had been dispelled, parents and students were quick to show their gratitude that teachers had come to the camps, that there would be schools preparing the children for their return to normal society. If Caucasian teachers and Japanese American families agreed about anything besides the uncertainty they faced, it was the exalted value of formal education for securing the future of the children.

These are essential characters in any school—parents, students, teachers. But like social institutions anywhere, the camp schools were subject to other contingencies. Administrative crisis was inevitable after an order to build instantaneous cities where none had existed. The suddenness of government policy soon bogged down in the lethargy of government bureaucracy. A librarian complained of the "red tape that seems to be the only crop that grows here at Topaz." Even more discouraging than the inanity of requisition procedures was the public opposition, the barrage of hectoring recrimination, that developed around the camps. Among the targets chosen by local politicians and the press was the construction of school facilities. Many schoolhouses remained plans on paper, as the U.S. Congress, influenced by constituent pressure, regularly cut back needed funds in the budget for supplies and services in the camps. Food, buildings, equipment, tools, and vehicles—all provoked controversy among people on the outside whose inclinations were more punitive than those of the federal bureaucrats and educational planners who saw the camps as an opportunity to do some good.[5]

One effect of these obstacles was a scarcity of supplies in the schools. "We were shocked to discover," recalled a Japanese American teacher, "that all the school barracks were absolutely bare." At first, students attended classes with few or no books, blackboards, pencils, chairs, tables, shelves, tools, art supplies, or typewriters. Science equipment was out of the question. "In the grammar school classrooms," reported a Caucasian principal to the Tule Lake community council that first autumn, "youngsters are to be seen every day sitting on the floor and using for desks cracked benches the surfaces of which are so rough that no decent performance can be expected of them." Edith Waterman at Poston recalled that younger students arriving to her class in the morning "carried chairs—often holding them up and saying—'See! see! My Daddy made this chair for me.' Older children made their own seats, three-legged stools, from mesquite trees fringing the southern-most part of the camp." At Heart Mountain a student later wrote in a composition about starting school that "some rooms had no desks and we had to sit on benches without backs like Abe Lincoln did." In the huge barracks room, he remembered, "you could hear the class on both sides and everything became just a jumble."[6]

Nor were these the only deficiencies: even shelter and the most rudimentary means of movement to and from places of learning were unreliable because of the places where the camps had been constructed. On some days the schools could not open because of the bad weather—dust storms, blizzards, swampy pools, clay mud. "When I finally got to the class, my hair was white with dust," recalled a ninth grader at Poston in a camp history written collectively by his class. The dust storms at Topaz were so ferocious that all movement and conversation stopped for the interim, whether for minutes or hours. Occasionally it was not possible to see from one side of the classroom to the other, so terrific was "this sultry heat and this inescapable dust," as a young Nisei woman described it. Lacking supplies, beleaguered by inclement weather, conducting large classes without sound insulation between adjacent groups of students of various ages, teachers started the year anyway. Inadequate schools, as an administrator at Manzanar pointed out, were better than unsupervised leisure for so many children without space to play and living in one room with their families.[7]

The problems of scarcity extended to teachers as well. The National Education Association (NEA) reported a nationwide teacher shortage of 50,000 to 60,000 at the beginning of the war. This figure increased rapidly as many teachers left for higher paying jobs in war industries. By the end of the 1942–43 school year, the number of teachers leaving their positions had increased from the normal yearly rate of 93,000 (about 1 in 10 teachers across the nation) to 189,000 for that year. Teacher attrition was a problem not limited to the camps for Japanese Americans; a major study of education during the war concluded that the lack of qualified personnel was one of the most serious problems facing the schools everywhere in the nation. In public schools, just as in the camps, one result was that many poorly qualified teachers, the least likely to grasp the

*Two children walking
on F Street in Heart
Mountain, Wyoming,
September 18, 1942.
The tooth-shaped peak
in the background is
the camp's namesake.*

many new opportunities created by accelerated wartime production, were instructing the nation's young.[8]

The WRA compounded the problem with bureaucratic bungling in the intitial recruitment and hiring of teachers. At first, its regional offices were given central authority for hiring, on the assumption that existing networks of federal programs and contacts with state departments of education could draw a cadre of experienced teachers. But camp officials rankled under this arrangement, for in every camp the policy of central control yielded too small a pool of teachers to staff the school system. Even by the end of the first summer, before the schools had opened, it became necessary to give greater autonomy to educational officials in each camp, allowing them to recruit on their own. The result was a fragmented process of recruiting that involved WRA regional offices, the U.S. Employment Service, the Office of Indian Affairs, and other federal agencies, state departments of education, local school officials, and contacts within universities. The composition of the teaching force reflected this fragmentation, juxtaposing rural traditionalists and urban Californians, Indian school veterans and retired schoolmarms from western towns, suspicious patriots and activist conscientious objectors.[9]

Side by side on the same staff one could find teachers with very diverse backgrounds. At Minidoka, for example, taught Helen Amerman, who was from Connecticut and had a B.A. from Michigan State and an M.A. from Stanford, where she had been a student in Paul Hanna's summer seminar that developed the progressive curriculum proposal for the camps. Her fellow teacher Albert Ficke, by contrast, was a westerner; he had received his M.A. from the University of Idaho and had worked previously for a New Deal program, the Soil Conservation Service of the U.S. Department of Agriculture. Other teachers from federal programs at Minidoka had come from the Civilian Conservation Corps, the National Youth Administration, the Indian Service, and the Works Projects Administration. Another teacher, Iona Sifton, was a native of the state, and her highest degree was a B.S. from the University of Idaho. Alma Plemmons had received her B.S. from the University of Texas and had been principal of a segregated "Mexican school" in that state. Ecco Hunt, a missionary type, had an M.A. from the Berkeley Baptist Divinity School and had been teaching before the war at a school for girls in Burma. Jessie Sistermans, a native of Berkeley, had been teaching high school in Los Angeles when the war broke out; like Edith Waterman, she followed her students into exile. Jewell Boatwright, of Jefferson, Texas, returned to teaching when the war came, having long ago earned a degree at East Texas State Teachers College.[10]

The administrators were just as diverse. The superintendent of schools at Minidoka, R. A. Pomeroy, was an Idaho native who had been principal of Boise Junior High School before the war. Minidoka's high school principal was Jerome T. Light, a Stanford graduate and staunch defender of progressive education; he went on to earn his doctorate at Stanford after the war with a dissertation under Paul Hanna on the school system at Minidoka. The director of industrial arts, in contrast to both the Idaho educator and the Stanford-trained progressive, was Charles Fleischman, who had a B.A. from Northern State Teachers College in South Dakota; he had been an educational administrator for the Civilian Conservation Corps before Pearl Harbor. Like the teachers, the school administrators represented an odd assortment of professional histories, subsequently reflected in their working assumptions about the nature of education in the camps.[11]

Miles Carey's experience (he was superintendent of schools at Poston) is one example of the extraordinary effort required to secure teachers. Concerned that the education of Japanese Americans not deteriorate because of the evacuation, he personally contacted nearly 700 teachers for employment in the first school year. He traveled around the West, partly at his own expense, to talk with prospective teachers. Unlike superintendents in the other camps, he was able to sign up more than enough candidates for the 101 positions authorized for Poston. Only 72 came, however, and 2 of those left as soon as they saw the place. Attrition compounded the problem; by December, Carey hired 19 more teachers, but 12 of those who came at the beginning of the school year had resigned by then. Only 55 teachers stayed the whole year. The average tenure of teachers at Poston during the first year was 4.8 months. Despite Carey's personal commitment to finding teachers similar to those who had taught Japanese Americans before the war, the administration at Poston later acknowledged that "a number of teachers over retirement age in other systems were hired, and almost no recent graduates of teacher training institutions were secured."[12]

While Carey searched far and wide for appropriate teachers, most of the superintendents recruited teachers more aggressively in states where their camps were located. At Jerome and Rohwer in Arkansas, for instance, almost all of the teachers were from the South, mostly from Arkansas. There were some good reasons for this strategy, not the least of which was the desire to give the camp schools a visible connection to the local school system. Ideally, this strategy would enhance the legitimacy of schooling under such unusual circumstances. Some early memoranda from the Washington office evinced a hope, never fulfilled, that states might eventually incorporate the camps as normal school districts by passing the necessary legislation. As it turned out, federal efforts to hire locally were vilified by the press. A frequent complaint was that teacher salaries were higher in the camps than in local districts (similar charges had been leveled at New Deal programs in previous years). A federal study showed this to be true in Arkansas, Idaho, Colorado, Utah, and Wyoming, but not in Arizona and California. Even in states where there was a difference in monthly salaries, critics failed to inform their readers that teachers in the camps worked continuously for eleven months of the year, since the schools operated on a year-round schedule.[13]

Encountering such local resistance to its hiring practices, the WRA continued to recruit selectively in other parts of the nation. This strategy, in turn, met with congressional and other opposition organized nationally, demonstrating how difficult it was to establish schools under centralized authority where no true communities existed. The response of the federal government to this predicament was to hire willy-nilly, taking whatever was available, losing most to attrition, then recruiting more from a shrinking supply. An administrator at Topaz remembered, "our judgement in the selection of personnel was tempered all too freely by the urgency of obtaining the needed employees."[14]

Even a take-all procedure did not prove resistant to the encroachments of red tape. Through its memoranda of agreement with state departments of education, the federal government had created a dual employment status for teachers in the camps. They had to meet federal civil service requirements, and they had to satisfy the certification requirements for teaching in the state where the camp was located. This original understanding became unwieldy in practice; at best, it seemed to many teachers an unrewarding complication for what in any event was only temporary employment. The allure of civil service employment vanished when it was discovered that no tenure or opportunity for promotion into other federal positions accompanied the teaching posts available in the camps. Being a civil service employee had disadvantages as well, such as the requirement that teachers work the standard office hours expected of other administrative employees. Unlike these other employees, they also prepared classes, evaluated student materials, participated in seminars and other activities designed for their continuing education, and attended instructional planning meetings on Saturday mornings.[15]

Disgruntled with the conditions they found at the camps, teachers then suffered a further indignity. Sometimes they were not viewed as peers by educators outside the camps because of their federal status and the "charity" stigma of social programs (again echoing earlier grumbling about New Deal jobs). Among some local constituencies this stigma was reinforced by negative attitudes toward any attempt to provide services to people of Japanese descent. These degrading features of employment in the camps, along with the general scarcity of teachers across the nation during the war, resulted in a small pool of eligible recruits and a high attrition rate, which brought a succession of inadequate and ambivalent teachers to many classes.

Teachers had not known what to expect when they came to work in the camps. "It feels like anything but a schoolroom," said a teacher at Amache after classes had started. Two teachers elsewhere wrote that they found the students "ambitious and cooperative, perhaps a bit more serious minded than their Caucasian contemporaries." To well-meaning teachers these were good students on the whole, flocking tentatively but not without hope into classrooms. The perception of this reality made their job all the more confusing, as they labored "to teach the fundamental freedoms upon which our democracy is based in a classroom from whose windows the guard towers are plainly visible." To teachers in the camps, no matter what their own views on Japanese Americans, this contradiction was unavoidable, a fact of life, fully present and immanent in every lesson. "The barbed wire fence, the guards standing at attention with their rifles poised, the reaction of their parents; these speak eloquently to these children and youth," reflected one discouraged teacher. For most teachers the situation was too confusing, the rewards too small, the hardship too great to merit enduring more than a few months.[16]

Despite the high rates of attrition, some of the camps reported that while many teachers soon quit their jobs, a small core group of those who remained became skilled at using the peculiar situation of the school to educational advantage. This group reportedly maintained strong morale and good relations with their students. Martha Hays, one such teacher at Poston, discerned two groups among the

Caucasian staff, one interested in the salary, the other devoted to the people. "In this camp," she observed, "there are also two groups of living quarters for Caucasians—one is separated from the camp by firebreaks and fields of broccoli, and is of white frame construction like the Administration Building near which it stands; the other quarters are black barracks in the middle of camp. The Caucasians may live where they choose," she continued, "and somewhat select themselves according to their reason for being here, those with the salary interest occupying the more remote but more comfortable quarters." Hays was one of several teachers who not only lived in the black barracks but opened their own living quarters to students after hours. "While the teacher graded papers," she recalled in a personal narrative at the end of the war, "there were lively discussions of the days in San Diego and Santa Anita, 'agitation' (good-natured razzing about the opposite sex), and talk of school, parties, and even the more serious business of religion."[17]

The room of Edith Waterman became a similar refuge for both students and their parents, stocked with cookies and candies she supplied at her own expense. "If the room were human and could speak, many a varied tragic story it might tell," she later wrote. "From my visitors, I learned that they, too, were not without fears, disappointments, sorrows and sicknesses." Several teachers who established such rapport with the children and their families tried to alleviate the bleakness of camp life by shopping for them in nearby towns, bringing back items not available in the messhalls and government supply rooms. A few Caucasian educators went even further than living in the barracks; they sent their own children to these schools, as did Jerome T. Light, whose son, Thomas Light, appears among the Japanese faces of his classmates in the high school yearbook, several pages after the picture of his father, who was principal of the school. Among other connections between the educators and the incarcerated population, some teachers at Poston worked with students and parents to build adobe schools, "mixing by hand this alkaline soil from the desert," recalled Katharine Sheckler, a seventh grade teacher, "and pressing it into molds to dry in the heat of the sun."[18]

Notwithstanding the compassion of some, all teachers worked in a context whose essential features had been defined by social policy. Even the most unprejudiced of them could not hope to change the disparate levels of status that existed in the camps. Some people were free to leave; others, often coworkers and sometimes profes-

*Nursery school children
playing with a class project,
a scale model of the barracks
at Tule Lake, California,
where they and their families
have been incarcerated,
November 9, 1942.*

sional peers, were not. Yet the working conditions of the camps set them side by side in cooperative relationships. All Caucasian staff enjoyed greater privileges, higher pay, superior housing, and, above all, freedom. Their Japanese American colleagues and students lived as restricted citizens.

Another constraint facing the Caucasian teachers who were sympathetic toward Japanese Americans was their own inequality of status within the administration of the camps. For teachers, too, the camps meant isolation, in spite of relative advantages over those who were not there by choice. While their status as Caucasians set them off from the incarcerated community, other factors set them off from the administration as well. Teachers worked at some distance from the central administration, immersed all day in the world of the barracks, exposed to its conflicts in the lives of children. When policies from above disturbed the community, teachers were on the inside, wrestling with the effects of parental anxiety on the emotions of the children. At the same time, teachers had little or no say about the policies affecting the camps. Day by day in their classrooms, teachers were not part of the office culture of the administration, having been relegated, both professionally and socially, to a secondary status between administrator and managed community. A social scientist at Amache observed that teachers were "neither of or with the administration nor are they of or with the Japanese." They were, in varying degrees, cut off from both worlds.[19]

Administrators wanted teachers to disseminate information about federal policy aims, so that the children could serve as a channel to the parents. But the teachers were not living up to their potential, the administrators felt, in carrying out the larger educational—that is, administrative—objectives of the camps. The teachers often did not understand these policy aims themselves. Moreover, they lacked, complained one report, the "fine points of accommodation" with the Japanese American community, the personal rapport and cultural understanding that had been exhibited by white church workers before the war. Caught between great expectations and a daily routine of teaching the ways of democracy to incarcerated citizens, most teachers bailed out as soon as possible. One teacher wrote after leaving Tule Lake, "I suspect Hell may be well-ordered, efficiently run with little friction, and be no less Hell for that. This thing is basically all wrong and all we can do on the project to make things run smoothly will not alter that fact."[20]

Under these circumstances, the ideals of progressive education sounded hollow to the average teacher in the camps. Most teachers—and especially those hired in rural states—were, by their own testimony, practical and straightforward instructors, of the traditional sort, accustomed to recitation, orderly rows of desks, children raising hands and waiting to be called upon. "We don't want any seminars on education," groused one of them after her first round of meetings with university consultants and administrators. "You don't learn anything if you know the Psychology of Education, Theory of Education, History of Education." Another proclaimed: "We don't want John Dewey—went in over my head and never did emerge." Parents tended to agree; they lobbied, through their advisory committees and community councils, for book learning and traditional subjects. They were not only being provincial. The closest thing to normal community life for their school-age children would be a traditional schooling program built around academic subject matter, not community-centered "learning by doing" behind barbed wire. While teachers in most camps incorporated some elements of progressive pedagogy into their classroom practice, very few held to the concept more comprehensively beyond the first year. Many did away with progressivism altogether and taught the state-mandated curriculum without adornment.[21]

Parents and teachers were often of the same mind that the progressive curriculum in the camps should be limited. Parents feared that given the environment of scarcity and involuntary detention, basing the educational program on the idea of a community school would not provide the learning opportunities that the children had experienced in their schools before the war. Teachers had other reasons as well for wanting to treat classrooms as relatively autonomous of the community. One was the sheer difficulty of teaching and controlling a class in the progressive manner that closely linked classroom activities and the productive life of the community. A further reason, stated openly in some instances by teachers and administrators, was a negative view not only of community schools in principle but of the culture of the families who made up the community. To integrate education more closely with community life under these circumstances—for example, to study a community government in which traditional forms of ethnic leadership were prominent—might mean reversing the process of cultural assimilation in which schools were supposed to play a central role.

The personal conflicts of being a teacher were even more difficult for Japanese Americans who taught in the camps. During the early stages of planning after the evacuation, it had been proposed that all teaching—all community services, in fact—be handled by the Japanese Americans themselves. When this idea fell by the wayside, it was replaced by the notion of a planned community, administered by Caucasian bureaucrats from social agencies, providing limited opportunities for management and self-government to the evacuated population. The schools, then, reflected this larger framework of social relations. Contrary to its democratic intent, community schooling incorporated the structure of authority that characterized the operation of the camps. An observer at Poston who watched the induction of 180 teachers reported that the Caucasians and residents stood in separate groups talking while they waited for chairs to arrive for their meeting. When the room was ready, the Caucasians filed in first and sat in the front of the room. They were followed by Japanese American female teaching staff, who congregated in the middle section of seats. Then came the Japanese American male teachers, who took the remaining seats in the back of the room. The observer who recorded this spontaneous event also noted that the Caucasians were generally middle-aged or older, the Japanese Americans much younger.[22]

The incident provides a glimpse into the behavior of Caucasian and Japanese American staff when they met as colleagues. Their assumptions about what seemed natural to do under the circumstances were based not only on courtesy and custom; what seemed natural was a reflection of the relations of power dictated by official policies of the planned community. The disparity occurred even as Caucasians and Japanese Americans worked together as virtual peers. Quite often the disparity seemed to dissolve into friendly informality. But formal inequality—the color line—was restored the minute conflict erupted between the managed community and the administration.

Japanese American teachers were in an ambiguous position, with and without power, working side by side with, but also under, their Caucasian colleagues, almost part of the administration, yet still members of the excluded group, never comfortably integrated into either. Their position made it impossible to ignore the realities of racial subordination, even as they advanced to higher status. Though assistant teachers often taught a full load of courses, they made only nineteen dollars a month and had no civil service status. Because of the shortage of certified teachers, they taught a large percentage of all the classes offered in the camps. For example, they were re-

*Third grade class at
Rohwer, one of the two
camps in Arkansas,
November 22, 1942.*

sponsible for 45 percent of the classes at Tule Lake at the beginning of the first year. At Jerome in Arkansas, the school year began with 12 Caucasian and 48 Japanese American teachers. In addition, they were required to take training courses, often from their Caucasian colleagues, to be eligible to teach at all. In Topaz alone there were reported to be over 800 Japanese American residents with college degrees. Some of them, like Henry Tani, had set up and operated an educational system at the Tanforan Assembly Center, but the administration at Topaz and the other camps had then mostly ignored early schooling initiatives of Japanese Americans, except in setting up nursery schools. Recruited within each camp by the administration, Japanese American assistant teachers were required to participate in in-service training led by Caucasian teachers who were sometimes less educated than they but who held teaching credentials. Young Japanese Americans had reason to doubt the enduring value of any teaching opportunities presented to them in the camps, for they knew they would probably be excluded when they lived and worked on the outside. The WRA made arrangements, nonetheless, with teacher training institutions, such as the University of Idaho for Minidoka and the University of Wyoming for Heart Mountain, to provide credit leading to certification for the "cadet teachers" trained in the camps. In Wyoming teachers of Japanese descent who satisfied the statutory requirements for certification received certificates that were valid only during the war and within the Heart Mountain camp.[23]

From the hundreds of personal histories compiled in WRA education reports it appears that the typical Japanese American teacher in the camps was a Nisei who had graduated from high school with honors in the late 1930s. Having received some art or music training privately while in school, this teacher had probably gone to college for two or three years by the time the war started. Either male or female—for neither predominated on the educational staff in any camp—this novice teacher was most likely a Christian who had prior experience as a Sunday school instructor, YMCA social worker, or helper in a city recreation center. If Buddhist, he or she had worked in social and educational activities for the Young Men's (or Women's) Buddhist Association. It was not unusual for Japanese American teachers to have worked before the war in a family business, perhaps as a part-time bookkeeper, or during seasonal periods of greater demand for labor in agriculture.[24]

During the 1942–43 school year, the WRA administration re-

ported that some of the best teaching was being done by these assistant teachers. Protesting at Heart Mountain, some warned that
they would do "only $19 worth of work." Parents, who wanted schools
at least equivalent to those in their home communities before the
war, expressed a strong preference for Caucasian teachers. Their
suspicions were often reflected in the attitudes of students, who had
been accustomed to thinking that all teachers were Caucasians.
Students and their parents occasionally petitioned the administration to have Japanese American teachers relieved of their duties by
certified Caucasian teachers. "Their inexperience," reported a Nisei
journalist about the novice teachers after surveying high school
students at Minidoka, "leads them into blunders which antagonize
the students." One assistant teacher imagined that the parents were
thinking, "these poor children are being taught by fumbling, inexperienced teachers who would not be allowed to teach anywhere but
in a Japanese evacuee center." But many parents soon came to
appreciate these teachers of their own race—and administrators to
disparage them, even as they admired their energy—because they
were very "subject matter minded" and insisted on formal mastery
of the written curriculum. Parents also remembered and appreciated
the heroic efforts they had made as teachers in the assembly centers
on their own initiative. Many students overcame their initial doubts
and grew to like these novice teachers, often only a few years older
than the high school seniors, for they understood more intimately
the problems created by evacuation. Some Caucasian teachers expressed gratitude for the help they received from such teachers in
learning about Japanese American family culture and the behavior
of the children. [25]

Because of their high level of education, the first wave of Japanese
American teachers and assistants were also the first to leave the
camps as the government began to permit limited opportunities for
resettlement and college study in 1943, while the majority of schoolchildren and their families remained in camp for the duration of the
war. With each passing month after the beginning of 1943, the new
assistant teachers drawn from the incarcerated population were
younger and less experienced than before. Of the well-educated Japanese Americans who taught in the beginning and remained in the
camps even through the first year, many chose to leave teaching
and do office or domestic work instead. They had found the classroom
instruction and extracurricular responsibilities too stressful for the
compensation they received. Once given the choice, the great ma-

jority of these young teachers found the excessive demands of employment in the camps no match for the more attractive opportunities in other professions and further training on the outside.

The students, in the midst of these crosscurrents of scarcity, ambivalence, and subordination, returned to school and made the best of it. "Life in camp started with excitement and regret," scribbled an eleventh grader at Amache in a composition for school. For these children the shock of segregation was not merely the presence of so many people with Japanese faces, but the variety of people brought together by racial exclusion. Like their parents, the children represented different social classes, educational backgrounds, and ambitions for the future. They were also from different places, different types of home communities. At Manzanar the 2400 students in 1942–43 had come from 212 high schools and 148 elementary schools before the war. Some had completed the previous year before being evacuated; others had not and were several months behind. At Topaz many students had been accustomed to midyear promotions, while others had advanced to the next grade at year's end in their home districts.[26]

Moreover, the school population in the camps was distributed unevenly across grade levels. The students beginning first grade were only half as many as those graduating from high school. Teachers found generally that elementary and junior high students adapted more readily to school life in the new setting. But there was a disproportionate number of high school students, and the problems most frequently cropped up in this group. The high school students showed a keener awareness of what had happened to their families when they were forced to leave their homes. These older students also had more to lose in the short term, being on the threshold of college and work. "You can't just *educate*," said one Nisei student; "you've got to educate *for* something." If this was a premonition among the young, it was a frightening crisis for older students. "My life's ambition was to be a nurse," wrote a tenth grader for one of her classes at Minidoka, "and though I think of it often yet, I'm afraid, very much afraid that I will be unable to carry out my plans . . . I have lost interest in school and in leaving; my desire for a nursing career has lessened; and I am a pessimist."[27]

Racial segregation produced new experiences for students. Some complained of the competition; after all, they had been segregated with many high achievers. Others found greater opportunities for being leaders in these schools than they had known before the war.

While experiencing physical hardship and mental anguish, the children were able to perceive the advantages and disadvantages of their new circumstances. They lost what had been familiar to them and gained sights and sounds that alternately bored and startled them: desert sun, lightning, long lines for meals, snakes, vast spaces, nooks among the barracks where they played marbles, dust storms, family quarrels heard through paper-thin walls. Many children spent more hours with their peers, away from the family, than they had been allowed to do before the war, both in school and out. At mealtime in the messhalls, people more often than not sat together by age and language groupings, the old speaking Japanese, the young English.[28]

As their social lives developed under these conditions, children pursued their studies as best they could. After each crisis in the camps—policy pronouncements, strikes and work stoppages, draft registration, demonstrations, and shows of military force—the children appeared disoriented, the adolescents tense, unable to concentrate. Some teachers opened probing discussions in class to release pent-up energy so that students could then turn to their studying, or they assigned compositions that allowed children to voice their discontent. A Nisei girl wrote of the evacuation, "This action will cause the history of the United States to have another black mark: first the Indians, next the Negroes, and now the Japanese . . . And then deportation? Wouldn't the other nations mock at democracy?" One Japanese American teacher at Poston made this strategy the driving force of the curriculum for his classes. "Knowing that repressed emotions are most dangerous in their effect upon clear, unprejudiced and unbiased thinking," he wrote about his approach to teaching eleventh and twelfth graders, "I have endeavored in the class discussions to bring into play all the curious ideas, prejudices, and warped views . . . For the only logical way to re-establish the faith and security of these frustrated and embittered people is through the preservation of the truth, positive and negative, about the various puzzling problems of the American scene."[29]

Sometimes the strategy of open dialogue backfired. A Caucasian teacher at Heart Mountain recalled that while airing opinions in her class, a girl began screaming, "Why did they do this to us? Why weren't they prepared for us when we came to the camps? Why were we treated like animals?" To regain control, the teacher shot back, "We were not prepared for Pearl Harbor, were we?" The tendency to identify these minority citizens with an enemy nation was a strong one, even in the minds of Caucasians who saw themselves as helping the displaced students. But the questions kept coming; at Amache a class discussion on *Working for Democracy,* a standard textbook, launched youthful forays into critical consciousness: "If we are citizens, why are we in concentration camps?" And another student: "Is the United States a real democracy?" One student elsewhere later wrote facetiously, "At Manzanar we had to skip the chapter on civil liberties."[30]

Though never implemented consistently, the progressive vision of schools rooted in community life did help to create dialogue about what was happening to Japanese Americans during the war. To recognize the authentic progressivism that occasionally exerted influence over life behind barbed wire is to grasp more subtly the conflicting social meanings that characterized all ten of the wartime camps. For example, high school seniors took a class called "Problems of Democracy," a highly idealistic part of the progressive curriculum rooted in the ideas of John Dewey and other educational thinkers after the turn of the century. A major concern of this class, and more generally of the combined English and Social Studies classes that were set up throughout junior and senior high school, was that children need to learn to experience their citizenship and develop a broader understanding of the struggle of their society to become free and democratic. Many teachers in the camps used the class to explore the background of evacuation. Most noticeably at Tule Lake in California and Poston in Arizona, they prodded their students to think about historical parallels in the mistreatment of other groups. Pursuing this course of study well beyond state curriculum requirements because they recognized the urgent need of their older students to gain perspective on the evacuation, some teachers introduced their students to the history of civil rights in the United States. At its best, the progressive curriculum encouraged students to think creatively about the status of minority groups in modern society. A frequent theme in student essays and commencement addresses was the hope for greater tolerance in the postwar world.[31]

At Tule Lake some idealistic strands of the progressive vision remained in the schools despite the coercive camp environment. Mary Barbul, who taught the "Problems of Democracy" course for Tule Lake's Tri-State High School, urged her students to come to grips with the experience they were going through and to develop the intellectual perspective for growing in healthy ways. "In the course of study," according to a report by a social scientist examining the school system, "the students have been introduced to elementary sociology and have been given an introduction into the meaning of research and research methods. In this class the seniors have made studies of the various social institutions of the community, the family, the church and the school." The student essays that have survived from such classes occasionally show a remarkable grasp of what was happening to Japanese Americans as a minority group. Some classes bound their essays together as books with original art to describe camp life. These handmade books offer some of the most vital testimony available for understanding the impact of the war years on the younger generation.[32]

More often, as the student essays clearly show, teachers channeled disaffection toward innocuous renditions of civic verities and Americanism. A teacher at Poston asked for papers on democracy, but first, in his own words, he "put a brake on long complaints" by asking only for a definition and brief statement of how the students could make their own contribution as citizens. Also in that camp, however, the students were allowed to vent their negative opinions at school assemblies—a rare occasion even in normal schools. When, at one assembly, a young student leader began, "We hate our teachers because they don't know how to teach," her words were greeted with a roar of laughter from the student body. The vice-president of the senior class told the assembled students and teachers, "We resent teachers who feel *so* sorry for us. We don't want them to feel sorry for us." In a parallel expression of something truly democratic occurring within the camps, the high school paper ran articles muckraking administrative attitudes and the malaise of the camp residents.[33]

Other expressions of criticism were more practical. Large numbers of boys left to work in sugar beet fields when work programs were established; so many, in fact, that parents lobbied for restrictions that would keep them in school. Another sign of disaffection in the schools was the increase of "juvenile delinquency" among the young. The phrase, although used frequently, was in truth too strong for most of what occurred, but it was taken seriously by parents because such things were almost unheard of among Japanese Americans before the war. Several Nisei made recommendations for dealing with the problem through student government, juvenile courts run by Japanese Americans, and special courses to channel aggression toward understanding and accommodation. Meanwhile, in several camps the parents pressured the administration to do something about the problem. One report cited a "worsening trend" of erratic behavior among the young people in the camps: "cheating, talking back to teachers, emotional breakdowns, lack of care of furniture, and general disrespect of faculty members." One camp resident said, "I never dreamed that Japanese children could be this bad," given their usual attitudes toward schooling. Youth gangs emerged in the camps, drawing primarily from prewar associations in cities of the West Coast, especially Los Angeles. Favorite activities included vandalism, petty theft, bullying young boys who attended class, and gate-crashing at parties. Many parents feared that the younger generation was out of control, that the experience of incarceration would do permanent damage to their families.[34]

By contrast, many students participated heartily in the school program and extracurricular activities after the beginning of the year. A great many showed appreciation and good will toward their teachers, and not a few teachers forged lasting friendships with their students. This dual reality, the layering of normal development and profound disjunction, must cast into doubt any one-dimensional depiction of the camps as either a benevolent salvaging of lives or an entirely nefarious oppression. At Amache the elementary students ran a successful cooperative store—a paragon of progressive theory in education—and in every camp there was a plethora of school activities, often seized upon by students as if they were lifeboats in the daily boredom of exile: student government, class associations, newspapers, literary magazines, yearbooks, honors societies, athletic clubs, agricultural groups, all the normal fare of students in schools throughout the United States. From the perspective of the administration, this participation was democracy in action. Perhaps there was, as claimed repeatedly by administrators in their education reports, a pioneering spirit among many students, as well as the more chaotic emotions induced by life in the camps. Students, especially those blessed with good teachers, sometimes embraced the ideals of progressive education. "If we can develop a cooperative spirit," wrote a college-bound Nisei, "we can make this community such a true community and at the same time so improve ourselves that the evils of a concentration camp are not only overcome but capitalized upon."[35]

Yet, as school progressed through the first year in the camps, these beliefs became more tenuous, the signs more disturbing that what was being taught about life in the United States could be

Taught by the progressive curriculum that schools should function as part of the life and work of the community, these children in elementary school at Amache, the camp in Colorado, are doing some landscaping in front of the barracks that is their school, April 24, 1943.

learned but not yet lived. Even social policies designed to be benevolent carried the stamp of authority but not of prior consent. They were being applied to a group so disadvantaged, in this case deprived of their rights by official action, that it had no choice but to submit at least outwardly to the procedure, or else rebel outright and bring greater repression, lacking the power to devise other means of advancement. Photographs in the National Archives show schoolchildren assembled outside their classrooms for the morning flag salute. From where they stood they could often see, in the distance beyond the black barracks, the fence, the watchtowers, and the barren land stretching far away. Under these circumstances the "democracy" of progressive education took on darker meanings than the planners had ever imagined. All the workings of the community were tightly meshed in one square mile within each camp; life and learning were one inside the fence, whether or not educators tinkered with the curriculum. Authority, the sanction of officialdom, was not distant or diffuse, as in most local communities. It was pervasive, close at hand. In practice, democracy meant orderly accommodation to social policies that sought to be as humane and efficient as possible without sacrificing goals determined outside the community. "We feel there is a helping hand coming from the administration," reported one Nisei to a visitor at Topaz, "but we also feel that there is another hand, which grabs this helpful hand and prevents it from reaching us."[36]

The schools in the camps were, like community government, teaching people how to live in an administered democracy for citizens who had been deprived of their civil rights. The analogy between community schools and community government is instructive because it suggests the paradox of an overwhelming authority trying to cultivate self-determination in a dependent population. Democratic procedure had a place subordinate to administrative policy in these planned communities. The WRA's own final report on community government summed up the record: "Community government became in actuality an adjunct of administration . . . It is true that many of the workers were drawn from the community, but the control rested in what came to be known as the 'appointed staff' . . . The result of such managerial control was the institutionalization of the people with almost complete dependence upon the controlling system for food, transportation, employment, housing, clothing, education, health, law enforcement, fire protection, maintenance, etc."[37]

An administrative order at the beginning of the school year prohibited the older generation from holding office and serving on community councils because they were not citizens. The anxiety of community leaders over this situation soon began to turn toward open conflict. The liaison between the administration and the incarcerated community became the inexperienced sons, who were citizens, and not the respected elders of the community, who were classified as enemy aliens. Resistance movements formed at the older camps in California and Arizona, accompanied by resentment toward those younger residents who were able to wield official power in the camps because of administrative rules. These people, Nisei males, were in a position to distribute administrative favors, articulate their own understanding of community opinion, and inform the administration of troublemakers. As children attended school, their family culture was in turmoil because of the impact of policy on traditional leadership and paternal authority.

This situation became a crisis in the fall of 1942 at Poston and Manzanar. The aftershocks of events in these two camps touched the life of the schools in all of the camps to varying degrees. In both Poston and Manzanar the Nisei males who had gained official power, many of them members of the Japanese American Citizens League, were suspected by other community members of having given information before the war that resulted in the internment of Issei leaders by the U.S. Department of Justice immediately after the attack on Pearl Harbor. Rumors circulated in camp that a few of the Nisei had taken advantage of other community members and benefited financially during the spring of 1942 by providing misleading advice while affirming the policy of evacuation, so that they could obtain the most favorable positions in the camps. Many residents also felt that a few leaders were engaged in corrupt practices in the camp enterprises, gaining money and favors from their key positions in the distribution system for goods and services. Whether or not these suspicions were all true, a beating of one Nisei male at Poston led to a general strike when one of the alleged assailants was locked up. The community seemed unsympathetic with the victim of the beating.

At Manzanar the causes were similar but bound up in a growing list of grievances from all sides: sugar rations, crowded housing, a corrupt cooperative store, inadequate clothing, promised school buildings, secret policy making, no understanding of community needs. These grievances were precipitated into threats of violence by the animosity that many people felt toward the young Nisei citizens who had apparently benefited from the administrative arrangements of the camp. After a Nisei was severely beaten, and a suspect was subsequently arrested at the behest of the administration, the military police overreacted to a protesting crowd and left two people dead at Manzanar, one of them a high school student, on the first anniversary of Pearl Harbor.

In the weeks leading up to the Manzanar protest, an underground movement had developed to oppose self-government and to educate people about the reasons for resisting the administered democracy in the camp. Hand-drawn posters in Japanese argued that the majority opposed self-government because they had lost everything and had no control of events. No one should believe the "sweet words," in one translation, of the War Relocation Authority; instead, the U.S. Army should supply the needs of its prisoners: "We fellow Japanese are all like fish on the cutting board, about to be sliced," declared one notice, tacked up surreptitiously in messhalls. "There is considerable weight to their arguments," conceded the project director at Manzanar, even as he tried to suppress the movement. Another notice, again in Japanese, warned, "Attention: We do not recognize any necessity for a self-government system. We should oppose anything like this as drawing a rope around our neck. Let the Army take care of everything." The press in western states seized upon the fracas to whip up animosity toward Japanese Americans, suggesting that unrest in the camps proved their disloyalty to the United States.[38]

Although the issues of community leadership and self-government did not produce such open conflict in the other eight camps, they did become focal points for discussing various frustrations. Councils resigned frequently when they could not carry out the will of their constituents. Cleavages developed between the formal apparatus of community government and the informal coalitions of Issei elders. Most residents came to see their barracks block as the primary organizational unit in the governance of the camps. Their frame of reference became its hierarchy of kith and kin, instead of the official power of the community government, much as would have been the case in a village, an isolated town, or even a big city ward. At Minidoka, the extreme case of apathy toward the idea of limited democracy, no community council could be formed until 1944. Before that, the community repeatedly voted down all charters presented to it.[39]

These community patterns added an element of unreality to the lessons about democracy in the core curriculum of the schools. An

illustration of how community frustrations entered school governance can be found in the case of Heart Mountain, where the teachers left a record of their own reactions to the democratic aspirations
of these involuntary planned communities. They had begun teaching
with a deliberate strategy of ignoring recent events in the lives of
Japanese Americans, but soon realized that their students could not
do anything until they began to make some sense of what was happening to them in the camps. Many teachers, especially those who
lived in the camps and not in nearby towns, overcame their initial
insecurity about teaching people of Japanese descent and made a
sincere effort to get acquainted with them and their parents. There
followed a few pleasant weeks, during the fall of 1942, when a great
deal of informal visiting took place, and many teachers felt that good
relations were being established.

In November a group of parents, considered leading members of
the community, called the teachers and administrators to a meeting
where they presented the community's viewpoint on the educational
background and needs of their children. It was an awkward affair,
marred by poor preparation and long speeches. Parents conveyed
their anxiety that the school system seemed inferior to the schools
their children had attended before the war. They criticized one cen-
trally important administrator who had treated any disagreement
with official policy as evidence of disloyalty to the United States.
This hard-line official had routinely punished community organizers
at Heart Mountain by sending them away from the relocation centers to more restrictive internment camps operated by the U.S. Department of Justice for enemy aliens suspected of espionage and
subversion.[40]

The meeting infuriated most of the teachers who attended. When
interviewed a year later, one of them recalled that she had thought
"the Japanese were attempting to impose their opinions and attitudes on us. I just felt as if they were stuffing them down my throat."
Far from leading to a cooperative democratic community, the orderly
expression of parental views made teachers turn angrily from sympathy to incomprehension, finally to disgust toward the parents of
their students. One teacher fulminated, "they should have realized
that they were expendable and consequently should try to . . . make
something out of the WRA program and the opportunities presented
to them." Teachers believed that they had gone more than halfway
in being as sympathetic as they had been at the outset, only to be
betrayed by parents complaining, telling them what to do in the

schools. After this episode, a "quiet settled antagonism" reigned at Heart Mountain; parents and teachers stayed away from each other.[41]

The ten camps had different educational histories and established many levels of communication between officialdom and the incarcerated population. What they had in common was a singular history of imposing policy aims on the schoolchildren and their families. At different times the camp administrations pressed for work programs, community government, draft registration, Americanization, resettlement, and other policies. The schools absorbed and reflected the community conflict that ensued. Some camps set up "rumor clinics" to quell negative opinion. Others used homemaking classes to teach children how to help their parents decorate their barracks rooms in "the American way." The prospectus for a course entitled "Learning the Way of Democracy," distributed to the superintendents of education in the camps by the WRA Washington office, stated that its purpose was to prepare Japanese Americans "to take a more prominent part than hitherto in normal American community life after resettlement." On closer inspection the drift of the prospectus was a curriculum to acquaint people "with the organization and functioning of the project." This meant—as in the scope and sequence chart of the Stanford curriculum proposal—that the democratic community was simply the camps themselves, the planned communities administered by the federal government. The course was supposed to review administrative authority and bureaucratic functions so that services could be managed more efficiently, all the while speaking of the small community as "the foundation of our democratic life."[42]

This is not to say that official authority crowded out participation entirely. Nor did the older generation consistently reject the progressive vision. During a meeting of a parents and teachers association at Manzanar, a respected elder commented as follows on a presentation by administrators of their plans for progressive education in the social studies program: "Sometimes we Issei don't understand this much. The Hearst papers in Los Angeles are always criticizing progressive education and saying it's no good. We know how the Hearst papers handle news and lie about us Japanese here. If the Hearst papers knock progressive education, then it must be all right." Within limits, parents did make their wishes known about community life and the aims of schooling, and to a limited extent they did take advantage of the democratic procedures available to them for that purpose. At Minidoka parents met with administrators to ask for greater restrictions, including the requirement of parental consent for youth under the age of eighteen who were going out on work leave during the school year. Parents wanted the boys to finish high school instead of harvesting beets: "Education is going to make a lot of difference after this war," said George Tani, a Nisei who attended the meeting.[43]

Such optimism is striking when seen in its context of racial exclusion and detention. In much the same way, at Minidoka the minutes of Parent-Teacher Association (PTA) meetings show the concerns of parents—many of them could not speak English and needed translators—that homework was not being assigned in the grade schools. They wanted more rigor in the school program, which was designed to promote and eventually graduate all students regardless of the grades they attained. At Topaz more than 700 parents attended a mass meeting of the association in 1943. Part of the program was conducted in Japanese for their benefit. The education staff later cited parental preference as one of the main reasons for shifting from a concept of community schools to a more conservative and traditional approach in the second year. Similarly, at its first meeting in Amache the advisory board of parents asked for strong academic training and diverse skills beyond current opportunities in the camps, so that graduates could find "some point of contact" with the occupational structure after the war.[44]

Parents had doubts about the vocational component of progressivism, especially since the WRA had decided not to provide opportunities in the camps for college or university work. "Instead," reasoned one memorandum in the national office, "we have emphasized the vocational program, especially that type of service which will equip evacuees to further the present war effort." Policy and planning tended to harness community institutions to the routine needs of production and camp maintenance. Some people, recognizing the pattern, felt that the vocational programs had been designed specifically *not* to train young people for job opportunities on the outside. As one analyst summarized the skepticism of parents, "anything that works in the line of training people for jobs on the outside is not vocational training, while everything that doesn't work is." Allen C. Blaisdell, an educational consultant who studied the problem, agreed with this view. He reported widespread suspicion in the camps that vocational education was a product "of political expediency and pressure from reactionary groups rather than the result of a statesmanlike analysis of the long-term problems which this minority group must be trained to meet." Blaisdell also reported that in several of the camps "it was felt that a program of education was needed to retard *too quick* response to economic opportunities on a submarginal level, and that emphasis should be upon training for more effective and thus more permanent relocation." Parents were dissatisfied with the idea of community schools partly because of the adaptability of such schools to inferior opportunities in an artificial community characterized by scarcity, segregation, and coercion. When, for example, the administration had pulled several hundred high school students out of class for three weeks to harvest potatoes after the beginning of the school year because of "unfavorable labor conditions," it represented the policy as an extension of the community school, involving students in the productive life of their community. Parents were not happy about the policy because it undermined the academic preparation of their children and because it sidestepped the more basic issue of work and economic independence for the incarcerated population. "Almost immediately after the potato harvest," commented one school report, "it became apparent that this was not to become a settled community nestled on the old lake bed between the hills for the duration."[45]

How did the Japanese American children interpret their own schooling experience after the first year? One answer—a misleading one—appears in the ebullient yearbooks produced by junior and senior high schools in the ten camps. The yearbooks are full of well-dressed and smiling adolescents, genial teachers, administrators with an air of decorum about them, plenty of sports and clubs, parties and pranks. The texts speak of pioneering faith and democratic living, emphasizing hopes for the future. But the true story contained more shadows. By the end of the first school year camp life had become more localized and insular, concentrated on day-to-day preoccupations and rumors. It was "a time of suspended expectations," recalled Yoshiko Uchida, a Nisei teacher, years later in *Desert Exile*. "No matter what I did, I was still in an artificial government-spawned community on the periphery of the real world."[46]

Worst of all, students were showing signs of losing their ambition, their will to succeed in the world outside. Surveying high school seniors at one of the camps in Arkansas, a community analyst found that nearly 46 percent had planned to go to college before they had been evacuated, but only about 14 percent planned to do so after the first year of school in the camp. The majority said they planned to remain in camp for the time being, even though by then it was becoming possible under government policies to leave for higher education. Likewise at Topaz, of the 219 seniors who graduated in the summer of 1943, only 20 had gone to college by the following autumn. Forrest LaViolette recorded his conversation with one boy at Heart Mountain who typified the more extreme form of the "personal disintegration" that plagued all students in the camps as they contemplated an unknown future. The boy found that the things he read had little meaning to him, and it took him so much longer to write even a personal letter that he came to the conclusion, "I can't think any more." In a composition for a tenth grade class at Minidoka another student wrote, "I cannot concentrate on study no matter how hard I try . . . I think that this strange, new environment is the chief cause of my decline." [47]

Standardized tests verified such impressions. Previously average students with a good number of high achievers in their schools before the war, Japanese Americans had fallen more than a year behind their grade level in basic subjects. George Sugihara, a documentarian in the reports office at Topaz, found evidence that students were aware of this loss when he surveyed graduating high school seniors about their year of schooling in the camp. Asked whether the high school curriculum fulfilled their needs adequately, two-thirds of the girls and three-fourths of the boys responded in the negative. "Of course not," scrawled one boy on his questionnaire. "With the fine collection of the most inadequate instructors, together with the scarcity of books and other necessary equipment it is almost an ironic comedy." Besides criticizing scarcity and the quality of teachers, some students questioned the school program. They disliked combining English and History into a nebulous core class aimed at general socialization and the inculcation of civic values. One student asked indignantly, "what in the world is the use of learning about 'Your Community'?—This is just like a grammar school course." While showing gratitude toward teachers who tried sincerely to help them, many students felt that the progressive program in the first year had placed them at a disadvantage in showing conventional credits for admission to college.[48]

At the end of the 1942–43 school year, students prepared for graduation ceremonies throughout the camps. The most remarkable aspect of the event was the spirit of good will evinced by students and parents in spite of the extremity of the situation. Despite their anxieties about the schools, parents offered an outpouring of support for teachers, often responding to the poor grades of their children with comments like these collected in one school report: "Send him home with his books. We'll make him study." "We shall see that Henry does a little more studying at home." "From now on I ask you to teach my child as if he was your own child and correct all his mistakes without hesitation." As graduation day approached, the difficulties of the year were put aside for the moment. Parents and students expressed their desire for a real event, complete with formal attire and the pomp and pedantry of graduation exercises. It was as if teachers and families had made a pact to ignore the presence of the fence and to make the ceremony a genuine rite of passage whose meaning and power would endure into the future. The graduation speeches and essays of the students reflected this willingness to imagine an event that might suggest a future reconciliation even though present circumstances appeared less than auspicious.[49]

Hope is the father of thought, averred one student in the graduation ceremony at Topaz. She reminded students that the future still lay within them, not in their immediate surroundings. Another urged fellow students toward the same conclusion, arguing that the true barriers to be overcome were within their own struggling selves, that "if our minds cease to be free, so will our world cease to be free." Was this merely forced optimism, an individualist credo of free will to paper over the collective predicament? It was, but it was also more than that, as one reads on. Since the flavor of graduation exercises is universally bland—in any community—one is drawn to the exception, the incisive, the insightful. Dogged by an incessantly euphemistic administration, faced with the sheer inanity of life in the camps, some students rose to the occasion and tried to fashion an intelligible critique of their position in the United States. At Topaz some of the graduation speeches were astute enough in their perceptions that the camp director, in transmitting them to the national office, appended a note saying, "The kids sound as tho they had been studying psychology. It doesn't sound particularly healthy to me. I should think it is about time to play down the minority group psychology."[50]

This "psychology" was an attempt to reach back into the origins of Nisei identity before the war and to take stock of the underlying patterns of culture and social conflict that had preceded their incarceration. Having lived "on the border line that separated the Orient from the Occident," one speaker observed, they had been caught between two cultures when the war began; they were citizens, but their status as Americans "had its beginning and ending with the spheres of our schools, and their immediate periphery." Reasoning thus at the high school commencement at Topaz, this speaker analyzed the response of his peers after evacuation: "On the one hand, we see a display of flamboyant, carefree, irresponsible behavior. On the other hand, we recognize those characteristics of despondency reflected in the mood of apathy and indifference, lacking purpose or aim." His antidote was the realism of people who have suffered and "can no longer take things for granted," but must rely instead on "keen objective thinking." He warned that "personal pities and illusory visions must be abandoned," so that the Nisei would be ready to face a difficult future and master it.[51]

Another speaker at Topaz, examining the Nisei's self-imposed barriers, argued that these barriers had been erected from within because of the tragedy of recent events, but that they could be changed if people willed it to happen. One barrier was "evacuation mind," the paralysis of spirit that arose from distrust and loss of hope. Another was a confused sense of judgment, a willingness to "take the easy way out" and live aimlessly. A third was fear of their own cultural origins, anxiety toward the racial community of which the Nisei were members, now more than ever before because of the evacuation and concentrated isolation of the group. Incarcerated with their families, the Nisei were forced to take stock of their collective identity as they looked outward to individual opportunities in the future. "Will the uneducated community become illiberal? Will they look upon us as quislings? Yes, fear has its claws." Equally threatening was the barrier of mental laziness as students learned to become content with their present status as wards of the government. Finally, contended the speaker, the Nisei had to become more willing to deal with the prejudice confronting them in the outside world, to "learn to face it and become its master," developing confidence in themselves and knowing that the "present quandary is a temporary one."[52]

"We stand for tolerance," affirmed another student speaker at Topaz in the junior high school commencement, "for we know the injustice and bitterness that can arise where there is bigotry and intolerance." The point resonated more deeply, it can be surmised, when in addition to the pain of evacuation the audience carried fresh memories of conflict in the life of the camps.[53]

After observing the high school graduation at Topaz, an anthropologist working there wrote that "here is a minority group which places a value upon formal education surpassed by no other segment of the American population." Students in other camps also evinced an expanding awareness of their development as a group in the history of the nation. At Manzanar a speaker reminded his audience that the war had displaced other populations, that Mexican workers and Appalachian sharecroppers were also living in temporary camps under government authority. Riots in Detroit and Texas, then the zoot-suit riots in Los Angeles, the speaker pointed out, had demonstrated that racism was everywhere inflamed during wartime, "when patriotism is emphasized on a large scale and tensions between races and nationality groups tend to grow." Turning the argument around, the speaker cautioned his listeners that racism was also prevalent among Japanese Americans, that everyone had much to learn.[54]

At Amache a speaker advanced to a higher ground of collective awareness when he offered an interpretation of U.S. history that differed markedly from the hygienic version of the textbooks. "Sometimes America failed and suffered," the speaker ventured. Thus commenced an argument that risked official censure in wartime, especially in camps where the government was demanding loyalty from incarcerated citizens. "Sometimes she made mistakes, great mistakes," said this citizen about his nation's history. For nations, like individual people, the speaker intimated, repentance must precede redemption: "America hounded and harassed the Indians, then remembering that they were the first Americans, she gave them back their citizenship. She enslaved the Negroes, then again remembering Americanism, she wrote out the Emancipation Proclamation. She persecuted the German Americans during the First World War, then recalling that America was born of those who come from every nation seeking liberty and justice, she repented. Her history is full of errors, but with each mistake she has learned . . . Can we the graduating class of Amache Senior High School believe that America still means freedom, equality, security, and justice? Do I believe this? Do my classmates believe this? Yes, with all our hearts, because in that faith, in that hope, is my future, our future, and the world's future."[55]

Realism, tolerance, and hope ran through nearly all the commencement speeches and essays that have survived from graduation exercises in 1943. As is customary on such occasions, the arguments opened toward the future. In the imagination of these articulate citizens behind barbed wire, it was a future in which the suffering

Two graduates standing in front of the high school where they have been studying at Tule Lake, California, probably during the summer of 1943.

of the camps would be converted someday into a more tolerant practice of democracy.

The first school year began with deficiencies and ended with caps and gowns. These were bona fide schools that deserved to be known as such, despite the location. And these were indeed planned communities, new towns replete with students and teachers enough to vie with most any school district in rural states. But the camps were not, after their first year, a product of social engineering that many people would feel inspired to replicate voluntarily in other parts of the United States. Shortly before graduation, a writer in the *Nation* called them a "Jap Crow Experiment." In a pamphlet called *Democracy and Japanese Americans* Norman Thomas deplored the world that policy had made in the camps: "We are creating an American pale like the old Russian pale for the Jews." Within the camps, meanwhile, there were signs both of "settled antagonism" and, still, of unflagging cooperation.[56]

Graduation, by all accounts, was a happy time, as such occasions tend to be. A guidance counselor at Poston quipped that the administration was blessed with "a much more tolerant student body than we have a right to expect." No single image or argument can convey the complexity of experience bound up in the institution of schooling within the camps. The history of exile included many fine gradations of hope and despair, the blending of cooperation and resistance among parents, students, teachers, and administrators. Once during the year, runs a story from the camps, a group of representatives from the Red Cross came to Manzanar to inspect conditions there. They commented to a librarian, a Japanese American woman, on how beautiful the scenery was around the camp. Beyond the fence, recorded well for posterity in the photographs that Ansel Adams took when he visited Manzanar during the war, the snow-capped Sierras rose splendidly above the dessicated valley, as they still do today. The woman listened with habitual courtesy and then responded, "I prefer the view of the Statue of Liberty."[57]

3
Loyalty and Its Lessons

OUTSIDE the camps, the U.S. Supreme Court was debating the limits of individual freedom in a democracy. In *West Virginia State Board of Education* v. *Barnette* (1943), it struck down a state law that had required students to engage in public affirmations of loyalty through compulsory pledges of allegiance to the flag. In the same year, while the Court also heard arguments on the constitutionality of the evacuation of Japanese Americans, U.S. citizens in the camp schools not only were required to salute the flag and sing patriotic hymns; they also watched and listened as their older siblings and parents went through a procedure of political confession that had far higher costs than failure to salute the flag. This procedure was the testing of loyalty by government officials early in 1943. Although children under seventeen years of age were not required to answer the questions, they experienced the impact of the loyalty crisis on their families. They also felt the side effects of the crisis each day in school, as the government's loyalty demands became enmeshed in the social meanings of Americanization, minority group culture, and education for democratic citizenship. The children continued to learn about democracy in their classrooms while the loyalty procedure and its aftermath of more restrictive policies toward the supposed disloyals were taking place. Although loyalty testing was not without precedent in the history of the United States, its application to a segregated racial minority was a new twist that had important consequences for the education of the children of war.[1]

The impetus for loyalty testing was twofold. First, the secretary of war reopened the army to Japanese Americans in January 1943. For Nisei males the questions were part of draft registration and were administered by military officials. In a letter to Secretary of War Henry L. Stimson, President Franklin D. Roosevelt praised this initial move to reincorporate the Nisei into normal citizenship: "The principle on which this country was founded and by which it has always been governed is that Americanism is a matter of the mind and heart; Americanism is not, and never was, a matter of race or ancestry. A good American is one who is loyal to this country and to our creed of liberty and democracy." Although it might seem disingenuous to offer equality of status in the responsibilities of citizenship, such as compulsory military service, after having denied it in the exercise of rights, the opening of the military to Japanese Americans was crucial to reinstating the group in U.S. society. Despite the anomalous character of the procedure, government officials sympathetic to the plight of Japanese Americans believed that the opportunity to demonstrate loyalty was a sign of the political system at its best, showing fairness toward a dislocated minority group. Once given the opportunity, it was believed, Japanese Americans could win favor in the public eye, and they would enter the postwar society on good terms with others who had fought alongside them in the war. From this perspective it even made sense to have a segregated unit for the Nisei in the armed forces, since the glory they won on the battlefield would demonstrate beyond any doubt that Japanese Americans were model soldiers and good Americans. The view of officialdom that the Nisei should go from relocation camps to combat zones was reinforced by the lobbying efforts of the JACL, which urged the government to give the Nisei a chance to prove their loyalty and regain normal citizenship status.[2]

The other impetus for loyalty questions was the government's interest in resettling the evacuated population. During the first few months after the transfer from assembly centers to relocation centers had been completed in the fall of 1942, government officials were well aware that the camps were not working as planned communities. It was thought to be far better, therefore, to resettle Japanese Americans eastward as much as public opinion would allow. Public tolerance for resettlement would presumably become greater as Nisei entered the armed forces and proved their valor. Then, as public opinion became more receptive, it would be possible to use the criterion of loyalty for selectively emptying the camps. As one WRA report noted, the loyalty questions "provided an opportunity for a wholesale job of leave clearance for a large segment of the center's population." This dispersal would make it possible to disband the abnormal communities at the earliest possible time, meanwhile pinpointing the location of agitators and others suspected of disloyal activities. Thus, while Nisei eligible for the draft answered loyalty questions to determine whether they would enter the armed services, the entire evacuated population except for minor children was asked to attest to its loyalty as part of a longer "leave clearance" questionnaire. Loyalty as construed by government officials became the key to rehabilitating the status of Japanese Americans as normal citizens of the United States.[3]

Among the items that appeared on the questionnaires administered by the government in 1943, two questions required an answer of "yes" or "no" from all incarcerated Japanese Americans who were at least seventeen years old: First, "are you willing to serve in the armed forces of the United States on combat duty, wherever ordered?" And, second, "Will you swear unqualified allegiance to the United States of America and faithfully defend the United States from any or all attacks by foreign or domestic forces, and forswear any form of allegiance or obedience to the Japanese Emperor or any other foreign government, power or organization?" Administered during February, March, and April of 1943, these questions were indeed instrumental in the creation of an all-Nisei combat team in the army, which opened the way for reincorporating the excluded citizens into one aspect of normal citizenship. And the questions did become central in liberalized leave clearance procedures for college study, work furloughs, and resettlement. They also made it possible, as administrators interpreted their meaning, to separate responses considered to be disloyal and place those persons in a separate "segregation center," thus relaxing the restrictions in other camps after the fall of 1943. Besides the initial evacuation and construction of camps, loyalty questions and the divergent opportunities and constraints they produced were the most consequential policy in the wartime experience of Japanese Americans.[4]

For those living in the camps, the loyalty procedure was sudden and unexpected. Without much advance notice, representatives of the army arrived with questionnaires for Nisei males who were eligible for the draft. As the draft registration proceeded, the camp administrations used WRA staff, including many teachers, to administer the leave clearance questionnaires. As people in the camps reacted, there were many recriminations against the procedure. Official and unofficial meetings took place day and night in the barracks. Families, often split apart by opposing attitudes of accommodation and resistance, tried to comprehend the meaning and implications of what was happening to them. Officials made some efforts to orient Japanese Americans so that they would understand the government's intent in carrying out the procedure. Nonetheless, the WRA administration—and the military even more—showed little awareness of the social and moral complexities of the loyalty questions when posed to those behind barbed wire. Throughout the procedure government officials insisted on a narrow, legalistic conception of loyalty, based on the formal questions being asked, and refused to consider the context and recent history in which these questions were being answered. This is perhaps understandable in wartime, when complex issues must be simplified for immediate action, but the result was a procedure that appeared to negate the humane rhetoric with which the WRA had been trying to soften the impact of racial exclusion.

At Tule Lake loyalty registration turned into an administrative fiasco, with much worse results than at any of the other camps, both in the severity of public authority and in the extremes of resistance. Providing little advance information and then taking a hard line when administering the loyalty questions, the administration was partly responsible for the fact that Japanese Americans at Tule Lake resisted the procedure more than those in the other camps. The rigid stance of the administration had an impact on educators there as well. Alert to the likely damage to the relationship between teachers and students, the superintendent of schools had opposed the use of teachers for the registration program, but his view did not prevail. Subsequently, teachers complained that they felt *used* as the procedure flared out of control and turned into the biggest crisis the camp had yet experienced. As resistance to the loyalty procedure increased, open divisions appeared in the ranks of administrators and teachers. Several conscientious objectors working as teachers refused to administer the loyalty forms at the registration tables. They were opposed by angry administrators and teachers demanding that they be fired. Among educators, conflict also emerged around the negative and qualified responses of many Nisei to the loyalty questions. Some teachers announced that they would not teach "disloyal" high school students, assuming that negative answers to the loyalty questions were equivalent to siding with the enemy. Others, troubled by the contradictory policy of demanding loyalty from people who were systematically being denied their rights, believed that public education—even in its most progressive form—could play no constructive role under such circumstances. Even more anguished were the Japanese American assistant teachers; they often understood more deeply the community's distress over the procedure, particularly the internal conflict of Nisei who answered "no" partly because they had learned the ideals of democracy in their past education in public schools. At Tule Lake the Japanese American teaching staff quit in droves because of objections to the administration's loyalty demands. They feared pressure and possible violence in the blocks where they lived, and they were upset over the additional affront of having to sign yet another loyalty oath, the one required of all teachers in California. In the teaching force as a whole, which peaked at about 200 teachers and assistants for the more than 4000 students in elementary and secondary schools, the attrition rate after the registration shows the devastating impact of the loyalty issue and the subsequent segregation on the educational system: 12 quit and 22 were hired in February; 49 quit and 19 were hired in March; 37 quit and 38 were hired in April; 40 quit and 58 were hired in May; 33 quit and 22 were hired in June; 35 quit and 19 were hired in July; 29 quit and 13 were hired in August; 78 quit and 6 were hired in September. After the crisis over loyalty registration, public schooling was no longer compulsory at Tule Lake.[5]

Throughout all ten camps, officials were shocked when many Japanese Americans—roughly 11 percent of those eligible for the questionnaires—resisted answering the questions, responded in the negative, or qualified their responses in unacceptable ways. Especially surprising was the fact that "no" answers were highest among young Nisei eligible for the draft. They had been raised from birth in American communities and educated in public schools. They were native speakers of English, often the most fully Americanized of the group. More than a fourth of all Nisei males of draft age did not answer with an unqualified "yes" to the question of allegiance to the United States. They were not pro-Japanese and the administration knew it, but they would not submit to the ritual of loyalty as it had been presented to them behind barbed wire. The recruitment drive was a dismal failure. Overall in the camps, more Japanese Americans applied for expatriation or repatriation (roughly 3000) than volunteered to serve in the armed forces (fewer than 1200) during the registration period. The army had hoped to recruit 3000 Nisei from the camps. In Hawaii, by contrast, where the army had set a goal of recruiting 1500, and where there had been no mass evacuation of people of Japanese descent after Pearl Harbor, almost 10,000 Japanese Hawaiians volunteered. They subsequently served in the 100th Infantry Battalion and then the 442nd Regimental Combat Team along with Japanese Americans. Emerging as one of the most highly decorated units in American military history, they earned the title of the "Christmas Tree Regiment" because of the profusion of medals and honors they received for their heroism in Italy and France.[6]

The issue of loyalty did not make sense to many Nisei citizens, incarcerated in the land of their birth. The wider social meanings of their resistance were not lost on educators in the camps. Realizing how many Nisei had answered "no" at Manzanar, Lucy Adams marveled at "the dark tangled conflicts which the categorical imperative of loyalty fished up, like the murex, from the deeps." She conceded that the procedure had gone "too deep into the roots of family and of race to be affected much by logic or eloquence." That it had was confirmed in reports by social scientists working in the camps. They perceived that loyalty was a practical decision influenced by immediate concerns, one of which was the question of whether the family would have to resettle against its will in a hostile outside world. Many feared further mistreatment of the minority group because of press statements and political rhetoric. Another was that the demand to fight for one's country was being made while one's parents and siblings were being denied civil rights. Some felt only a genuine desire not to take sides in a fracas where one is bound by blood and friendship to both protagonists, a war not only between nations but between cultures, languages, and histories. "The loyalty they understand and express is family loyalty," complained Adams.[7]

Although this perception contained some truth, it reflected certain racial attitudes that the white majority and the government held toward people of Japanese descent, whether citizens or not. The notion that Japanese Americans could not understand *political* loyalty was widespread among Caucasians. In the camps there were numerous copies of the Tolan Committee reports from the spring of 1942, containing testimony gathered before the evacuation by a congressional investigation of opinion about the feasibility of "national defense migration." Earl Warren, then attorney general of California, had reasoned in his testimony that "when we are dealing with the Caucasian race, we have methods that will test the loyalty of them," but "with the Japanese, we are in an entirely different field and we cannot form any opinion" due to "ingrained differences and an unacceptable mode of living." During 1943 this view was substantially accepted by the U.S. Supreme Court in the *Hirabayashi* decision, which upheld the curfew imposed by the Western Defense Command on Japanese Americans prior to the evacuation. Japanese cultural practices and language schools received judicial notice as indicators that the loyalty of the group was not readily ascertainable, and that therefore the claim of "military necessity" was valid as the justification for evacuating the group. Newspaper editorials and statements by hostile politicians during the war expressed similar views, reinforcing the conviction of dissenting Japanese Americans that affirmations of loyalty would make little difference when they seemed destined to be treated as outsiders no matter what they did in service of their country.[8]

As the loyalty testing proceeded, schools absorbed the uncertainties of the camp environment. The children went to class; in most of the camps they were given time to discuss what was happening around them. At Minidoka new teachers in the lower grades received instructions, entitled "Philosophy of the Elementary Schools," urging them to recognize that their students "wait hopefully for some assurance that those fundamentals which you are explaining are workable principles of democracy necessary for post-war readjustment in a world where minorities have equal rights with majorities." While promulgating such instructions, however, the administration also showed a penchant for identifying disloyalty with family ties in an immigrant culture: "We must choose whether or not through adequate schools we are going to attempt to save these young Americans for America or whether we are going to push them steadily and irretrievably back into the welcoming arms of their parents and Japan." Reflecting this view, one teacher wrote in her evaluation of the school year, "I knew that the children were being swayed by their parents . . . The children showed a conflict between loyalty and filial piety." Since they were predisposed to see the family and the school as opponents in a struggle to mold the culture of the children, administrators were doubly concerned about the Kibei, the more than 9,000 members of the second generation who had received some education in Japan. Many teachers saw themselves as protecting younger children from the influence of the Kibei, often the oldest male in the family, as well as from the parents. A researcher studying Tule Lake early in 1943 found that the high school had instituted remedial English classes for the Kibei. This form of educational tracking was intended to address the language needs of students who spent part of their lives in Japan, but it also negatively labeled them. It placed on the Kibei a social stigma in the peer culture of the school and separated them from the more assimilated Nisei.[9]

A similar stigma fell on the culture of the parent. To many educators the traditional authority of the Japanese American family seemed averse to the political socialization contemplated for their students. This view rested on the assumption that the cultural traits of the elders were inimical to the American way of life, that the forms of cohesion which had permitted the group to take hold in a hostile society must be washed away. "Democracy is under attack," fulminated the *Community School Forum,* a WRA publication. "Our American marriage customs, for instance, are not understood by the older Japanese. They are part of our democratic pattern of living." In traditional Japanese communities, parents arranged marriages for their children through intermediaries who made sure that the match was a proper one according to custom and the status of the families. Teachers in public schools told their students that they should choose for themselves. At Manzanar the administration surveyed high school seniors individually, asking them through their teachers, "Do our Issei parents have the right to arrange or approve our marriages?" The survey probably has no value as a social indicator, but more students answered yes than no. Other cultural lessons in the classroom that aimed at reeducating families through their children included the unit "A Barrack Becomes a Home," essentially an introduction to the material culture of the white middle class, and another called "American Table Manners." The latter argued, "Politeness is the same in any country," and then proceeded to summarize the conventions of the majority culture in the United States.[10]

Culture and kinship were in danger of becoming symbols of disloyalty inside the camps. The schools played an ambiguous role in the loyalty conflict, partly opening the way for broader discussion, partly closing the range of perspectives and insisting on the official view of the government. In the latter case the authority of teachers was coupled with a strong distrust of the social and cultural orga-

*High school students
running between classes
at Rohwer, Arkansas,
November 17, 1943.*

nization that had kept Japanese Americans together in the past and helped them to survive. War on the traditional culture of home life took the form of personal battles against incorrect habits and incongruous ways, as social planners and camp administrators sought to develop the "loyalty" of individuals so that they would leave behind the traditionalism of their kin and community, dispersing into the freedom and the new roles that would soon be theirs in the larger society around them. In the minds of many administrators, the enemy became the family itself.

Whether individual teachers chose to adopt this point of view or to reject it in their own classrooms, education began to take on a different aspect after the loyalty procedure. There is no better evidence of the change than the school files that contained extensive information relevant to determining the eligibility of families for resettlement. Indeed, one way that the administration learned more about the background and habits of parents, who frequently were poor speakers of English, was through their children and the routine contact between schools and family culture. The gathering of information and the creation of detailed files about every student contributed to the penetration of governmental authority into the authority of the family. This, of course, would be true in normal communities as well; but there the difference would be that families could exert some control over their schools through democratic processes. In regular school districts extensive record keeping on students had achieved legitimacy in recent decades because of the professional norm among educators that called for careful study of the child in order to socialize students while meeting their educational needs. In the abnormal communities of the camps such files were another way in which authority was being exercised without prior consent or community control. The information thus gathered represented an attempt to classify, evaluate, and influence the development of children and their families.

A description of the student files at Poston includes, besides school and health records, extensive personal and family information. The "anecdotal record sheets" bring together typed transcripts of teacher comments, reports of home visits, and student interviews in chronological order. Interleaved with this material are "confidential rating sheets" that describe "special needs and weaknesses" of each student and the "direction of changes taking place in student behavior." The files have in them samples of the written work of each child for each year in the camps. Among the kinds of personal data

Dancing in the high school gymnasium at Heart Mountain, Wyoming, November 24, 1943.

collected were student responses to WRA Questionnaire 1815, which asked for the following categories of information.[11]

Personal Adjustments Found Most Difficult
Conditions Considered Most Important to Future Happiness
Three Wishes
Things in Former School Missed Most
Gains
Parents' Use of English

A similar emphasis on comprehensive school records appeared in every camp. The reasons were educational, tracing the development of students in the social context of family and community. But as the issues of loyalty and minority group culture began to overlap in the minds of many administrators and teachers, the files became more than educational. Placed in the hands of relocation staff and leave clearance boards, whose membership included school administrators and teachers, personal files could become part of dossiers for or against political rehabilitation to a condition of freedom in the outside world. When seen in this light, the detail of the student files is striking. The assistant principal of the high school at Tule Lake suggested the following universe of information for such files, in addition to school and health records and the personal and family data from WRA questionnaires.[12]

Delinquency
Family Background
Food Habits
Handedness
Home Duties
Honesty
Individual Case Study
Leadership
Nail Biting
Notable Accomplishments
Observations
Outstanding Number of Books Read
Part-time Employment
Personal Traits—Cooperation, Responsibility, Work Habits, Working to Ability
Punctuality
Reason for Irregular Attendance
Major Reasons for Not Attempting to Graduate
Recreation
Reinstatement
Self Direction
Self Support and Support of Dependents
Sleeping Habits
Social Attitudes
Special High School
Suspension
Thumb Sucking
Unusual Experiences
Use of Tobacco, Alcohol, Tea, Coffee

Can the concept of loyalty and an abundance of data in administrative files be used to shape the behavior of individuals? Writing about asylums, one form of "total institution" designed to change individuals, Erving Goffman traced the "moral career" of the inmate, the planned changes that mark the passage of an individual through stages created artificially by the institution. Robert A. Mossman has studied in detail the analogy between the camps and total institutions as defined by Goffman. Mossman's analysis highlights leave clearance policies and camp rules as the structure of social control in a coercive setting. Loyalty, from this perspective, becomes a therapeutic goal of an institution created by the government to change undesirable individuals to conform to a new pattern. The daily routine of life is designed to rehabilitate them according to criteria imposed by the government through its employees. The control of "release" from the institution defines the moral career of the inmate, setting the terms on which reincorporation into normal society is made possible.[13]

The analogy is suggestive but not without limitations. The politics surrounding the establishment and administration of the camps did not lead at any time to an efficient use of internal controls to produce specific individual changes—except through the schooling program, and this would be true in any immigrant neighborhood where children attend public schools. Even the notions of planned communities and community schools fell far short of any recognizable extant form of therapeutic institutionalization. At all times there was contention within the administration and the camp community that fragmented any efforts to bring about fundamental changes in behavior. The active politics and resistance inside the camp, moreover, belie any label of totality, in spite of the spatial concentration and coercive perimeter of the environment. The concept of total institutions does serve well as a metaphor for one tendency of the camps. But as social scientists working in the camps made clear in their many reports, life inside was contested and political, often utterly unpredictable, following no imposed design of moral suasion, much as administrators might have wished for subjects more amenable to benevolent coercion. The word "colony," which was used frequently by administrators, comes closer to the daily reality of the camps than does "total institution," especially after the first year.

The loyalty controversy offers the key to understanding the particular brand of institutional totality that appeared in the camps for Japanese Americans. For the most part the administration saw itself merely as managers of a relocated population, not therapists working within an accepted paradigm of individual rehabilitation. As far as social services were concerned, the New Deal was the paradigm, and the purpose was simply to move the group to secure niches in society. By their own testimony, administrators saw the Japanese Americans as mostly loyal but containing some problem cases and a few outright disloyals. The office records of the WRA Community Management Division show a dawning realization, by late 1942, that the task of running a social program for the group of people under its control was turning out to be a great deal more difficult than administrators had expected. To begin with, the administration knew little about the people it was managing. The surprises of the fall of 1942 had not been pleasant ones: the strike at Poston, the protest demonstration and deaths at Manzanar, the crumbling of JACL leadership in the camps. Far from being total, these institutions were veering out of control. Even the most manageable were failing to emerge as workable planned communities on the scale imagined by the planners, and with growing social conflict the educational program was in jeopardy.

Reviewing the situation, the top administration of the WRA was impressed by the difference between Poston and Manzanar when disturbances took place in the two camps. It was noted that in Poston there had been a social science research unit in the fall of 1942, whereas in Manzanar there had been none. The strike at Poston had been settled peaceably and the riot at Manzanar had not, even though there had been similar grievances and patterns of agitation behind the two events. It seemed clear, especially to the social scientists who proposed it, that some form of community analysis was appropriate for all ten relocation centers. The activity would be based not so much on a therapy of individual intervention along the lines of asylums, as on a more generalized program of cultural observation to facilitate the management of these dangerously concentrated wartime communities. This recognition led to an administrative initiative that had major implications for defining the acceptable limits of family culture, community leadership, and socialization of children in the camps.

"Many of the difficulties and crises of administration in industry, in colonial government, and in the War Relocation Authority," wrote John Embree in *American Anthropologist*, "are due to clogs or gaps or perversions of the information that should be communicated up and down within the structure. Once this problem is recognized—

and it always is, eventually, after time, tempers, and lives have been lost—some form of Community Analysis is established. It may take the shortsighted form of a spy system as in some industrial situations and some colonial governmental situations, or it may take the more enlightened and in the long run more practical and efficient form of open and scientific attempts to provide administrators with a knowledge of the complexities of human relations as they develop and change in the organization. Examples of this latter solution are, for industry, the Western Electric Company; for colonial government, the British in New Guinea and parts of Africa; and finally in our American parallel to Colonial Administration, the War Relocation Authority."[14]

The social scientists who recommended the arrangement were intending simply to apply the wise management practiced at Poston, which relied on social expertise instead of an obvious show of force, to other camps. The proposal met with approval and was put into effect early in 1943 with Embree directing the community analysis unit, just as the conflict over draft registration and leave clearance procedures reached the boiling point. Administrators were sympathetic to the idea of community analysis, in part because more authoritarian measures, not to mention more open participatory schemes such as community government, were failing to keep order. They knew from past experience during the New Deal that social scientists could help where coercion could not. "The fact that some form of social analysis had been used in the Indian Service and in the Department of Agriculture for at least a decade," commented Embree, "doubtless facilitated this general acceptance of the new proposal, inasmuch as many of the WRA staff were former Indian Service and Department of Agriculture men."[15]

Using applied anthropology and sociology to manage conflict (as had been done in industrial workplaces, penal institutions, foreign colonies, public works projects, and Indian reservations), the social scientists quickly gathered information on the evacuated population—their characteristics, social cleavages, customs, reactions to policy, expectations, loyalties. Even while administering the loyalty questions, those in charge of some of the camps began to change their management strategies to harmonize the demands of authority with the culture and social organization of Japanese Americans. In an early report called "Dealing with Japanese Americans," later published in *Applied Anthropology,* Embree recommended using go-betweens drawn from the camp community instead of face-to-face communication between WRA authorities and the people whose lives they were managing. To do this, he suggested relying on intermediate committees, which would spread personal responsibility away from those who were cooperating with WRA. This strategy would also create an opportunity for unanimous action by respected members of the community. At the same time, drawing on the observations of cultural anthropology, including his own classic study of a Japanese village, Embree also told project directors that their own communication with the traditional Issei and their families on major policy issues should be in the form of direct address before large groups on the most important matters, thus replicating the personal authority of a village head or the center of power in a farming community. He and other social scientists urged administrators to study the factions coalescing within the camps, using differences of opinion and natural coalitions for leverage in implementing policy without social strain. They should avoid open conflict, he recommended, by creating meaningful roles for "out-groups" like the disaffected Issei who had lost power during the evacuation.[16]

Filtering down to the emotional and educational world of the children of war, community analysis became part of the configuration of education and political socialization in the camps. The analysts mediated between the hardened attitudes of WRA staff and Japanese Americans. These "court interpreters," as a university-trained Nisei called them, believed that both authority and culture were malleable if sufficient information could be made available to show that a harmony of interests existed. For example, many administrators had wanted to suppress Japanese language in the camps, in newspapers, religious services, language schools, and so forth. Some of the proposed regulations would have been more severe than those in the internment camps for enemy aliens rounded up for suspected espionage and subversion. Broad-minded administrators who resisted such urges were confirmed in their views when community analysts stressed the need to communicate within the social structure of the evacuated community. This could take place only in the Japanese language for many of the older generation. Many parents spoke Japanese with their children, and though the children spoke English in school, part of the schooling success of the children sprang from the parental control that was exercised in Japanese. After community analysts began to join the administration of all ten camps early in 1943, the formal and informal rules touching upon Japanese cultural practices relaxed in most of the camps. The noncitizen Issei were given the right to serve (and therefore to control) the community councils. Reports from the social scientists showed administrators how to operate as effectively as possible within the boundaries of communication that emerged from the new arrangements.[17]

As administrators adopted these methods, the traditional Japanese American family appeared to them in a more sympathetic light. It was not the enemy, but a potential ally whose cooperation could be won if its own needs were properly understood. From this standpoint, the gathering and use of information became important not so much for evaluating loyalty as for seeking actively to cultivate it, locating areas of mutual interest where accommodation might be possible.

The WRA instituted community analysis to gain more information and greater control, but the aim was not merely to restrain the incarcerated population. The disturbances at Poston and Manzanar had sparked adverse publicity that threatened the entire basis of humane treatment of the Japanese Americans as envisioned by federal planners. Social services, including public education for the children, had their problems, their coercive side, especially when implemented in the camps. But if suddenly overruled by less sympathetic forces in the political arena, they could have been replaced by practices vastly more coercive and punitive. Senator Albert B. Chandler of Kentucky, who chaired the Senate Military Affairs Subcommittee, "investigated" the camps after the disturbances at Poston and Manzanar, mainly capitalizing on newspaper interest to denounce the WRA and demand that the army take over the administration of the camps. If this had occurred, the experience of the children of war would have been more like the initial months in the assembly centers, where educational programs were voluntary and unfunded.[18]

A darker scenario would have been even harsher action against Japanese Americans. The American Legion's national readership learned from its excitable journal, in an article entitled "Japs in Our Yard," that the camps were powerful "Little Tokyos" where the enemy was well organized to undermine the war effort on the home front. The Hearst papers and the eager battalions of anti-Japanese columnists in western states seized upon internal dissent in the camps to point out the activity of "pro-Axis" groups in a population they had known all along to be disloyal. Failing to find any traces of spying or sabotage among Japanese Americans, the reconstituted anti-Japanese lobby dredged up the old argument that people of Japanese ancestry could not be assimilated, that they were culturally subversive. Deprival of citizenship and deportation were the answer, according to some. Nor were visions of more extreme treatment unknown within the camps, particularly among the military guards whose task it was to imprison, not to assist, the population under their control. In April a man named James Hatsuaki Wakasa was shot dead near the fence at Topaz while apparently walking toward the center of the camp, one of several deaths at the hands of guards during the incarceration. To those who sympathized with Japanese Americans these were unconscionable moments in the work of reconstructing a future in America for this dislocated group. But to others the violence could as well be taken as a sign that these people were making trouble and should be dealt with more severely.[19]

Politically, both the WRA and the camps were fighting for their lives. Though it was a latecomer among social programs launched by the New Deal administration, a wartime mutant of earlier efforts to ameliorate the nation's miseries during the Great Depression, the WRA faced the ire of an ever more powerful opposition in Congress that had finally gained enough votes to confront the president directly and scuttle his plans for social welfare. Early in the war the Civilian Conservation Corps was dissolved, the Farm Security Administration began to collapse under attack, and the National Youth Administration was first converted to serve war industries and then put out of business when it failed to receive appropriations. The anti-administration coalition in Congress was already irate over the administration's attempts to deal liberally with racial minorities, especially blacks. Now they began to depict the WRA as disloyal and subversive in its own right, a mollycoddling dole for a race of spies and saboteurs, people obviously opposed to the war aims of the United States because they were protesting even the soft treatment they were already receiving at public expense.[20]

The falsity of such charges did not detract from their effectiveness. The WRA urgently needed arguments for assuring politicians and the public that it was doing the right thing, that its aims were loyal to the American way of life. The key element of the WRA's rationale was essentially an educational one, that it was proper to treat Japanese Americans as loyal subjects who would again become part of American society and join the postwar world as equals alongside other citizens. In making this argument, WRA officials were defending one of the most controversial principles of the New Deal: the idea that displaced groups should receive public assistance until they can gain the skills and resources they need to reestablish themselves in the economy. The defense was being made—inauspiciously—as other social programs from the depression era were being destroyed by the majority opposition in Congress.[21]

By late spring of 1943, after the loyalty controversy was well under way, Congressman Martin Dies of Texas and his Committee on Un-American Activities in the U.S. House of Representatives began to make the WRA another target of their persistent hectoring of the liberal policies of the Roosevelt administration. Conducting hearings in June and July, and then again in November and December, the Dies committee fanned media hysteria during the months when U.S. prisoners of war were being executed publicly in Tokyo, when race riots were occurring in Texas and Detroit, when the public was finally beginning to sense the turning tide of battle in their favor on the Pacific front, and when many state and local jurisdictions where the camps were located were moving quickly to pass restrictive measures designed to keep resettling Japanese Americans out of their communities. Dies and the jingo press held to the notion that the Nisei could not be Americanized and that the Issei were dangerous enemies on American soil. By attempting to restrict the social services of the camps because of such imputed disloyalty, the opponents of Japanese Americans were treating the camps symbolically as centers of Japanization, mere holding pens until deportation and expatriation could be arranged. The implications of this social philosophy for education in the camps were grave. It infuriated these critics that the WRA was using public authority constructively—even if coercively—to keep Japanese Americans in the United States and bring them back into the economy and polity.[22]

Community analysis, viewed in this larger political context, was more than the mere application of social control in a coercive setting, for that control was also a thin membrane protecting the incarcerated Japanese Americans from determined forces acting against them outside the camps. The close observation of culture, brushing aside popular insistence upon racial traits, offered concepts that, when placed in the right hands, translated into power to persuade and to conserve humane principles in the political arena, as well as into authoritarian policies to shape the destiny of Japanese Americans. Community analysis was accompanied generally by liberalization of policy. In June of 1943 the central office issued a memorandum declaring that library policy in the camps was to be determined freely by a board of Japanese Americans named by the elected community council, and that books in Japanese would circulate on the same basis as other books. When work slowdowns and soldiering on the job became common, the community analysts were set into motion to discover causes and to suggest strategies for improvement or for stimulating resettlement. Instead of showing hostility toward Japanese culture in everything from hairstyles to marriage customs, as many administrators had done in the first year of the war, the community analysts probed new developments with interest. They looked for points of leverage, ways of building compliance with the needs of administrative authority, while also communicating to the authorities the needs of the managed population.[23]

The WRA moved ahead in 1943 with its policy of sending "disloyals" to a separate "segregation center." Tule Lake became the camp redesigned for that purpose. Government officials and camp administrators encouraged the majority of Japanese Americans in the other nine camps to resettle as soon as possible in communities outside the restricted zone of the Western Defense Command. While this message was spreading, the community analysts faithfully reported what they saw: that the elders were reasserting their power; that the Nisei leadership, prematurely empowered by government policy, left the camps first; that stable patterns of community authority were emerging in the camps; and that individuals, both old and young, were coming to see themselves again as part of a cultural and social organization. As the analyst at Manzanar noted, "the Issei are extremely important in the formation of opinion here and react strongly, though from behind the scenes, when they feel slighted or ignored."[24]

This undercurrent of organized parental and community power influenced the schooling of children in the camps. By the end of the 1942–43 school year, the greatest shock to the Nisei—registration for the draft and the liberalization of leave clearance policies—had passed. Many older members of the second generation, more than 15,000 of them, were now on the outside, while many others had opted for segregation as disloyals at Tule Lake. The great shock for the Issei, the opening of the West Coast and the announcement that the centers would close, still lay far ahead in what seemed to the older generation a distant and uncertain future. Meanwhile, as the analysts began to record and the administration to acknowledge, the majority of the Issei were determined to stay put and keep their children by their side, behind the barbed wire fence, inside the delicate membrane of benevolent coercion that separated them from the outside world at war.

Exiled within these planned, managed, analyzed communities, those who remained at the end of 1943 were becoming cautious about the prospect of leaving. Segregated into the camps, segregated again after the loyalty review, the great majority of Japanese Americans were still incarcerated by the middle of the war, and they were suspicious of any claims being made about life on the outside. Ambiguously, life went on inside. Mired in uncertainty, parents, children, teachers, administrators, and community analysts all grappled with the tangled meanings of racial segregation.

As families were broken apart by the draft, by opportunities for resettlement, by segregation of disloyals at Tule Lake in the fall of 1943, by classrooms where their civic lessons contradicted the visible environment around the school, teachers (as shown by their instructions and evaluations) looked for growth of self-control, responsibility, cooperativeness, and the ability to work independently. Sometimes they felt they were waging a losing battle against the strength of families in a time of crisis. The children were in some ways becoming part of school and society on American terms, but they were also members of their families, deeply influenced by a collective history of which most teachers knew next to nothing. One little boy drew airplanes covered with Japanese flags on his tablet, until the teacher lost patience, tore up the pages, and declared, "We will have no more pictures of any flag but the American flag." Another teacher discovered that one of her students had drawn a picture of the Statue of Liberty waving a Japanese flag in its hand. Some teachers saw that these were not two worlds for the children, but one confused reality.[25]

Not all teachers were sympathetic to the inner conflicts they were witnessing among their students. "Sometimes I wonder," said one teacher at Amache, "whether or not our efforts may take an interminably long time to become really effective with these people." This teacher reasoned that if the race of Japan, which was older than that of modern Europeans, produced leaders as bad as Hitler in Germany, then there was danger of being overrun by "these so prolific ones" who would cause great misery on earth. "However that may be," she continued, "we have dealt with these children who are sweet and lovable as all children are, on a purely democratic basis, and have done much toward putting the mantle of democracy upon them." A social scientist, commenting on such attitudes, expressed concern about "a number of Caucasians on the staff who have found a stimulus in the realization that they are members of the dominant racial group." Enjoying the power to decide for themselves whether the people in their charge were loyal or disloyal, many of these people "have come to accept the situation as good and reasonable, giving substance to their feelings of superiority." Other teachers, however, believed unequivocally in the citizenship and dignity of their students. More willing to understand the ambiguous lives of second-generation immigrants, they were surprised at the perspicacity of some students. Polling high school students on issues of tolerance and respect for others, Gertrude de Silva, a teacher at Poston, wrote in an education journal that "these seniors have been sobered and have become sensitive to justice through their own privations at an age when most youth find boring the study of the principles of our American Constitution."[26]

The loyalty crisis and segregation of disloyals placed a great strain on schoolchildren. Incomprehension and distress had seized their families as the government went forward with its procedure. Neither the loyalty questions nor the political segregation that followed the racial segregation addressed the underlying question of why parents had been forced out of their homes and into camps. Once the government had invoked its loyalty-disloyalty distinction to bring about this further segregation, many people remaining in the camps were struck by the absurdity of transferring disloyals to Tule Lake. As an administrator at Poston commented after the transfers were completed at that camp, "The segregation of those 'oriented toward Japan' by emotional, political or economic interests has not led to the happy clarification that was hoped for. Just as Tule Lake is not all Japanese, neither are the Issei of the other centers ready and eager for assimilation to Main Street. Even as the Tule Lake trains left Poston, the most disturbing sense one got was that no one, staying or going, was aware of any clear difference between stayers and goers." Young people saw their friends, and occasionally members of their own family, among those leaving for the train.[27]

In the months leading up to the transfers in late summer of 1943, schoolchildren acted out the frustrations of the incarcerated population. Absenteeism rose dramatically during the loyalty testing, and signs of disorder followed each related announcement of policy throughout 1943. The superintendent of schools at Manzanar, which

After the loyalty testing and the government's decision to segregate the "disloyals," this boy goes by train with his parents from the Minidoka Relocation Center in Idaho to the Tule Lake Segregation Center in California, August 9, 1943.

had the largest school enrollment of all the camps, reported serious discipline problems with "children who are disrupting and excited about the segregation movement of their families." A few students blatantly defied their teachers and announced in class that they were no longer under the authority of the school since they were going to Tule Lake. Obscenity, vandalism, and intimidation of "loyal" students by youth gangs punctuated school life with reminders of the cultural politics engendered by loyalty classifications. Hiro Katayama, who wrote "Our Younger Generation" for *All Aboard,* a Nisei publication at Topaz, observed that the camp environment itself, more than student loyalty or disloyalty, "contributes toward lazy and sloppy habits in the children." To speak of loyalty at all in such institutions was more than unfair; it was tragically irrelevant. "During their most impressionable years," wrote Katayama, "the young students sing 'America,' salute the flag, and learn about democracy in the classrooms and then return to their dingy barracks 'Homes' and wonder why they can't go back to their America."[28]

Students in the camps saw one development that taught them a great deal about loyalty in 1943. Community leadership was becoming more organized and assertive in the camps. This leadership built upon the prestige of the older generation, rather than the temporary and officially sanctioned insurgency of older Nisei, as had been the case in the assembly centers and the more permanent camps during the first months. The Issei had answered the loyalty questions with a higher proportion of "yes" responses than the adult Nisei, but they were much more hesitant about resettling. As many older Nisei left the camps, the Issei settled down to a less conflictive life with high concentrations of older adults and younger children. Except for a wave of draft resistance at Heart Mountain in 1944 and a drastically different history that unfolded at the Tule Lake Segregation Center, protest in the camps became more muted, the resistance more absorbed into normal functions of self-government and petitioning committees of influential Issei.[29]

The WRA, eager to disband now that the way for resettlement of "loyal" Japanese Americans had been smoothed, buzzed with impatient strategizing and propaganda to stimulate relocation. Showing little interest in WRA plans for them, the older generation dug in its heels to remain for the duration of the war. "Relocation is more difficult than it has ever been," conceded the director of community management to a conference of school superintendents from the camps in 1944. "I think there is more Japanization in the centers than there ever has been. I think we are losing ground rather than gaining . . . and it will get increasingly harder to get these people out as time goes on."[30]

Among both the "loyal" and "disloyal" who remained in the camps, Japanese cultural practices flourished, offering a lesson quite different from the aims of government policy. This was a sign not of disloyalty but of a resurgence of community organization on the terms that had existed before the war. Families resisted social surveys and family counseling administered by the WRA; they identified these activities with the threat of forced relocation, with the barracks searches that had intimidated families during the first year, and with the many promises that they felt had not been kept by officials. Operating independently of WRA policy initiatives, community organizations were linked efficiently to the administration through Issei-dominated committees. These organizations often duplicated WRA services but provided them in ways considered acceptable to the Issei. They also served to maintain distance and provided channels for cooperation, making official discretion more advisable than direct action for most administrative policies. As the WRA cut down the work force to encourage relocation, the community networks forming across barracks blocks became more adept at pooling scarce resources, accommodating unmet needs, persisting in an organized way while maintaining order within. Encouraged by the strengthening of community ties, parents attempted to reassert traditional controls over the children remaining with them, shaming and ridiculing, praising good behavior, dealing with problem cases through their community organizations in a discreet manner so that the Caucasian officials would not become aware of difficulties. Meanwhile, parents were also pushing their children toward busy application to worthy tasks instead of what they perceived as the levity of Nisei social life. Traditional family controls, paradoxically, at once resisted cultural assimilation and strongly supported school learning. Parents wanted academic excellence in the public schools along with closely regulated personal relationships and consultation with the family in making choices for the children.

Education—of the official kind—went on in the midst of this quiet struggle to regain control of the destiny of the minority group from within. Numerous adjustments were necessary to make it possible for teachers to sit in front of a class of students day after day as they came into contact with this struggle. Many Caucasian teachers restricted their contact with students by giving Japanese American assistant teachers a disproportionate share of extracurricular activities, thus widening the gulf between school and family. "Such advantage-taking is perfectly apparent to our students," complained a Caucasian teacher who wanted the best for the incarcerated population. But it was a hard life for teachers, "a forgotten people" as one analyst recognized them to be. They continued to suffer from low prestige in the caste system of the camps, and they were still isolated from administrators and Japanese Americans alike. Teachers knew little of the policy decisions from above that shaped their work, nor of the family and community life into which their lessons flowed.[31]

School life embodied the conflict between administrative goals and community self-determination. At Manzanar, for example, the administration fancifully launched a program to have high school students teach English to their parents. The effort showed how little the administration understood, or was willing to understand, the patterns of authority and communication in the families under their care. In another camp the superintendent of schools threatened that the school system would not reopen in the fall of 1944 unless twenty-two Japanese Americans could be found to work as assistant teachers. Caucasian teachers were close enough to the grind of daily life in the schools to know why recruitment would be difficult, but their voice was rarely heard in the administration. It was obvious to them that the Nisei who were willing to teach had either left camp for the outside world or had gone to Tule Lake, while those who remained and were able to work in the schools had no desire to do so because they saw no future in it. The less mature Nisei remaining in the camps found little satisfaction in policing unruly classes. They knew well that the parents resented the hiring of people who had just graduated from camp high schools to teach children not much younger than themselves. A group of parents suggested recruiting college-trained Nisei from the outside to return to the camps and teach with full civil service status like the Caucasian teachers, but the WRA rejected the proposal.[32]

Teachers did manage to communicate to the administration that without the mature and more assimilated older Nisei around, parental influence over the schoolchildren was growing. Confronted by the determination of the Issei to maintain control over the upbringing of their younger children, an administrator fretted in the summer of 1944 that education "has fought a sometimes losing battle for possession of the children's minds and habits." Administrators could hear all around them that Japanese was the lingua franca of the community. Significantly, though, language study in both Japanese and English was common for old and young alike during the war. The Issei, relieved of work responsibilities, studied more English than they had in the past. They were exposed in their leisure time to radio broadcasts, newspapers, adult education classes, letters in English from their children and friends. The younger generation, thrown into close quarters with their parents, learned more Japanese than they might have in a mixed setting on the outside. As the rich vernacular bridging the distance between the two languages continued to proliferate, even the most hard-bitten assimilationists among the camp administrators began to see that this was not a virulent form of Japanese nationalism. What had seemed a dichotomy during the loyalty registration became a living reality of coexisting cultures. "The Japanese children should learn about the Japanese culture and become good American citizens," said a teacher in a Japanese language school. "This is not impossible."[33]

In fact, it was exactly what the parents were striving for. "The American government did limit our activities in society," recalled an Issei pioneer many years later, "but it could not limit or confine our beliefs . . . the Japanese culture flowered in the desert." Fueled by such conviction, another education, altogether different from the aims of official policy, was under way behind the barbed wire. The total education of the children proceeded at many levels, taking in the experience of the parents along with the lessons of the public schools. Besides witnessing the power of community institutions, the children lived amidst the flowering of more delicate lessons. In poetry and other cultural forms the older generation continued to build without apology, as in this satirical *senryu* poem, later translated for the *Journal of American Folklore:*

Here stands our metropolis
once we dwell long and feel
at home in sand and dust.

The older generation had its own lessons to teach about loyalty, and chose its own forms in which to discover and express the truth of its experience. Clubs formed to write and judge *senryu, haiku,* and *tanka.* Attended by the Issei and the Kibei, they provided vehicles for mobilizing the emotions of the group and for developing forms of criticism as well as escape. Wakako Yamauchi translated this one from the camps, signed "Toshu," and published it in 1979:

> Loyalty, disloyalty,
> if one should ask
> I cannot answer.

"They ask me to take a stand," Yamauchi comments on the poem and the plight of its author. "I can only divide myself. The ancestral land that could not provide for me still holds all those things dear to me: the ashes of my father, my mother, memories of my boyhood, *Yamato Damashi*—the spirit of Yamato. My brother is a soldier in the Imperial Army. They ask me to deny these. They ask me to commit myself to a country that will not accept me. And yet . . . and yet in these years here, I have found a measure of happiness and comfort. I have invested my children here. I stand divided." Such feelings deepened into a tragic affirmation through the cultural forms preserved by the group in exile. The poetry was a way of responding to that which could not be helped, to preserve identity while seeking solace. In the language of the home a part of life moved freely, its energies not subject to the dictates of public authority. Writing in *Amerasia Journal* in 1976, Constance Hayashi and Keiho Yamanaka brought into English the living contradiction of this spiritual freedom in the desert camp, as it was expressed in a poem of the Issei:

> With such a wide sky
> the Japanese
> have no home.

Often beyond the ken of administrators and teachers, invisible from the vantage point of official policy, the spontaneous mobilization of the cultural resources of the group was among the most significant educational achievements of the war years.[34]

Other forms of expression emerged, forms of teaching and learning outside the ambit of public policy. Several accounts depict the long lines of women at dawn, sifting the desert dust for tiny seashells at Topaz, the camp built on a dry lake bed. These shells became flowers, birds, winter landscapes. Taught by the skilled Issei craftsmen in the camps, Japanese Americans produced carved furniture and sculpture, wooden carts and whirligigs, rocking horses and trucks for the children. They made stage sets for *shibai* and *kabuki* drama, miniature landscapes, mailboxes, nameplates. Despite the wartime animus of many Caucasians against the traditional culture of Japanese Americans, calligraphy, weaving, embroidery, pottery, painting, and other expressive arts became part of camp life, lacking official support and sanction but commanding respect from residents. Dry gardens and arrangements of found objects appeared around and within the barracks, accompanied in some places by cactus gardens, portulaca, and locust hedges. Pieces of wood, hand-rubbed and polished, called *kobu,* showing the work of human hands that have brought out the beauty from within a natural form, became common sights. These could be seen in any number of interior spaces alongside fishes of brightly colored paper, arrangements of artificial vines and flowers, panels for poetry and painting, and a home shrine for worship. For many of the Issei, life in retreat meant salvaging the familiar world as they watched so much being swept away. As the war progressed, their years in exile were punctuated not only by official dictates, but by classes in traditional arts, by religious holidays and festivals, by plays and parades, by drama and singing, by *sumo* and *judo* and other sports.[35]

This cultural activity was educational—in the sense of the word that extends far beyond schools and formal instruction—but it was not merely teaching people to go back to a Japanese past. Cultural expression offered a means of mobilizing the energies of the group to cope with change and develop initiative to build a new life. Some of this dynamic change in the community spilled over to the schools, particularly where the remaining progressive teachers continued to encourage self-exploration and community consciousness. The children, too, wrote poems, staged plays, pursued traditional arts and crafts, and developed forms of expression to represent the complexity of their family world behind barbed wire. Ruth Tanaka, a student at Poston, exemplified the urge of many Nisei to come to grips with their past as they sought future opportunities through education. In her poem "Saga of a People" she probed the deeper structure of loyalty as understood by the children.[36]

> They have sprung from a race as old as Time,
> Their backs are bent, their hands are wrinkled and brown,
> For they have toiled long years under a harsh master-Life;
> Each passing year has left its mark
> Upon their seamed and weathered faces
> That show as other faces do,
> A heart-deep yearning for a far-off land;

Loyalty and Its Lessons

A land of frail houses, stunted trees, a sacred volcano
Sleeping under a blanket of snow . . .

Lest they forget the islands of their fathers,
They have brought their little treasures with them—
A miniature chest of drawers, lacquered dragon-red;
Two dainty fans gay with dancing girls;
A bamboo screen with a tiny arched bridge . . .

The seeds they sowed took root and sprouted,
Grew tall and straight with bursting pods;
Giving rich promise of fulfillment.
So grew their black-haired children
Straight and tall, drawing nourishment from the free soil
Their lives were like a deep, peaceful river
Formed by the mingling of two streams,
The old familiar customs of their ancestors
Mixing with the new bewildering ones of their foster country
And slowly giving way before them:
Eating a breakfast of crisp bacon and scrambled eggs
Instead of the hot soup and rice they had eaten
In the home of their fathers;
Raising a huge paper carp on Boys' day;
Awkwardly tying a silver star to the tip of the family Christmas
    tree . . .

They have come to a new home
Living in a single room
Behind barbed wire—
They know that peace has been shattered throughout the world
By heavily laden bombs of terror and destruction;
But they who love the deeply tranquil soil
Are stunned, bewildered by it all,
By the cold wall which their American friends
Have built around them.

Now they are standing on the beloved soil of their western mother,
Their wizened bodies huddled together
Against the bitter cold.
Rising they look toward the sea
Vainly striving through the mists of the past
To live again the dreams of their youth,
Thinking of a pleasant land where cherry blossoms
Warmed their hearts in spring . . .

Then they turn towards each other with eyes full,
Unashamedly,
Understandingly;
For deep in their almond, brown eyes,
Deep in the innermost depths of their souls
There shall always glow a hope,
A hope that peace shall come one day,
A peace forging with understanding and friendship
The islands of their long-lost youth
And the far stretching land of their children's birth.

Paralleling the earlier school life of the Nisei, a few Japanese language schools and tutors were introduced in the camp. These were a sign of mixed loyalty to many Caucasians, for they persisted in teaching the children, as had been the case in the language schools before the war, that the Japanese spirit would unite the people and help them to prevail against adversity. Many parents continued to hope, as they had in their communities before the war, that education in this spirit, rooted in ethical and moral precepts, would someday bring together the two warring cultures. This reconciliation would also sustain the peace of the family, of children and parents living across two cultures. It was difficult for many Japanese Americans to imagine any genuine strength without community institutions, the social and cultural organization that had sustained them ever since they came to the New World. One Japanese language teacher recalled, years later, when five Nisei volunteers for the U.S. Army had come by to bid farewell to him in the camp. He told them simply, "You are warriors inheriting Japanese blood . . . You will work hard and serve this nation well." Two of the five died in battle on the European front.[37]

As Japanese Americans struggled to come to terms with their wartime predicament, the issue of loyalty created divergent destinies for the Nisei, some leaving the camps right away, others remaining in exile. Teachers expressed surprise that those going to Tule Lake Segregation Center in the fall of 1943 included many of their best students. Many of these students did not want to go but were following older siblings whose defiance carried the family into deeper exile and, for a few thousand, expatriation. As exclusion proceeded another increment, placing the members of a racial minority into different categories under public authority, teachers and their students spent their days in class, teaching and learning the lessons of citizenship. In February of 1944 the U.S. House of Representatives passed a resolution to deport Japanese Americans who renounced their citizenship, even if renunciation was made under duress and behind barbed wire. In July of that year Congress passed a law that had been drafted by the Department of Justice, making it possible for Japanese Americans to renounce their citizenship. The administration at Tule Lake permitted groups of agitators to organize a drive for signatures to initiate the procedure of renunciation, and more than five thousand signed. At the same time, increasing numbers of Japanese Americans were relocating from other camps to American communities. School life continued in the shadow of these larger developments.[38]

Speaking at a youth conference sponsored by the Nisei of Topaz early in 1944, John Embree identified what he saw as the crux of the debate when he told his listeners that they should do everything possible to make themselves part of larger groups in society, rather than trying to find their way as a highly visible minority living together at close quarters as the Issei had done. He urged the second generation to relocate and take the jobs that were available, or to go on to further study, and not to degenerate in the camps. He encouraged all those who had an education to disperse themselves widely across the United States, concluding, "Don't go west, but go east, young Nisei!"[39]

4

Educating "Projectiles of Democracy"

"To TRAIN these people not just to make a living or pass the time until the war ends, but to make them ready to hurl as projectiles of democracy into the maelstrom of postwar readjustment—this is the sober demand of common sense, as well as the high demand of justice," wrote a camp administrator at Poston. That the second generation would rapidly disperse across the nation seemed inevitable to WRA officials as soon as leave clearance policies were liberalized. The median age of the Nisei was about eighteen in 1943, time to start college or a career, neither of which was possible inside the camps. Although some Nisei had been born as early as 1910 and others were still being born in the 1940s, a great many entered the camps during the throes of their transition from youth to adult life. For a large portion of the group, their age was ideal and their education adequate for swift mobility from racially segregated enclaves into colleges and the war economy. A sociologist writing for *Social Forces* identified a key assumption of relocation policy for the younger generation when he argued that "selective dispersion" was part of the solution for the "Nisei problem" of racial isolation. Another assumption for Japanese Americans as a whole was that the parents would follow their successful children to new homes away from the West Coast.[1]

Much to the disappointment of WRA officials, most remaining evacuees were not ready and willing projectiles. In June 1943 a community analyst had predicted that an effective program could resettle the whole population of the camps within one year. The probability of rapid dispersal had seemed especially high in light of the great demand for workers in war industries. One year later only about 20,000 Japanese Americans, or 18 percent of those in the camps, had relocated, and they were mostly young and single. Only 13 percent of the Issei had left. The reasons for this hesitation were obvious as far as the Issei were concerned; their losses had been the greatest and they were the least prepared to shift to new careers and communities. The discouragement of the remaining Nisei was less intelligible to WRA administrators. It was as if the graduating Nisei who remained in the camps did not understand the value of education. In a speech to the residents of Poston in 1945, two years after the resettlement program had been launched, WRA director Dillon S. Myer fretted that "these children are not going to school, I hope, with the idea of learning how to live in relocation centers all their lives."[2]

The federal government created elaborate channels for resettlement in 1943. The WRA hired relocation officers in numerous cities and negotiated for jobs, housing, and fair treatment. Other staff members conducted studies of opportunities and attitudes in places considered promising for resettlement away from the West Coast. The central office of the WRA developed a public relations campaign—speeches, films, radio broadcasts, national speaking tours, articles, legislative testimony, booklets. These activities were designed to advocate reinstatement of Japanese Americans in the normal life of the United States. At the same time, the WRA publicized outside opportunities within the camps to encourage the evacuees to venture forth. Building on New Deal precedents and again drawing many employees from earlier social programs, the government was attempting what it considered to be a humane feat of social engineering, since the West Coast was still closed to the group. Still, it was clear to all that resettlement was proceeding slowly. A generation of students was growing up in families that were reluctant to disperse into the society that had so recently forced them into the camps.

The ambivalence of the younger generation about the future was closely intertwined with the contradiction of teaching an incarcerated population about democracy. For young Japanese Americans during World War II, the value of education depended, in part, on deciding whether freedom might possibly exist in the future, even when their current investment in learning was being made under circumstances of manifest oppression. This decision about the future, unlike the order to build the camps or the administrative policies that ensued, had to be made by the Japanese Americans themselves, and it could be no more than a guess, whether informed by hopeful conviction or bitter disillusionment. Educators, social scientists, and camp administrators, no matter how gracious their motives, could not promise that the future would be free. The Nisei had to decide whether accommodation would make them patriots or quislings, whether the future would make their people Americans or "another Indian problem." Without knowledge of how it might turn out, no one could say for sure what the future might bring, which agenda was most plausible, or to what extent present beliefs might influence future success.

For the older children, the decision to resettle was often a choice of whether or not to continue their education beyond high school during the war. Of the approximately 2,500 Nisei attending college in western states at the beginning of World War II, only about 200 were reported to have transferred to other schools in the Midwest and East before being evacuated. If the rest were to receive no higher education, it was not clear what was to become of them, nor what hope their example would offer to the many other Nisei students who were graduating from high school each year. In 1942 more than 28 percent of the evacuated population was between the ages of fifteen and twenty-four, compared to slightly more than 17 percent in the same group for the entire U.S. population. From the rising generation of Nisei almost 4000 boys and girls had attended twelfth grade in the 1941–42 school year before being evacuated. Within the camps there were few opportunities beyond high school, and nothing approaching a genuine college education. The best alternative was work, but in the camps they could earn no more than nineteen dollars per month regardless of skills or productivity.[3]

As students inside the camps realized that "all we held dear to us could be swept away," outside, a few liberals, educators, and religious groups worried that concentrating citizens and their immigrant parents behind barbed wire was inimical to democratic ideals. The *Christian Century* featured an editorial in the summer of 1942 asserting that there was a "strategic necessity" for immediate action to protect "a whole generation of young Americans in one of our minority groups." The editorial spoke to the conscience of the white majority in American society: "To validate our many declarations of purpose and goal in this world struggle, all the rest of us must extend to them every chance for fuller assimilation into our national life." During the evacuation in 1942, a small coalition had formed to help the dislocated Japanese Americans, giving special attention to helping the college-educated elite, partly because they were seen as a vanguard leading the group into the mainstream of American life, but also because other strategies of assistance seemed impossible in the face of the anti-Japanese hysteria and the so-called military necessity in western states.[4]

Educators and concerned citizens working to help the Nisei from outside the camps were also protecting the norms of open competition and individual freedom that gave higher education its legitimacy as a democratic institution in American society. The list of advocates included nationally known educational leaders like Robert Gordon Sproul of the University of California and Ray Lyman Wilbur of Stanford University. Besides advocating the interests of the Nisei, educators were defending their own position in the moral order of U.S. society as keepers of enduring values, sorters of intellect, managers of assimilation. In support of the student relocation from camp to college, educators argued that it was essential to avoid the waste of human resources brought about by the evacuation. The Nisei were citizens who would play a role in American society after the war. Sending them to college would cost no more than maintaining them as wards of the government in the camps. Those who went to college, the argument continued, would symbolize to their families and friends in the camps that education was still the best route to a successful future. Finally, the process of assimilation would be enhanced among young Americans in midwestern and eastern communities, where the relocated students would be received more generously than on the West Coast.[5]

For many Nisei students there was little doubt that the brighter prospects were *outside*. This word acquired new meanings for those forced to live inside the fence. As one student had written from Amache early in the war, while awaiting leave clearance so that he could go to college, "this is taking on more and more of a concentration camp atmosphere. Spotlights will start glaring soon . . . a fence is being built . . . closer and closer the net winds. And we sit speechless . . . either in astonishment or from lack of interest, or from lack of any direction to the voices raised here and there." Some people complained that family authority had been so damaged by the evacuation and camp life that it left children without the discipline needed to prepare them responsibly for the future. Those within the camps, deprived of movement, unsure whether their former communities on the West Coast would remain forever out of bounds to them, were now in danger of losing their capacity to imagine where they might go and what they could do to rebuild their lives after such a collective catastrophe.[6]

The organization of special channels for student relocation had proceeded quickly as soon as the government began moving Japanese Americans from their home communities to temporary assembly centers. During the confusion and uncertainty of the mass evacuation, it helped considerably that the plea for fairer treatment of the Nisei found a sympathetic audience in the nation's capital. On May 21, 1942, Assistant Secretary of War John J. McCloy wrote to Clarence E. Pickett of the American Friends Service Committee: "Anything that can legitimately be done to compensate loyal citizens of Japanese ancestry for the dislocation to which they have been subjected, has our full approval." Successive meetings of educators and concerned groups in the spring of 1942 led to the formation of the National Japanese American Student Relocation Council, with offices first in several cities, then centralized in Philadelphia during 1943. The council, a voluntary agency operating on private funds outside the government, became a strong advocate for the interests of Nisei students eligible for college. It played an aggressive role in persuading institutions of higher education to participate. It set up standards and procedures for college application, then screened candidates and coordinated communication. It raised funds to help the Nisei pay for college, since the government would provide no support. The council also pressured federal authorities for expanded educational rights for the Nisei, and it tried in several ways to boost the sagging morale of young people in the camps.[7]

Some colleges right away refused to participate. One would not even issue transcripts of former students of Japanese descent, arguing that they should all be treated as prisoners of war, whether citizens or not. Despite such occurrences, the response from colleges was favorable enough overall that hundreds of students were able to relocate in the year following evacuation. By the fall of 1942 the council had administered and collected from the camps more than two thousand questionnaires filled out by Nisei interested in attending college. Japanese Americans matched this energy with their own as they raised funds—more than three thousand dollars, no mean sum in those days, from Topaz alone—to give scholarships to Nisei students leaving the camps for college. Philanthropic groups and church organizations contributed funds for scholarships and the operations of the council. The effort to get students out of the camps became known as an "underground railroad" among those who kept it going during the early months of the war. The metaphor suggested a transit not merely from camp to college, but from slavery to freedom.[8]

For students, thanks to the council and the willingness of the government to cooperate, there was a way out of the camps, though only for some during the first year of incarceration. For a select few early in the war, college was one of the only available niches in normal communities outside the fence. The journey from camp to college was a quest for educational opportunity and for a brighter future, but it was also a choice offered on terms set by those who directed higher education, terms that were at the same time checked and controlled at every step by the government. Social advancement was to be had through sponsorship by designated officials who selected students according to cultural criteria as well as cognitive aptitude. A committee of deans, registrars, and personnel administrators evaluated the Nisei applicants, reviewing scholastic performance, character, professional ambitions, contacts with Caucasians, and special interests or unusual talents. This sponsorship by a philanthropic organization working to create opportunities for a disadvantaged group—an arrangement new to the Nisei and, in fact, to most minority groups—operated within the constraints of government policy and the receptivity of communities and local institutions. To obtain leave from the government to attend college, the Nisei aspirants needed proof that they had been accepted at an institution outside the Western Defense Command. The government required evidence in advance of adequate financial resources, testimony from a public official that the student would be acceptable to the local community, proof that the institution had been cleared by the U.S. Department of War, and certification that the Federal Bureau of Investigation had completed a security check and granted the student a clearance. In the first two years of student relocation, Nisei students were not allowed to attend most major universities because of defense research and production on campus or in the cities where these institutions were located. When the restriction was lifted in 1944, Nisei students applying to such universities were subjected to an additional "personal security" questionnaire.[9]

Beyond these general policies controlling the selection of college Nisei, notes taken by the field staff of the student relocation council reveal that government officials took a keen interest in regulating the process of selection and sponsorship. Early in the war, outside educators and staff of the council found their movements constrained and monitored when they tried to gain access to evacuated students. Within the camps the government allowed only narrow interviews, focusing on the college admission procedure, and not even touching on family or community life. At first, the presence of a member of the internal security staff of the administration was often mandatory in meetings between students and field staff of the council, and all communication had to be conducted in English. Perhaps most important, those given indefinite leave to go to college found it difficult to go back to the camps, except for one small group of college Nisei who returned under the auspices of the student relocation council to recruit other students for college.[10]

In summary, three features stand out from the first years of student relocation. First, educators and humanitarian groups organized a system for selecting and sponsoring individual Nisei to leave the camps to attend institutions of higher education. Second, the system of sponsorship functioned within constraints set by governmental authority and local willingness to receive Nisei students into the community. Third, the conditions placed on the admissions process and on college attendance impeded communication about the family and community life of Nisei students, and for the most part prevented those who attended college from returning to the camps for the duration of the war.

The people on the outside who helped Nisei students in the camps were nourishing the hope, which persisted among Japanese Americans, that educational opportunities still existed, that equal citizenship and social mobility were still plausible images of the future. In working to keep alive such hopes, educators and other Caucasian allies created a system of sponsorship that, by design, scattered individual aspirants from the concentrated community and impeded their return. Exactly when the second generation was on the threshold of college, individual students faced a difficult choice: either they pursued academic achievements, thereby allowing themselves to be dispersed and isolated from their racial group, or they remained segregated in the slow, dispiriting, but nonetheless recognizably communal life of the camps. This was how educational opportunity was presented to college Nisei and shaped their relationship with the rest of the incarcerated population.

One student, writing from Smith College, said she knew what it was to fly from a cage. She soon found that this was also to fly into a chasm between two worlds. Many Nisei students realized the contradictions of their sudden dispersal and acknowledged their ambivalence as they tried to untangle opportunity from oppression. They wrote hundreds of letters to the few Caucasians they felt were genuinely working to help them. These letters piled up at the offices of the American Friends Service Committee, for the Quakers had reacted to the evacuation in 1942 by extending what they called a "spiritual handshake" to the victims, helping in various ways to soften the impact of anti-Japanese hysteria during the nation's mobilization for war. At the invitation of the federal government, the Quakers had played a central role in setting up the National Japanese American Student Relocation Council. Perhaps because these pacifists had offered unequivocal support to Japanese Americans at a time when even most liberals were rationalizing the oppression as a regrettable consequence of military necessity, they were privileged to hear voices among the Nisei that others could not hear. The letters offer glimpses of self-awareness during an extreme crisis for Japanese Americans. Such evidence could be seen as limited by the fact that the Nisei students were writing to enlist the sympathies of Caucasians who had power to help them, but the range of written reflections in the letters suggests that a deeper and more authentic communication was taking place. To read these letters is to realize that later explanations often leave out the role played by the Nisei as subjects of their own experience, not merely as the objects of history. The college Nisei, vanguard of a minority group that excels in higher education, helped to construct their place in American society in part by how they chose to understand what was happening to them.[11]

Even good fortune spawned bizarre predicaments for those who went from camp to college. Riding trains eastward across the country, the Nisei students traveled with servicemen returning from such places as Pearl Harbor and Guadalcanal. Arriving alone to college towns where Japanese Americans had never set foot before, these young people immediately confronted their own insecurities, the fear of having the wrong face and being in the wrong place. Venturing forth as a tiny elite, the Nisei students saw themselves as "ambassadors of good will" whose charge was to open the way for racial tolerance. In the words of a play staged at Amache, they were "eastward pioneers," their frontier good relations with the white majority. "Living in the same dorms as others and studying together," wrote three Nisei students from a college in Missouri, "we are testing a type of relation that we were never able to experience on the Pacific coast." Writing from Wellesley College, a student told her friends in camp that "those who have probably never seen a Nisei before will get their impression of the Nisei as a whole from the relocated students." Relatively free to move about in their new lives, those who went first were clearing a path for others to follow.[12]

Education presented the college Nisei with opportunity, but it also impelled the select few into a diaspora. Before the war most of the college group would have been concentrated in half a dozen universities on the West Coast, near their families and communities. Now, they were far away from what they had known before and from their families in the camps. Although their movements were not restricted once they were on the outside—except for excluded zones established by the military, such as the West Coast—they found themselves constrained by their own lack of knowledge about the larger world of the majority culture. Often the Nisei students lived with Caucasian families and roommates at college, an arrangement that intensified the separation from their ethnic origins. A Nisei wrote from Ohio that "seeing America, the larger America, for the first time . . . we are creeping out of a shell that we have unconsciously been in." Once on the outside, the college Nisei confronted a stark dichotomy between past and present, children and parents, school and home. Quite often they found themselves to be the only Japanese Americans in an entire college town of Caucasians. For most of them the separation from what they had known before was total, since during the war they could go back neither to the camps nor to their prewar homes.[13]

While the college Nisei savored new experiences, shadows intruded upon their good fortune wherever they went. The sole means of escape for these students was an exceptionally high level of performance and verifiably conventional behavior on terms set by their Caucasian sponsors in the new world they were entering. Having been instilled with a strong commitment to education by their immigrant parents, the Nisei now found it necessary to prove themselves worthy of equal treatment for fear of being sent back to the enclosed communities where their race had been concentrated. In this way, the cultural affinity of the minority group for educational achievement was channeled by racial oppression and liberal sponsorship, first into a pattern of dispersal, away from parents and the concentrated community, then into an obligation to maintain high levels of achievement and conformity to justify the second generation's status as citizens in American society.[14]

This predicament added a frightening dimension to the usual concerns of students about success and failure. A quest for confirmation replaced the self-evident truths of citizenship; and for the time being, the alternative to assimilation was not the familiar ambiance of an ethnic neighborhood and family businesses, but existence as wards of the government in a controlled environment. The Nisei were aware of this predicament: "The long stay in the camp has etched in my mind the value of freedom," wrote one of them from Salt Lake City. "So I say again," she continued, "life begins with freedom." But ever since the shock of evacuation, freedom was no longer an inalienable right; it depended on successfully managing the perceptions of others, persuading them that one deserved to be free. One had to gain recognition and the approval of whites to be selected and sponsored to leave the camps. Once free to go to the place approved by the government, one still had to convince others that this freedom was appropriate, having not yet secured enjoyment of it. While one Nisei journeyed to the Statue of Liberty and marveled that "she still carries a torch for me," another remarked that "the fellows out here treat me very well so I haven't got a kick coming anywhere."[15]

In spite of the risks and disenchantments, higher education was a channel to the free world. More than four thousand Nisei students were allowed to leave the camps to study at institutions of higher education outside the restricted zone of the Western Defense Command during World War II. The group served as a living example for the entire racial minority, suggesting a transition from camp to college, from oppression to opportunity even in the darkest of times. For many students it was a journey across space, time, culture, and class position. Education brought the Nisei into contact with people whose alliances could help them overturn public acceptance of the intolerant assumptions that had swept Japanese Americans out of their homes at the beginning of the war. While a history of both accommodation and resistance developed inside the camps, the college Nisei fought for connections with the outside world, a mixed world of oppressors and friends and mostly indifferent people. Even when they met with hostility, the college Nisei were in a position to learn more about the circumstances that were causing their oppression.

"As we face the future," wrote a Nisei woman in an education magazine, "our horizon is darkened by the possible threats of movements taking place to exclude all the Japanese from the United States after the war and to deprive us second and third generation American citizens of our citizenship." Southern and western congressmen were indeed pushing to keep all Japanese Americans, including the college Nisei, inside the camps. The bills proposed to deprive the Nisei of their citizenship did not pass, but the threat remained. The fortunes of Japanese Americans were not secure amidst the violent movements of public opinion and the machinations of special interest groups. In an editorial in its *National Legionnaire* the American Legion found it "hard to understand why, at this time, men whom the Government does not see fit to trust with rifles are permitted to pursue uninterruptedly their college and professional courses . . . There is a rankling hurt in the bosom of good, honest, patriotic, loyal, and devoted Americans when they see their sons come to the crossroads—their sons take the road that leads to war and the battlefields. The Japanese boy takes the road that leads to college and, to use a trite phrase worn rather thin and threadbare, the abundant life." Many traces of this resentment remained even when Japanese Americans were allowed to serve in the U.S. Army after the second year of the war.[16]

Colleges wishing to accept the Nisei students at times encountered a fusillade of local protest. When politicians and pressure groups agitated against the presence of Japanese Americans on campus, they were guided by reasoning that pronounced guilt by racial association with the enemy. In some places trustees feared sabotage and fifth column activities from these people of Japanese descent. Enterprising administrators wanted military personnel studying in special programs within their institutions to boost war-depleted enrollments, and the presence of the military in programs designed to further war aims would mean, because of government regulations, that no Nisei could be admitted to the institution. Among educators, though, many instances of resistance to the relocation of Nisei students probably stemmed less from prejudice or from self-aggrandizement than from timidity, a fear of undermining the prestige of their institution among conventionally minded citizens who, excited by the war emergency, had little patience with the nuances of educational opportunity in a democratic society. It is remarkable in retrospect that so many college officials welcomed the Nisei and defended their rights even when highly vocal segments of the surrounding community disapproved.

Recognizing that the challenge was, above all, one of persuasion and public relations, many college Nisei spoke far and wide to community groups while attending school. A star pupil who became class president in his college and served on the executive committee of the local YMCA spoke nine times a month to different groups around the state where he lived. Another was elected student body president at a college in Kansas, but decided, without prompting from college officials or fellow students, to step down when local politicians staged a fiery meeting to denounce his election and decry such subversive activity on the campus. It was a delicate process for the Nisei students, balancing self-determination and accommodation under these circumstances. "Understanding will have to come through seeing, feeling, experiencing—and then believing," reflected one of them. "I know we Japanese Americans will first have to develop a philosophy of understanding others and their reactions in order to *be* understood and to comprehend in a small way our own problems in relation to others." In spite of some instances of public resistance to their presence in college, it was still possible for this group of young people to believe that "our acceptance in the American community must germinate from us, from our activities." They realized that they were struggling not only against external oppression but against self-imposed limits, their own assumptions about what was possible.[17]

Some of their deliberations touched upon the appropriate response to injustice—and to success when it came. The college group was well aware of the doubts among Japanese Americans in the camps that anything but discrimination and exclusion could be expected in a racist society. One young Nisei wrote that he preferred to be treated badly because "the race situation is what it is and there isn't anything we can do about it. I expect prejudice." Another asked her peers rhetorically, "What can you and I expect in a country where they tolerate slums like those of Chicago, or the Okies in California, or the poor whites in the South and the lynching of Negroes?" Many others among the college Nisei felt that the only answer was total assimilation and one-hundred percent Americanism. For some, however, this doctrine raised the specter of Nisei racism as the college-going elite adopted the racial attitudes of the dominant white majority. One student warned that "our hope is to gain equality with the Caucasians, and the Negro is forgotten in the rush . . . We've got to combat this racial feeling . . . any group in trouble finds it so much easier to shove the blame onto some other minority group, and we are as guilty as any other racial stock."[18]

There were also signs of solidarity between the races. Those who went east found friends in various stages of nascent critical consciousness about the democratic promise of the United States. One Nisei student reflected on the patterns of prejudice standing in the way of other minority elites attending college: "There were several Jewish boys who tell me that they cannot enter medical school; the Catholic boys here have similar problems to tell, the Negro chap can talk endlessly of the south, the fellows of Italian descent speak of the disparagement they often receive, and on it goes." In Chicago a Nisei woman attending college lived in a cooperative house that was battling its landlord to allow a black student to continue living there. The example was one among many of how the college Nisei were learning to recognize the contradictory position of education—and educated elites—in a society that continued to be sharply divided along lines of race and class. It was a poignant reminder of the burden of race in America when blacks offered expressions of sympathy as government propaganda attacked Japanese racial characteristics.[19]

The racial stigma would not wash away easily. Many Nisei student, prodded by WRA briefings encouraging separation when they left the camps, wrote of the need to avoid forming cliques when several Japanese Americans attended the same school. Yet, this strategy was not enough. Social acceptance could not be achieved merely through rapid dispersal of the race. One problem was sheer indifference, the tendency of the majority to lump minorities into a single insignificance as far as the dominant culture was concerned. One student complained that a teacher "actually asked me whether the rest of the Niseis spoke English, and another *history* teacher asked me why the Isseis were not citizens." These more subtle forms of prejudice were cause enough for desperation at times: "I feel like tossing my books into the fire and taking the first train to Topaz," the camp in Utah. This melancholy correspondent confided that he had begun to discover "something unreal" about his experience at college, a "slow, subtle change . . . it seems harder to make Caucasian friends . . . I can't help feeling that I am putting a wall deliberately between myself and others."[20]

Such feelings of powerlessness no doubt recurred as the scattered elite graduated from college. For they often moved on to job discrimination, dual wage scales for white males and for minorities and women, and further exclusionary policies set in their path, education and the good will of some Caucasians notwithstanding. Even so, the college Nisei also felt empowered as they advanced. Accepting an unfair challenge and proving themselves, through education, to be fully part of the nation at war with the nation of their grandparents, many of them gained an appreciation of the larger arena of contending forces that made the United States so paradoxical in its freedoms and tyrannies. The letters they wrote suggest another gain as well. Inasmuch as the college Nisei were leaders who saw themselves as clearing a path for others to follow, they recognized that part of their task was to create a shared understanding beyond themselves, a way of symbolizing to others the social faith that would turn tragic events into a future reconciliation.

"When misfortune falls we tend to wallow in it," wrote the Nisei who expressed such an understanding with the greatest eloquence, "and completely ignore the forces working to counteract this situation; we concentrate on those who brought about the misfortune and forget those who under severe handicaps are fighting to ease and correct the misfortune; one suddenly realizes the gross injustice one has done to those who have kept faith and courage in the ideal he himself has given up for lost and useless. The ideal becomes more beautiful and real than ever because it is now devoid of its superficial members and we see it in its purer working forms. It becomes clearer than ever before and finally we grasp the inner meaning of such terms as 'faith,' 'courage,' and 'democracy.' The course of the past two years has been thus with me."[21]

Whatever hopes or fears the college Nisei might have had, were they not still the chosen few? What did their ideals have to do with the lives of others who were not so fortunate? Life in the camps, it must be remembered, had a history of its own, marked by such high points as protest demonstrations, work programs, strikes, loyalty testing, segregation of supposed disloyals, the drafting of young men into the army, draft resistance, and a family resettlement program that met with resistance from Japanese Americans because they were wary of what might happen to them in the outside world. While some of the college Nisei wrote ecstatically about barbecues and pillow fights with their Caucasian peers, many young Nisei in the camps were losing heart. In late 1943 the field director of the student relocation council was appalled by the contagion of "lose-fight," the slang word in the camps for the hopeless apathy felt by many young people. Most disturbing, the percentage of graduating high school seniors who were applying for leave clearance to attend college was declining as the war progressed.[22]

A Nisei poet in the camps despaired as others on the outside professed hope and promise:

Oh—
Is it only a vanished mirage
That I thought the land of the future—
Hope, success, happiness, fulfillment of humanity?

In the falling dusk—
I hear discouraged, disillusioned voices—
"Why is it wrong to be colored?"
"We have served, and want to serve! Are we given
  no place in this land?"[23]

The educators and government administrators involved in student relocation had thought of ending the council in 1943, since by then it seemed to many that the path to college had been cleared. But a new problem had arisen, reinforcing the need for active sponsorship of students, and thus, as it turned out, extending the life of the council for another three years. Now that the energies of the council were not needed so much for persuading colleges, communities, and all levels of government to make way for the Nisei students, the focus turned inward, to the camps, where it appeared to those on the outside that the younger generation was "thinking up reasons for staying put," perhaps even losing its will to live in the United States. Worse yet, it was becoming evident to some advocates of Nisei educational interests that the schools inside the camps were contributing to the problem.[24]

Touring all ten camps in the summer of 1943, staff of the student relocation council learned that many Caucasian teachers were advising Nisei students not to go to college. "Some of this hostility," observed the field director, "is born of race prejudice, particularly among the teachers who are attracted to the projects by the relatively high salaries paid by the Federal Government." But, he added, the lack of support for Nisei educational aspirations also arose from "an attitude which the teachers describe to you as realism. They will tell you that it is a mistake for a Japanese American to think in terms of a college education since he is destined to be only a manual laborer anyway. They point out that if he goes to college and gets 'high falutin' ideas about what he can do in life, it will only lead to unhappiness and disillusionment when he finds that the fields for which he trained are not open to him."[25]

Such attitudes became an even more serious factor in 1944 when the college placement function of the student relocation council was absorbed by the counseling staff in the camp schools. This policy change meant that the council would henceforth engage only in supportive activities such as raising funds and coordinating communications. In that year the field director of the council discovered that students at Topaz were not able to take more than four academic subjects in school. One of the thirteen college Nisei who returned to the camps under the auspices of the council in the summer of 1944 said that the evacuated students "sensed a diabolical plot which had as its end the un-education of the Nisei, in the hope of having our mental processes compete with the Digger Indians of yore in excavating for a living."[26]

There were other reasons as well for the drop in college applications. Many students in the camps who could have gone to college refused to do so. If they were the oldest children in their families, they often felt a responsibility to care for the young and for their aged parents. An illness in the family was enough to keep many students in the camps, since parents often depended on their children to communicate with authorities in the English language. Many boys preferred to wait and show their loyalty with derring-do instead of sitting in college classes. "Maybe after the war when Freedom comes, I might again ask you for advice," wrote one lad to the student relocation council as he enlisted in the army. More than sixteen thousand Nisei from the mainland United States served in the armed forces during World War II. Some Nisei males, however, refused both college and military service. From Heart Mountain, the camp in Wyoming where the draft sparked bitter and organized resistance, one student who spoke up probably reflected the attitude of others who remained silent: "It is true that I applied for student relocation . . . but I did so under the influence of another man, and I was not sufficiently independent in my thinking. I had left college toward the end of my sophomore year because of a distaste for the methods and philosophical bases evident in the educational system in practice—and also because of a basic readjustment of my views wherein lay true service in life and wherein lay right and wrong." Though girls were often preferred by colleges (they aroused less suspicion), many were discouraged by their parents from leaving camp for fear of what might happen to them in distant places. Other young people stayed in camp to help their families eventually resettle in outside communities instead of using scarce family resources for their own education. A smaller number merely awaited the end of the war and expatriation.[27]

The college Nisei who returned ran into a wall of questions from those who had remained in the camps—about the future, social life on the outside, reasons for the council's altruism, and a sense of foreboding that one interviewer summarized as follows: "I wonder if there's any use going to college in these kind of circumstances. Broken down: How will they treat you? Eats on the train? Call you a Jap? Stare at you? Cost a lot?" Encountering resistance, one of the college-educated elite complained of students in the camps that "they do not see the whole problem of democracy, and therefore, cannot argue constructively, and when pressed, fall back onto the constitutionality of the evacuation as a basis for disbelief in America." There was also the issue of guilt for the college Nisei. To witness the lethargy of the "colonists" inside the camps while they, the racial pioneers and ambassadors of good will, advanced to new occupations and a more normal life on the outside, was deeply disturbing. As one student wrote, it was "heartrending to think of the 100,000 others who should have the same opportunities I have, but who are instead being subjected to that environment of mass internment." A returning Nisei admitted that "defeatists in the Center have expressed their disapproval of my beliefs and I can feel the effect of their words digging into me."[28]

Hoping to expand family resettlement by creating a positive impression of the outside world, the camp administrators allowed the "returnees," as the college Nisei visiting the camps under official auspices were known, to circulate freely in the barracks and speak with parents as well as children. The reason for this belated liberality is to be found in the predicament of the government after it had built the isolated camps. Once people had been excluded, dispossessed, and concentrated together against their will, it was no easy task to disperse them. From the perspective of the government in 1944 and 1945, not enough Japanese Americans were leaving the camps to resettle in American communities. The total population of all ten camps in January of each year went from 110,240 in 1943 to 96,576 in 1944 to 80,878 in 1945, even though there were few obstacles to obtaining leave clearance in the last two years of the war. The remaining population within the camps showed a higher and higher proportion of young and old people, as the most employable and educable left for opportunities outside.[29]

Thus, the complement to elite sponsorship for the few, the other side of opportunity and dispersal, was an even greater concentration of those members of the evacuated population who, having lost the security of their prewar ethnic communities, did not have the resources, the attitudes considered appropriate, or the will to master the channels of sponsorship that were available for reincorporating themselves into the world outside on favorable terms. Those of the college elite who returned to the camps, sponsored by the same Caucasians who had helped them to get out, now faced the incarcerated community and tried to persuade its younger members that they should disperse themselves widely, as the vanguard had done, into niches that awaited them in places they had never seen. The records of the student relocation council suggest that the returning college Nisei were successful in making known their views and reaching many ambivalent high school students in the camps, but that they also encountered varieties of resistance that were deeply rooted in the crisis of the generations and not likely to be resolved through individual opportunities for exit and dispersal.

Among school-aged Nisei who remained in the camps, one of the chief obstacles to higher education was parental objections. Knowing how much the parents supported the education of their children under normal conditions, the college Nisei who returned saw right away that this was a more complex problem than it had appeared from the outside. A torturous communication was taking place between the remaining Issei and Nisei in the camps. After experiencing the imposed authority and opportunity that had divided the generations in so many ways, those who still inhabited the camps by 1944 were, paradoxically, moved to consider what they had in common. The demand of many Issei for family solidarity, even when they believed strongly in the value of education, became a way of negotiating the future on their own terms. The reports of the few college students who returned to the camps suggest that the Issei were calling for an awareness of collective needs as the college-bound Nisei pursued individual opportunities.

The students who returned came to see, therefore, that their role was not merely to persuade fellow Nisei to enter the channels of outside sponsorship so that they could leave the camps and attend college. Their role was also to serve as examples to the Issei, showing them that a settled life in America was again possible through the education of their children, that families would surely benefit from new opportunities in the postwar world. Returning students found that the prospect was not an outlandish one to the Issei if it was presented in the right way. "Parents will listen," concluded one who returned, "to children who show determination and initiative in their thoughts about education. It is the Niseis who waver like a pendulum or toss like corks in a sea who succumb to the objections of their parents." The educated Nisei, returning to the camps as children of character and accomplishment, exemplified the possibilities of the future to the older generation. They gave Japanese Americans inside the camps an occasion to speak directly with those who had ventured forth into the outside world and showed that it could be done.[30]

Certain nuances in this message made the returnees' conviction about the future at least plausible to many high school students and their parents—in a way that the rhetoric of educators, administrators, and social scientists in the camps was not, no matter how altruistic their intentions. The written reflections of the college Nisei indicate that both assimilation and resistance were involved for those who sought higher education through the sponsorship of the student relocation council. The college Nisei had demonstrated through great effort that future success was not ruled out by present suffering in the camps. But they had also encountered isolation, fear of rejection, marginal status, all of which interfered with their social mobility. They were forced to acknowledge these experiences, even as they achieved greater acceptance than in the past. Theirs was, they believed, a path that many others would follow in the postwar world.

Watching the new generation on the rise, the Issei had mixed feelings about the opportunities of their children, a spectrum of emotions ranging from disgust to adulation. The legal isolation of the elders remained unchanged, reaching back to the permanent denial of citizenship or any right of naturalization that had conditioned their lives in the United States from the beginning. There is no shortage of evidence of the tensions between old and young over the cultural consequences of assimilation. "I find myself stumbling over words," said one Nisei son, "as I make vain attempts to talk to my father. I don't understand him; he doesn't understand me. It is a strange feeling to have such a barrier between my father and myself." Yet, many Issei did enter into an unstated pact of reconciliation with their children, or at least one of tragic acceptance. "My father is old, 78 years old," wrote one of the Nisei students after departing from camp, "and he knew I would miss him greatly and that he may never be able to see me again. But as I left," continues the letter, "he strengthened me with these words. 'I am old, someday you will hear that I am dying, perhaps while you are still in school. Forget about me. Make my dying days happy in the knowledge that you are studying and preparing yourself for service. My life is in the past, yours is in the future.' "[31]

Apart from the college students, the young men and women who entered the armed forces, and the first wave of older and more mature Nisei who took outside employment, relocation outside of the camps proceeded at a sluggish rate. After a certain number of individuals had left as soon as opportunities were available, it became clear—to the community analysts if not to most administrators—that families were part of what was holding the rest back. This pattern of resistance called for special efforts to do more than provide opportunities for individual release. It was necessary to make family resettlement more plausible to the reluctant families. While the WRA hired relocation officers to persuade local communities to accept Japanese Americans, it also expanded its relocation efforts within the camps. In all of the camps except for Tule Lake Segregation Center, family surveys, adult education, and relocation counseling added new pressures on those remaining behind barbed wire to consider relocating as soon as possible. The administration also hoped to use the relocation of college Nisei as a wedge for bringing families into the communities where the students had settled. For students ready to leave the camp for college, the administrative handbook advised that "the selection of a school should be coordinated with a future relocation plan for the family." This strategy probably had a retarding effect on student relocation, though it did encourage collective instead of individual planning among hesitant families.[32]

As the 1943–44 school year began, more than ninety thousand Japanese Americans languished behind barbed wire. About as many were living as supposed disloyals at Tule Lake as had managed to leave the camps after the first full year of operation. The top WRA administrators were determined to use every resource at their disposal to stimulate greater movement out of the camps—everything from bringing in respected outsiders to reducing incentives within the planned communities. The latter strategy included keeping wages low, preventing productive enterprises from becoming self-sustaining, reducing job quotas, withholding building materials, restricting community services, and keeping Japanese Americans out of the controlling administrative positions in community management. According to the "reconditioning procedures" added to the WRA administrative handbook, "Evacuees must be stimulated to a healthy discontent with the limitations of the center, or they will never move." As official planning increasingly stressed the dissolution of the camps, schools were viewed as essential to the policy mandate of accelerating dispersal by changing people's attitudes and preparing them for the transition. "You should make every effort to establish *positive* attitudes toward relocation," teachers were instructed by their superiors. "Evacuees should be indoctrinated so that they want to go."[33]

The schools had to become instruments of the policy of resettlement, administrators believed. They held meetings with teachers to infuse the entire school curriculum with the message that it was time to resettle on the outside. Readings, student reports, compositions, map study, and class discussions centered on different places where families could resettle. Teachers coached students to talk with their families about the temporary nature of the camps. Across all subject areas, teachers received instructions to frame the material under study in terms of the family's imminent return to normal life. One set of guidelines provided the cues: "When you relocate . . . " "On the outside you will . . . " Classes routinely set up a "career corner" and relocation folders on desirable cities that students had studied in their class projects. Often the students clipped articles from newspapers and magazines during class to assemble materials favorable to resettlement. With some assistance from relocation officers on the outside, they corresponded with pen pals in normal communities. In every way possible teachers were supposed to inculcate the desire to leave the camps and resettle away from the West Coast. At Amache a community analyst helped to redesign the Social Studies curriculum to stimulate relocation; in his syllabus he emphasized social skills such as applying for jobs, communicating with fellow employees, "how to eat, drink, and be merry gracefully," getting the most out of banks and insurance agencies, learning to take good advice, "dealing with trouble," and how to make friends. Relocation lessons often included a reassurance that other groups had suffered discrimination and then achieved success in the United States. "After the democracies have won this struggle," wrote one administrator at Jerome in Arkansas, "the privations and inconveniences of the present will be recognized as a purifying process, making us more appreciative of the opportunities that will be ours."[34]

This use of school curriculum to stimulate family resettlement ran up against hardened skepticism of many Japanese Americans remaining in the camps. The WRA pressed on with its goal, certain that early resettlement was better for them than continued existence as wards of the government. Broadening the justification for bureaucratic intervention into the lives of the incarcerated population, the WRA handbook reasoned that the people in the camps had developed "psychological blocks" to relocation, such as "lack of self-acceptance" and "inability to face reality." It was the job of teachers to dissolve these with proper instruction. From the perspective of the administration, symptoms of unreality in the minds of Japanese Americans included "lack of desire for information concerning the major issues of the war," "demand of rights which are unattainable at this time," "a tendency to cling to the security of the parent-child relationship," and "satisfaction with life" in the camps. On the last point the handbook warned that "satisfaction of physical needs without effort becomes increasingly attractive to some the longer they live in the center." The danger of people remaining behind barbed wire and losing their will to leave was growing in the camps as "life within them ceases to be intolerable." Teachers were told to emphasize how much better conditions on the outside would be, through "constant repetition" of the most promising aspects of resettlement. They were also told explicitly to stress "movement to the Middle-West, East, and South," that is, to use the schools purposefully to reinforce a federally induced pattern of migration away from the prewar homes of Japanese Americans.[35]

The word "relocation" had been used to designate the evacuation and thus came freighted with meanings. The word was distasteful to Japanese Americans; in its previous incarnation it had meant calamity. The administration persisted, nonetheless, directing community analysts to isolate relocation problems and help design curricula to change behavior both among children and adults. In January 1944 the directors of the camps received an "emergency instruction" from Dillon S. Myer, WRA director, calling for meetings with education staff in each camp to review relocation objectives. Each camp was to create at least ten new organizational strategies within one month for carrying out the objectives. Relocation should "permeate the curriculum," Myer wrote. The management plan to meet this goal was to involve every member of the education staff in direct action. As for specific objectives, educators were to introduce more information about the outside world, instead of lessons oriented to the camp community; and they were told to redouble all efforts to inculcate American cultural values and the English language. Using responses by camp administrators to this official communication from Myer, the WRA compiled a guide to applying the school program to federal relocation policy, organizing the directives under several headings that reflected the chief administrative preoccupations: staff attitudes, psychological blocks to relocation, Americanization, vocational training, and the use of the English language.[36]

Most parents, feeling the pressure of these policies through their children and occasionally through WRA surveys, social work, and communications, were adopting a wait-and-see attitude. They read the newspapers and knew at least some of what was going on outside. They were aware of the persistence of negative attitudes that would greet them upon their return to U.S. society. In September of 1944 a national poll asked Americans, "After the war, do you think Japanese living in the United States should have as good a chance as white people to get any kind of job, or do you think white people should have the first chance at any kind of job?" Sixty-one percent of those asked replied, "White people first." Shocking stories about the mishaps of relocating Japanese Americans were standard gossip in the camps, frequently confirmed by western newspapers that were passed around the barracks and read eagerly for evidence that the government was not telling the whole story in its propaganda. The proportions of rumored disaster were usually false, but the emphasis was not entirely misleading. A memorandum by the WRA solicitor at the end of 1943 had tallied anti-Japanese legislation and ordinances in twenty states, among them prohibitions against Japanese Americans buying land (including citizens), intermarriage bans, restrictions on the right to transact business, bans on licenses, nullification of inheritance rights, exclusions from civil service, voting restrictions, and exclusionary clauses in standard real estate contracts. Although there was growing evidence that communities would receive Japanese Americans, bad news was more believable than good news. When a parent-teacher association was organized at Amache in 1944, the state PTA refused to recognize it. When cooperative enterprises were set up in some of the camps, they soon foundered because of objections and fear of competition from the outside. Each humiliation and rejection weighed more heavily on the scale of opinion than any amount of official encouragement.[37]

The slights from outside were especially hurtful when they called into question the lessons being learned inside the classroom by the children of war. When Amache High School planned a football game against the nearby Wiley High School in Colorado, the event was called off shortly before it was to begin because parents of some of the boys from Wiley said their children could not play. A student leader from Amache wrote to students at Wiley that her brother, like their brothers, was in France serving in the U.S. Army. She noted that the game was to have taken place on Armistice Day, which commemorated a previous "war to end all wars." She implored, "How can we show the world the road to brotherhood when we at home do not practice it?" The effect of such an incident was to reinforce the anxieties of the incarcerated population about life on the outside, far in excess of positive evidence to the contrary, and despite the constant reiteration of hopefulness in the educational program. For teachers, the hostility of local communities was deeply damaging to their lessons about American life because it destroyed the only possible contact with normal institutions in the vicinity of the camp schools, and it undermined the assumption that life would be better for Japanese Americans on the outside. "It was extremely difficult," wrote one teacher, "to teach the ideas and ideals of democratic society and to urge their relocation when constant reminders confronted boys and girls with evidence of prejudice and undemocratic procedures."[38]

Many of the teachers came from rural states where the majority of the camps were located. As the field director of the student relocation council had noticed, their attitudes toward providing the relocated population with opportunities in communities away from the West Coast were not as positive as the language of WRA policy. Outright prejudice was only one ingredient of the educational dilemma. Whatever their attitudes, teachers had classrooms to control, conventional lessons to teach. As one administrator discerned, conflict was inevitable between camp administration pressuring families to resettle on the outside and teaching staff trying to persuade children that education inside the camps was important and worthwhile. Like teachers everywhere, those who taught in the camps for Japanese Americans were routinely overloaded with grandiose expectations about their role in socializing children. Individually, they could persist only by working out a manageable set of activities organized around what they were able to teach. Many of them, of course, did not persevere. Attrition continued at high rates. Those who did stay on inhabited a world behind the classroom door that was profoundly different from the efficient planned communities sketched by policy and publicity.[39]

The discrepancy between policy and practice also appeared in the uses made of Japanese Americans as teachers. A substantial portion of those who taught in 1943–44, as in the previous school year, were Japanese Americans. More and more, however, these were not older Nisei, who had been the first to leave the camps for jobs and higher education. Rather, they were increasingly drawn from recent high school graduates who had not relocated because they lacked skills and credentials. These young teachers were disgruntled because their work was not preparing them for future careers. Their students were often unruly and aggressive since the young Nisei lacked cultural authority over their peers. The turnover continued to be rapid, but it was constantly the most mature and highly trained who left— the best role models, the more mature leaders of the second generation.[40]

Variations appeared from camp to camp, but everywhere the educational system was at best an inefficient instrument of central policy directives. The Herculean task facing the schools was no longer to form ideal communities or even to carry out an enlightened program of dispersing a racial minority into new homes. Merely to survive as minimally productive educational institutions was enough for the mortals who sat face to face with their classes each day. The teachers were struggling to bring the educational level of their students back to national norms in basic subject areas. This was probably the most important goal in the minds of most teachers by the middle of the war; and it, too, was formidable. They ran up against practical impediments to creating new futures—crowded living quarters, lack of sleep, family tensions, community conflict. The teachers witnessed daily the limits of their own effectiveness in changing the lives of their students within the confines of the camps. They did not necessarily understand much about the discrepancy between policy and practice or what had caused it, but they saw regularly the glaring difference between official euphemism and living fact. Teachers worked on the edge where authority touched real lives and took the form of interaction instead of directive. An anthropologist observed that because of the loss of older siblings, the cultural distance between parents and children, and the paucity of contact between teachers and families, "teachers had a most difficult job instructing because the students had psychological tendencies to reject learning, and to obstruct cooperative relations between teacher and class."[41]

Within these limits, teachers responded to the challenge as much as they were willing or able. They consciously shifted the emphasis of instruction in their classrooms to raise the hopes of students about opportunities on the outside and in the postwar world. As relocation became the guiding principle of Social Studies for high school students, one student remarked dutifully, "We should find out the problems that would confront us in each state . . . and we should study culture, history, and other traits of that particular section." The social problems under study continued to include the need to learn such things as the etiquette of introductions and invitations, and the social graces of travel. "After all," imagined one student, "hatred is built on ignorance and at close quarters most everyone is not as unpleasant as they are supposed to be. We must be prepared to sell ourselves and our people by knowing how to do the little things gracefully." The WRA handbook stated explicitly that the educational program should "lead each individual to practice American manners and customs." This was taken literally to mean such things as "shopping" and "desirable forms of recreation" as well as etiquette and mores. The emphasis also extended, intriguingly, to "the American ideal of the equality of women," both in the classrooms for schoolchildren and in Americanization programs for adults. Teachers were supposed to carry forth the battle of Americanization on the cultural as well as the political front. The evidence from curriculum guides, teacher narratives, and educational reports suggests that to the extent that they were able to, they often did.[42]

Administrators had difficulty understanding the resistance of Japanese Americans to the policy of relocation. John Embree, the anthropologist who headed the community analysis staff of the camps, had called it "resistance to freedom" and described the administrative problem in some detail for a professional journal. Community analysts worked diligently to find alternative ways of communicating the policy to families in doubt. They knew well that morale in the schools was visibly falling by the middle of the war. Teachers, for their part, had no difficulty seeing that the push for relocation was traumatizing their students because of the confusion and opposition it was creating in their families. After hearing her students talk about family attitudes toward relocation in 1944, Mildred Standing, a teacher at Poston, recalled that "we were unable to help some of the children in losing their fear of the future. The younger children, especially, have almost forgotten what life is like outside the camps; the older ones hear discouraging reports and discussions by their elders and worry about them." The administration tried an experiment of allowing some high school students to leave the camps by themselves to attend school on the outside, hoping the families would follow, but the trend toward dispersal did not accelerate. Except for the declining size of age cohorts entering school, the school population was remaining fairly stable as the war progressed. This meant in effect that families with children were generally not relocating.[43]

Despite the intensity of WRA policy initiatives, the schools were not stimulating relocation. Indeed, their presence, though substandard, was probably helping to slow down the desired movement outward. The administration faced a dilemma by establishing public schools and purporting to teach about democracy inside the camps. On the one hand, allowing schools to deteriorate might well stimulate relocation, bringing about more rapid dispersal into normal communities and their democratic way of life. But inside the camps this strategy would also communicate to the incarcerated population a message of hopelessness, a lack of conviction about their futures in the United States, and a duplicity in any attempt to defend school programs as preparation for responsible citizenship. If, on the other hand, the schools were improved, as parents wished, students would be better prepared for a future in which they would live as equal citizens on the outside. But this would also make the camps more livable, more desirable as communities in which to remain until the war was over and the West Coast opened up again, or perhaps even beyond the end of the war. Far from being democratic, such a policy would foster dependency on the government. Either way, the administrators, despite their barrage of propaganda, could not impose their own construction of social reality upon the minds of Japanese Americans. The majority was inclined to remain in the camps and seek educational opportunities for their children there for the duration of the war.

A Japanese American who served as a block manager at Poston suggested that the camp culture had become organized around two poles. One was the "California-Japanese culture," the social organization of immigrant communities, which was similar to, but several decades behind, the culture of Japan. The other was the "professional Americanism of the schools," their curricula, activities, and teachers from the larger world of American society on the outside.

The first pole was the core of the camp community in all ten camps. "The process of relocation," said the block manager according to an administrative report, "has simply drawn off the individuals who were farthest from the core—like molecules escaping by evaporation from the surface of a liquid. Relocation . . . has de-Americanized the core community. The young who are left . . . are increasingly reabsorbed into the culture of the core."[44]

By the end of the 1943–44 school year, John W. Powell, the WRA administrator at Poston who reported this view, adopted a similar image for the resistance to relocation. Writing about the conviction to stay in the camps until the end of the war after the older Nisei had left, he wrote, "we can see whole clusters of individuals, like molecules in a solution, flowing forward and escaping into the free condition, or flowing back and settling into crystallized attitudes of inertia." Looking around at the little world that the policy of racial exclusion had made at Poston, Powell believed that "the Authority is underestimating the genuine institutions of the California-Japanese family community, and overestimating the potentialities of individual Nisei escape into urban assimilation."[45]

Federal planners had succeeded in creating an elaborate social machinery of dispersal, demonstrating that the relocation centers could channel individuals outward into opportunities waiting beyond the fence. But the core community, the family authority and social organization that Japanese Americans had brought with them at the beginning of the war, endured and resisted federal plans for resettling the majority of Japanese Americans away from the West Coast. Despite the erosive effects of policy, this core community mobilized to protect its cultural institutions within the camp, there to hold the children until the outside world might appear more propitious for the group as a whole.

5

"The Children Don't Do It That Way"

WORLDS apart on many issues, parents and school officials were united in their concerns about the youth culture of the camps. The strengthening of family bonds, an important development in the social history of the camps after many older Nisei had departed, stopped short of taming adolescence. Parents recognized that the cultural and emotional distance between them and their children reduced the effectiveness of traditional community institutions in controlling adolescents. Officialdom, too, was perplexed that it could not motivate the older children. The public culture of the schools had no more purchase in this respect than did the ethnic culture, once so many young people had been concentrated at close quarters without constructive purpose. The camp environment intensified the solidarity and disaffection of youth. Parents as much as administrators and teachers felt the reins of authority slipping from their grasp. "Once I told my daughter to do something," said one mother to a teacher, "and in a flash she says, 'Why mother, the children don't do it that way.'" Many parents did not see their teenagers between the time they got out of bed and the time they went to sleep. "When parents are not providing food and shelter for their children," suggested a community analyst at Minidoka, "the children do not 'owe' them that much, and consequently have less

respect for them. Often children make this remark, when repri-
manded, 'You don't pay my room and board.' "[1]

The older children were often engaged in a dual struggle against
official coercion and traditional authority. At times they evinced a
cavalier attitude that offended the sensibility of the parents as deeply
as it did that of the administration. In school student resistance was
on the rise in 1944. Parents and the administration tried to intervene
in different ways, the parents through family pressure, block committees, and community councils, the school through the insistence
of teachers and the use of formal discipline procedures. But young
people often followed their own impulses anyway. At Topaz mass
walkouts of classes became widespread in 1944. Students did this
for fun as well as to resist teachers they disliked. "Last Thursday,"
reported a student after one such strike in April, "we walked out
on one of the teachers. She is egocentric. Everything she says is
right and not to be judged or corrected. One boy corrected an obvious
error she made. He was sent out of class because of it. The class
thought this was unnecessary injustice. We all walked out on her."[2]

Similar protests cropped up throughout 1944. Many students pro-
tested at Topaz when a favorite teacher, a conscientious objector,
was suddenly fired. Pressure developed at Minidoka to oppose the
firing of a principal who was loved by the community. Also at Minidoka students went on strike in the junior high school because a
teacher slapped a boy after class. They returned only after the principal of the school called an assembly and explained the situation
publicly, coaxing the teacher to make a formal apology in front of
the students. In short, students made it known that they were part
of the politics of education in the camps. They sometimes drew the
line and resisted openly when they did not like how they were being
treated.[3]

An event that rocked the youth culture with violent frustration
was the lifting of the blanket exclusion of Japanese Americans from
the West Coast. The Western Defense Command rescinded the exclusion order on December 17, 1944, effective the second day of
January. On December 18 the U.S. Supreme Court handed down its
decisions on two key cases that legitimated but also limited government policies toward Japanese Americans. In *Korematsu* v. *United
States* the high court upheld the constitutionality of the evacuation
on the basis of military necessity; but in *Ex parte Endo,* it held that
the government could not legally detain citizens who had been deemed
loyal through official procedures. Although the government retained

the power to exclude individuals thought to be dangerous to the nation's security, for most Japanese Americans the year 1944 ended with unequivocal signs that the fences would soon be coming down.[4]

In the months following the opening of the West Coast, a wave of vandalism struck the schools, latrines, and recreation halls in the camps. At Minidoka students broke into school the following spring and caused major damage, destroying property, supplies, and irreplaceable files. The community analyst, summarizing what had been a growing tendency to vent frustration on the schools, thought it had to do with discontent, dislike of some teachers, poor use of leisure time, and a longing for excitement. Underlying these sources of frustration, he suggested, was a lack of intimacy between parents and children when the big decision about relocation had to be made. There was also a fear that the remaining evacuees would be pushed out of the camps and left to cope with both poverty and the hostile world outside. For young people the immediate future was more certain than it was for adults; they would continue in public schools. Yet, they would do so in families that had been forcibly relocated out of and then back into U.S. society.[5]

The strains of this unusual rite of passage to normal citizenship were greatest of all for the young people at Tule Lake Segregation Center. Tule Lake had its own youth problems, its own tumultuous educational history after 1943. Although strikingly different from what occurred elsewhere, that history in many ways reveals the heart of the educational experience for children in all of the camps. The segregation of "disloyals" was central to the government's strategy for selecting and dispersing the other Japanese Americans into normal communities. For this reason, Tule Lake after 1943 could be viewed as the mainspring of the government's entire sequence of mass exclusion, incarceration, and selective resettlement. Tule Lake Segregation Center was designed for harsher applications of official sanction and force against the minority group than were used in the other camps. As a social institution, the segregation center not only complemented but made possible the increasingly generous policies of relocation in the other camps after 1943. At its most extreme, Tule Lake became the point of no return, the last exit from life in the United States for the several thousand people who chose expatriation or repatriation to Japan. It also represented the threat that hung before residents in all of the camps, the alternative to satisfying the government's loyalty demands. The educational forms that arose at Tule Lake to confront and defy that threat require special attention to understand more deeply the experience of the young.

As Japanese Americans deemed "loyal" had moved on to other camps and to the outside world, Tule Lake had received from the other camps those who had answered the loyalty questions inappropriately, requested repatriation or expatriation to Japan, or otherwise aroused the suspicion of the government. Transformed by the further segregation of people who had already been racially excluded, Tule Lake plunged into a bitter history of riots, organized protest, military repression, factional conflict, beatings, and murders. The camp became front-page news even as 1943 drew to a close, tantalizing the public imagination with symbols of race conflict and retribution while the larger war against Japan raged on the Pacific front. A double "manproof" fence, guard towers with spotlights and machine guns, six "baby tanks," and a battalion of soldiers had surrounded the camp by the winter of 1943–44.

As the official segregation center, Tule Lake became the most severe and the most tragic of the camps. To government officials who believed that the loyalty questions had been appropriate for identifying Japanese Americans ready to join the armed forces or resettle in normal communities, the segregation of "disloyals" merely established the conditions necessary for a humane policy of relocation. According to this view, which dominated the WRA and the war department, the people who remained at Tule Lake after the "loyal" were cleared to leave for the other, less restricted camps had cast their lot with Japan for the future. But to those who held the opposing view and resisted the loyalty questions, either by answering "no" or by qualifying their affirmative responses, the procedure represented yet another oppression beyond the evacuation and subsequent camp life. Once the supposed disloyals had been concentrated at Tule Lake in the fall of 1943, many continued to resist in ways that tended to confirm the view of the administration and a hostile press that they preferred Japan: they participated in language schools, Japanese cultural practices, paramilitary drills, repatriation requests, and pro-Japan organizations. Between these hardened positions of authority and resistance, a complex cultural history took form at Tule Lake, and youth cultures played a prominent role in the conflicts that ensued. The meanings of such disputed terms as "loyalty," "disloyalty," "America," and "Japan" grew out of deep-seated disagreements over how to interpret present policies and how best to prepare Japanese Americans for an uncertain future.

Before reviewing educational initiatives and the responses of young people, some background on the camp is in order. The WRA completed its segregation of all the "disloyals" from other camps, along with their families, to Tule Lake Segregation Center after the summer of 1943. Some 6,200 people left Tule Lake for other camps, while 10,800 came to the segregation center. Beginning with a population of 13,000, Tule Lake grew eventually to almost 19,000 by the end of 1944. As it carried out its segregation policy, the federal government created a new variety of planned community. These people, negatively labeled and concentrated in a separate institution, were expected to "relocate" to Japan after the war was over. But again the plan bore little resemblance to reality, since this was not the purpose of the camp for the majority who resided there, despite national publicity directed at pro-Japanese activities inside the fence. Most of the people at Tule Lake were waiting for circumstances to change on the outside, just as in the other camps. They were resisting public authority over their lives and fortunes, hedging their bets to be able to make the most advantageous decision to restore themselves in the postwar world. After the war was over, most of the people at Tule Lake remained in the United States.[6]

The question of what sort of schooling took place at Tule Lake Segregation Center is easy to answer with regard to the first few months: none at all. Public schools held no classes at Tule Lake between the summer of 1943 and the end of January 1944, even though WRA schools were on a year-round schedule. From October through January the camp was electrified by successive crises, mass protests, the appearance of tanks and heavily armed soldiers around the perimeter, then labor disputes, serious accidents, a work stoppage, and the shooting of a Japanese American by one of the sentries. In the midst of these events, officials opposed the formation of a representative body, the Daihyo Sha Kai, after self-government had been banned from the camp, along with a smaller negotiating committee to present needs and demands to the administration. This spontaneous rise of self-government won a camp-wide vote of confidence in the representatives of the people, but to little avail because camp life deteriorated into the declaration of martial law and the invasion of the army after some fights and a beating.

As tensions mounted, residents at Tule Lake witnessed the imprisonment of the negotiating committee, as well as others thought to be "troublemakers," in a specially built stockade in the administrative compound, then the imposition of a curfew, the separate fencing of the ward with the most troublesome blocks of barracks, and the beatings of *inu* or informers (literally "dogs") by fellow residents. There ensued another vote of confidence, this time under army surveillance and control, resulting in a narrow victory for those who wanted to end the status quo of passive resistance and return the camp to civilian rule. Subsequently there appeared a gradual increase in accommodationist tactics, shadowed by an underground of uncompromising resistance, culminating in the murder of the Issei who directed the camp's Cooperative Enterprises, and who was thought by many to be collaborating with the WRA and distributing favors and profits to his friends. This action was followed by widespread fear of engaging in any kind of communication with the administration lest one be branded an inu and beaten or killed.

Public education was not compulsory at Tule Lake Segregation Center, but it became one of the major issues of camp life after martial rule ended early in 1944. Schooling remained a matter of contention not only between residents and the administration, but increasingly between vying groups of residents. All the problems of providing education for a segregated population in the other camps were concentrated yet further at Tule Lake because of the additional segregation that had taken place; the contradictions of progressive practice and minority resistance were brought out into the open. Less than two years earlier Paul Hanna's graduate seminar from Stanford had visited Tule Lake and used it as the prototype for designing a progressive curriculum for all the camps. Now it was the segregation center, an even more extreme exclusion of the racial excludees, containing people defined by policy, but not by any crime they had committed, as inimical to the interests of the United States.

The people at Tule Lake developed their own symbols of opposition and their own forms of schooling to maintain social cohesion. They created private schools, some designed to complement and others to supplant the teachings of public schools. The intentions of public schooling became more distinct, in turn, to those who sought its benefits as an alternative to the institutions being created privately by the resistance in the camp. The most interesting issue from an educational standpoint is how culture was used to symbolize the struggle of the Japanese Americans attempting to reconstruct their beliefs in an imagined future where they could live with dignity.

Educators continued to play a role in that struggle as far as the young people were concerned. Long promised, a new high school building was finally completed at Tule Lake in 1944. Situated in the firebreak between the "colony" and the separately fenced administrative compound, Tri-State High School opened in February after repeated delays—and after having been commandeered by the army for housing troops during late summer and autumn. During the weeks of mounting conflict after the segregation had been completed, teachers had urged the authorities to finish construction and open the school. Some of them, arguing that schooling was still a good investment for the children, had "donned overalls and began to install the roof-jacks and connect the stoves themselves," reported the superintendent of schools.[7]

When the WRA schools reopened after the second vote of confidence, they had only 68 percent of their previous enrollment. Two of seven wards at Tule Lake had forbidden children to attend these schools. After segregation, the high school program was cut back, eliminating extracurricular activities, drastically restricting vocational education, and reducing academic subjects to a half-day period aimed at meeting the minimum requirements of the North Central Accrediting Association. But teachers continued to tell students that their future was in the United States, and the public schools showed a "spirit of cooperative good will," reported one administrator, which stood in marked contrast to the pall of coercion in the camp. Recalling years later his feelings as the construction came to an end on the public high school, a Nisei student was glad that the buildings "actually looked like a school. They did not resemble the barracks in any way. Tiny [a friend] and I went to look at the new school and were both pleased at what we saw. It felt like a school and the smell of fresh paint was still in the air."[8]

The high school became a social center for many Nisei who found little solace in the paramilitary drills and cultural preparation led by the Kibei, the minority of the second generation who had received part of their education in Japan. Unlike many of their Kibei siblings, most of the segregated Nisei were relatively Americanized youth in their cultural preferences. Despite their outrage at having been mistreated by public authority, as a group they tended to like baseball and jitterbug more than *sumo* and *utai* (the Japanese art of singing). Habitually, the older Nisei students spoke English with each other. They often talked about movies and life on the outside. Among themselves, they generally felt as uncomfortable with the ways of the Kibei as they did with the more traditional ways of the Issei. Given the choice, the young males who sought refuge in the cultural milieu of the high school appeared to prefer their hair in the Hollywood style of the day, not in the *bozu*, or shavehead style, of the early morning drills. Although high school enrollments fell precipitously between the end of the 1942–43 and the 1943–44 school years, three hundred Nisei still graduated in 1944. One of the students, when interviewed by the Japanese Evacuation and Resettlement Study, epitomized the cultural confusion of many other Nisei at Tule Lake when he asked: "What are we going to do if we stay in here?"[9]

High school was a cultural enclave for many Nisei within the segregated camp. They used its protection at their own risk, avoiding visible leadership roles, for the danger of retribution from the "pressure boys" was real and present. When a group of high school Nisei held one of their jitterbug dances in 1944, the building was surrounded by Kibei vigilantes who had come to stop the event. "Why break us up—we're not hurting you any," said one Nisei according to a witness. "You're going back to Japan," responded the leader of the vigilantes: "You're just Japs. Get these ideas out of your heads." But, in the account of the witness, the high school kids stood their ground: "You wouldn't want us to break up your gambling games. If you like, stay here, and we'll teach you how to cut a rug. If not, go away and leave us alone as we leave you alone."[10]

Most often, the more Americanized Nisei suppressed the ways of being that brought them into outright conflict with the cultural demands of the resistance. They kept a low profile because these ways had taken on perverse connotations in the segregation center. Once officialdom deemed Japanese culture disloyal and contrary to Americanization, the resistance movements in Tule Lake developed the symbols of disloyalty as part of their continuing protest against unjust treatment. They vilified the administrative conception of American loyalty by initiating a collective quest for identity as excluded people who were irrevocably Japanese. Thus, for the Nisei living in this highly charged ideological confrontation, to flaunt aspects of the assimilated culture was increasingly risky, since the resistance had hardened its determination to use symbols of disloyalty for maintaining group cohesion. Many Nisei lived furtively in their peer culture and avoided public exposure. "I spoke to seven high school groups and had a wonderful response," wrote Thomas R. Bodine, the field director of the National Japanese American Student Relocation Council, after he was allowed to visit Tule Lake in 1944. "I went to two high school dances and met a lot of the kids off the record. I've floated around elbowing kids and chatting with them. But *not one* has come to see me or sign up for an interview."[11]

Against the revived program of the high school, many parents chose to organize their own forms of education. Their resolve was reinforced by a movement in the camp to "resegregate" yet again the residents, establishing a camp-within-a-camp, separately fenced and administered, to house those who had made definite expressions of their will to go to Japan. Six thousand residents signed a petition in April 1944 that called for resegregation for "the discipline and education of our children adapted to the system of the wartime Fatherland." The WRA refused to act upon the recommendation, but Congress added momentum to the resegregation movement that summer by passing the law that made it possible a few months later to renounce American citizenship during the war. By the time official procedures were developed, organized groups within the camp were applying great pressure to renounce, and more than eight thousand residents did so. The great majority of these later revoked their applications, relocated after going through Justice Department hearings, and finally managed to reinstate their U.S. citizenship after years of litigation in federal courts. Paralleling the movement to pressure residents to renounce their citizenship in preparation for the return to Japan was an efflorescence of private schools in the camp, reflecting a spectrum of belief and disbelief in the collective symbols being forged for the group.[12]

By the fall of 1944, roughly 4,300 students were enrolled in Japanese language schools at Tule Lake, while enrollments in WRA public schools had fallen to about 2,300, down from about 4,700 students two years earlier. The cleavages among resisting camp residents appeared in the organization of the language schools. The first schools to appear with substantial enrollments were under the Japanese Language School Board, composed mostly of the people called "old Tuleans" by Dorothy Thomas and Richard Nishimoto in *The Spoilage,* the first major study of Tule Lake. These schools, condoned by the administration, showed the propensity of the "old Tuleans" (those 6,000 or so segregees who had been in the camp since presegregation days) to seek limited forms of accommodation as they resisted public authority. The WRA granted such schools space but not resources, and in return the board kept records of students, teachers, and courses. Members of the board encouraged parents to send their students back to the public schools when they reopened. Some cooperation with the authorities occurred in making the hours of officially recognized language schools complement those of public schools, thus imitating the role of these schools before the war. Residents in the participating blocks contributed financially to have materials mimeographed for use as textbooks, and the schools collected small tuition fees from parents to pay the teachers. Led by accommodationist trustees elected by the people of the wards, this school board was able to reduce friction between its system of instruction and the public schools—again, much as leaders of the Japanese language schools had done in immigrant communities before the war. Many of the constituents served by the Japanese Language School Board wanted both Japanese cultural training and American schooling for their children, while openly resisting the loyalty classifications of the government.[13]

These officially condoned language schools made it convenient for families to keep their options open. Parents could support their cultural milieu while also making sure that their children continued the studies they had begun in American schools. In this respect language schools were an expanded version of the Japanese cultural activities permitted by the WRA on a smaller scale in all of the camps, coexisting with the public schools. The differences at Tule Lake came first in the magnitude of the language schools as an educational movement—embracing several thousand young people and dwarfing the public school enrollments—and second in their heightened ideological significance in the history of the camp. Despite the vigor of the Japanese language schools, there were limits to official tolerance. Equally important, there were limits to the willingness of the segregated population to confine its cultural resistance to arrangements that did not supplant the public schools. On the one side, these limits became apparent in the campaigns of the authorities to root out resistance leaders, including some who controlled cultural organizations and language schools, and imprison them apart from the rest of the camp residents. On the other, the clash of factions at Tule Lake created strident alternatives to the officially condoned language schools, suggesting to many families that those schools were not sufficient as a form of resistance and cultural preparation.

The equilibrium of the accommodationist language schools was upset by escalating demands of the resistance for their plans to make "return" to Japan a program of actual denationalization rather than merely symbolic protest. With the petition to resegregate the camp, a movement directly challenging the fence sitters by labeling them "loyals," there emerged a broken front of eight underground "school republics" operating as self-contained systems against WRA regu-

A girl studying in one
of the Japanese language
schools at Tule Lake,
California, November 19,
1945.

lations and without any relation to the Japanese Language School Board. These schools and private tutors relegated many of the older Japanese cultural practices cherished by the Issei to a secondary role and instead tried to emulate the current curriculum and military exercises of modern Japan. The explicit purpose of many of these schools and tutors was to prepare youth for immediate "return" to Japan. Still, for many parents, despite the stridency of the rhetoric, this was a protest movement. The "return" was a local metaphor heavily freighted with emotional meanings, essentially a symbolic protest within the bounded political economy of camp life, not yet a final move to break all relations with the United States.[14]

But the hardening ideological lines of protest and the inflexibility of the government were raising the stakes with each passing month. Increasing pressure was placed on parents to keep their children out of public school and to repudiate the officially condoned school board in favor of autonomous organizations in several wards. Some of this pressure took the form of persuasion and threats, while some erupted as beatings and destruction of property. Months after the era of martial rule was over, a WRA documentarian observed that the conflict between official and renegade schooling systems was "at the root of many of the disturbances . . . which the [evacuee] police and the WRA internal security officers have had to control."[15] The reason for this conflict was that many people—a growing number after it was announced at the end of 1944 that the West Coast was again open to Japanese Americans and that the camps would soon be shut down—were resisting the organized resistance around them. Many families were still trying to keep their options open by sending their children to both public and private schools, but the ideological vise was closing in many parts of the camp, demanding a choice of one or the other. In contrast to the public schools, where attendance was now voluntary, the locally controlled private language schools of several wards were declared compulsory by the local ward leadership, which had fallen under the domination of extreme resistance factions. Families risked intimidation and injury if they patronized either the public schools or the officially condoned language schools of the camp-wide Japanese Language School Board.

Some understanding of the most entrenched resistance against the administration and its schooling institutions can be gained by examining the operation of a particular private school. A Kibei informant reported to the community analyst on a language school in ward 7, a bastion of resistance to WRA policy at Tule Lake. Only one WRA nursery school had started up in the entire ward because the language schools had supplanted them in all but one block. The language school observed by the Kibei informant was designed to imitate as closely as possible the entire program of the Kokumin Gakko, the national elementary school system of Japan in the 1930s, including nationalistic teachings and martial arts. Unlike WRA schools in the fenced camp, which were authoritarian institutions teaching individuals to live in a democracy, the language school was governed democratically by a board elected from parents of the ward; yet, it was teaching students to live in an authoritarian society. The school was in session five days a week, with day and evening sessions, in recreation halls and ironing rooms. Teachers placed overwhelming emphasis on "discipline, conformity, and respect to superiors." Students were, for example, instructed to snap to attention and then bow with respect when any teacher approached. The school was dominated by Issei and Kibei, though it was not tied formally to the political system of the ward.[16]

Young children, noticed the Kibei informant, preferred this full-time language school to the public school, finding the stories of Japan "remote, curious, and idealistic," quite in contrast to the stultifying routine of the camp. Water running in an irrigation ditch became a fabled river; perhaps the young men goose-stepping across the firebreak might call up images from tales of adventurous samurai in the medieval past. In contrast, the high school students, according to the Kibei informant, tended to prefer the American public school for its freedom of choice, its depth in specialized subjects, and its respect for individual development. "Teaching methods are superior and more flexible," commented the Kibei on Tri-State High School. "And the Nisei is notoriously no friend of either paternal or scholastic authoritarianism." For disgruntled Nisei, the daily fare on "the invincibility of the militant state" was made even more unbearable, as an educational experience, by the sheer amount of rote memorization required of students. In one language school it was reported that a Nisei girl astounded her classmates and the teachers when she refused to sing Japanese patriotic songs and, instead, while the class was singing, belted out "Pistol Packing Mama" at the top of her lungs.[17]

Inasmuch as education in general is a way of constructing the social future of individuals and groups, the question arises what were these people preparing for? Some were truly getting ready for a return to the land where their parents had been born. An obedient

Nisei was reported as saying: "When your future is washed up here, and you're just a green kid in your parents eyes, there's plenty to learn, plenty to master." Reflecting on his status and theirs, he continued: "They never had a place here, never even had citizenship. Now we're put in the same boat and we're not prepared, their own children." Nevertheless, for the majority of children in the camp, a Japanese cultural education was not for future life in Japan; it was to satisfy parental wishes that they affirm their Japanese heritage, irrespective of where they went after the war. The Issei were caught between societies, prepared to make their way neither in the authoritarian Japan suggested by the early morning drills nor in the jittery democracy that had caused them to lose most of their property and placed them behind barbed wire. In the ambiguous years of exile, between worlds, between leadership by one generation and the next, between noncitizenship and citizenship, many members of the older generation at Tule Lake wanted to make sure their children were at least Japanese like themselves. For them, this was a cultural more than a political goal, and their schools were, to a fault, merely cultural in most respects.[18]

One WRA community analyst noticed this fact after a few months, remarking on the many antagonistic communities of the camp, each "busily purveying cultural wares" according to their varying amount of assimilation and disaffection. Except for the most extreme schools, such as the one observed by the Kibei informant in ward 7, which was in the minority, most of the curricula of the language schools, both official and unofficial, stressed the "familiar *cultural attributes* of a person of Japanese background: ability in Japanese language, manners, tea-ceremony, flower arrangement, etc., in short the very things the poorly educated Issei found most strangely wanting in his Americanized child." For women at Tule Lake this meant pressure to be more traditional and to accept patriarchal authority; they took classes in sewing, etiquette, and household arts. For boys the missing elements of character were those of discipline and deportment. Most fundamental, even with hard work most boys and girls could not speak Japanese well enough to converse fluently with their parents by the time they were in high school. Once the parents had been progressively segregated and concentrated with their children by official policy, many responded by attempting to reverse the acculturation that had taken their children from them in so many ways without bringing any reward. The dispute over loyalty and disloyalty became a "mental battlefield," in the words of one Nisei reflecting on the vehemence of his elders. School life—both public and private—became enmeshed in elaborate strategies of cultural survival.[19]

Like the Nisei who served valiantly in the U.S. Army, went to college during the war, or received leave clearance before the surrender of Japan and were able to resettle and work in normal communities, the people who stayed behind at Tule Lake also had hopes for the future. Japan symbolized these hopes, and the language schools embodied them to some extent for the segregated parents and their children. The Japan of the Issei imagination was in part a cultural promised land of communication between parent and child. This "Japan" was not so much a place as it was the coveted gift of future success for the child, recognized and appreciated by the world at large, but on terms that would honor the entire family and again make it whole. It was, above all, the yearning for a just reward of human dignity and social acceptance based upon the traits instilled in the old when they were young. "Japan" became the actual Japan for several thousand as they went through with denationalization, once the way was opened by Congress. But for the rest, the majority, "Japan" was an imaginative construct, a cultural strategy of self-preservation in U.S. society, where they remained after the war. Education in this sense protected the identity of the group against individual dispersal, against the policy of relocation and the "freedom" it offered after having first taken everything away.

Who were these thousands of people who educated for "Japan" and then stayed in the United States? Their story is different from the families of the some sixteen thousand Nisei from the mainland United States who joined the armed forces and it bears little resemblance to the experience of the more than four thousand who entered college during the war, although many parents at Tule Lake also had children who did these things. The answer suggests a deeper structure of selection inherent in both the loyalty questions and the progressive policies of acculturation, selection, and dispersal. Compared to residents in the other camps, the people at Tule Lake were more likely to be rural, poor, Buddhist Californians, either unmarried farm laborers or members of large families with many children, and possessing no property after the evacuation; Thomas and Nishimoto called them the "residuum" in their study of Tule Lake. However labeled, these people were the dispossessed for whom "disloyalty" spelled temporary safety from the prospect of a worse fate on the outside.[20]

Official policy and communal reactions to it had unwittingly selected the most powerless of this immigrant group for the segregation center, where they were pressured, both from within their
own community and by official actions, to leave the United States.
Some did, creating a form of education designed to equip them for
a remembered Japan that no longer existed by the time they arrived.
The majority of those incarcerated at Tule Lake stayed behind in
the United States, relocating en masse to the West Coast. The Japan
they educated their children to respect was a vision that helped to
empower these families to persist and to maintain their culture and
kinship in the postwar world.

For the remaining Nisei at Tule Lake, the contradictions of education spawned acute personal dilemmas when relocation became
the policy even of this camp in 1945. Their parents had been pushing
them toward the Japan of language and cultural niceties, if not the
more strident blend of camp protest and Japanese nationalism. Now
it became brutally clear to them that most would soon be relocating
into American communities. The dissolution of the camps forced the
Nisei, citizens all, to confront again their powerlessness to alter the
rules by which public authority had classified them and managed
their lives during the war. "Well, then," one Nisei was quoted as
saying after he had heard that relocation into normal communities
on the outside was official policy for Tule Lake, "does this mean that
they're going to call off the whole party, that the last few years have
been just kidding around, that repatriation and segregation and
everything we were told to take seriously is just a big joke?"[21]

Between the promise of education and the "big joke" of segregation, these students lived in the uncertain world of their families.
Temporarily concentrated, enclosed within barbed wire, under heavily armed guard, that microcosm was now being propelled outward
at alarming speed into the larger world around it. Confronted with
the inevitable dissolution of the camps, parents and children who
remained inside in 1945 were taking stock and trying to decide what
to do. Resettlement was imminent for the incarcerated in all the
camps, though it would take longer at Tule Lake because of a cum-
bersome process of hearings and individual relocation decisions.

From all the isolated wartime camps Japanese Americans had
already gone forth into the larger world beyond the fence. They had
often settled in communities they had never even visited before the
war. Finding work and education, they had demonstrated that it
was not unreasonable to hope for a future in the United States. Soon

the government would turn out the remaining residents, whether or not they could find their way to jobs and homes. While WRA officials, camp administrators, teachers, and community analysts worked to dissolve continuing pockets of resistance in the camps, to persuade fearful residents that it was time to rejoin society, another stocktaking was under way. Educators were anxious to record their own vision of those years. They gathered information and developed arguments for reports and publications to justify what the schools had done for the children. This attempt to control the symbols that might be used later to judge the incarceration was, in its own way, a sign that the years of exile were drawing to a close.

Writing in the *American School Board Journal* in 1945, N. E. Viles, head of the WRA education section in Washington, characterized the schools in the camps as a successful experiment in intergovernmental relations. He reported that all but one of the thirteen high schools had been fully accredited in the seven states where they were located; the exception had been the segregation center at Tule Lake. In all but one of the states, Arizona, the work of the schools had been enhanced by outside boards of state officials and educators working with federal administrators to plan and evaluate the schools. Relations with outside communities improved as the war progressed, boasted Viles. The educational establishment in the various states contributed to the camp schools by recommending teachers and working as administrators during the crisis. This collaboration had made a great difference, he argued, in coping with a difficult situation during the national emergency. The final reports from the camps reflected this sense of achievement in spite of the many problems that had been encountered.[22]

Educators were aware of the political value of their achievement in building a school system while the nation mobilized for war. "During the evacuation period," wrote Viles, "these children, American citizens by birth, had been promised and under our national pattern they were entitled to make normal educational progress during the time they were detained in government camps." By October 1945 the movement out of the camps had reached flood tide after the announcement that all of them except for Tule Lake would be closed before the new year. Viles reflected with satisfaction that the "federal-state-local co-operative plan brought most of the results anticipated ... There were few difficulties. Other than having an enrollment of a different racial group, operated behind guarded barbed-wire fences, and being housed in temporary buildings, there was little to distinguish the center schools from those in neighboring communities."[23]

Administrators were more frank about the problems in administrative reports than in articles published in education journals. At Amache, for example, they conceded that the program was a compromise between local conditions and recommended educational practice. The result, noted the superintendent of schools as he looked back over the experience, was "a curious blend of successes and failures, high hopes and disappointments, laughter and sadness, idealism and stark reality." Teacher shortages had undermined the programs at Gila and Topaz. In other camps the gulf between WRA administrators and the educational staff continued to isolate the schools from allied social services. Isolation plagued the schools in numerous ways, alienating them from family, community, and society. Schools were also cut off from channels to productive work. "It was most unfortunate," concluded one report, seconded by others in many of the camps, "that training opportunities requiring the approval and support of state officials and departments did not materialize." Equally common was the conviction that in spite of the hardships, public schools had helped to keep alive the promise of American life during hard times. As a teacher handbook at Amache declared, "These unattractive, ill-equipped rooms and these fear-filled newcomers have been built into a school of which we are proud."[24]

To most educators, the dilemma of the camps was solved by relocating the Japanese Americans into normal communities. The problems of young people, even those of an unruly youth culture that neither the parents nor the administration could control, were then reassuringly administrative: how to convert subject-by-subject promotions into grade-level promotions to consolidate fractional credits, or how to develop comprehensive records on the students before and during the war. The teachers who remained in the camps at the end of the war were neither progressives nor missionaries for the most part. At Manzanar the core cadre of teachers was called "sensible" and "sincere" in the final estimation of administrators. They were professionals who stayed on relatively good terms with their students "without going to extremes as crusaders for causes." From staff rosters and teacher narratives it appears generally that the teaching force in the camps evolved from its initial diversity into a fairly typical blend of rural and small-town professionals, products of state teacher training institutions, with a sprinkling of teachers from elite institutions and urban centers. During the last two years of the war, in 1944 and 1945, the central administration in Washington became more adept at setting its expectations at a level that could be achieved in the camps as they were, leaving behind utopian visions of what might be. A set of instructions to be used in the teaching of reading, for instance, furnished "translations" or paraphrases in simple sentences of articles appearing in popular magazines. One called "How the South Feels about the Race Problem" was tailored to provide a lesson in realism to the children in the camps: "Certain small groups have had to be treated unfairly at other times in our country. If not perfect, this is still an improvement in the situation. It may be the best we can do." The emphasis had turned away from idealism. Maintaining adequate instruction for people returning soon to U.S. society was enough.[25]

Despite their disaffection, students in the camp schools had produced higher levels of academic achievement as the war progressed. Educators tested their students yearly and found some overall improvement between 1942 and 1945. "In general," a summary report concluded, "the pupils in the WRA schools were equal to or slightly above normal in scholastic achievement at the time the schools closed. They had some losses in status from March 1942 to March 1943 but the better than average programs in 1943–44 and 1944–45 made up for these losses." This pattern was one found to be emerging from various tests, including the widely used Stanford Achievement Test. At Manzanar, which had the largest school population of all the camps, the explanation for this improvement was that the school system had evolved toward a synthesis of academic rigor and some remaining progressive methods in the classroom. In 1945 the elementary schools reported, based on diagnostic tests used by the state, that state standards had been equalled and often surpassed, "especially in the skill subjects" like reading and arithmetic.[26]

At higher grade levels there were more problems arising from poor language skills and lax study habits, in the view of the educators who administered the tests. As in the studies conducted more than a decade before of Japanese American children in California, the testers found deteriorating academic achievement in the higher grades. This trend was heavily influenced by the scores on tests involving complex uses of the English language. At Amache the Progressive Achievement Test found overall that whereas high school seniors were performing at six months behind their grade level in 1943, by 1945 they were performing at one year and three months ahead of grade level. Shadowing this improvement, however, from 1944 to 1945 the scores for seniors in one area that was tested, reading comprehension, fell from four months behind national norms to one year and four months behind for the grade level. In the camps generally, concluded the WRA in its summary report, students were "normal in mental ability" but had "language difficulties."[27]

Tests administered at Poston revealed an intriguing pattern besides the often noted aptitude of Japanese American students for quantitative problems. The testers observed that the students seemed "handicapped" in acquiring specific vocabulary, but that they showed remarkable ability to "grasp meanings from context in spite of this handicap." Educators at Poston quickly brought young readers to grade level on the Gates Primary Reading Test by intensifying the traditional emphasis on spelling, vocabulary, and reading fundamentals. This emphasis was blended into a generally progressive program, so that rigorous drills and individual and group projects coexisted productively in the classroom. Here is but one example among many of how the schools maintained educational momentum even when the relations between the community and the schools had been deeply disfigured by the official policy of racial exclusion.[28]

Touring camps in 1945, the field director of the National Japanese American Student Relocation Council found students less apathetic about the future than they had been a year before. This, too, was an acheivement, mostly the result of opportunities opening up on the outside for many students and families, he believed. At Gila the students in Butte High School echoed a complaint that had surfaced frequently in the camp schools during the war. They charged that the examination standards were becoming too high because of the competition in a segregated school with students of superior ability and diligence. When it was argued by some of the students that they would be rewarded more for the same levels of achievement when they were in public schools on the outside, the community analyst now took this to be a sign of rising morale in view of the imminent prospect of relocation to normal American communities. Such evidence from the camps was mixed, however. A study at Poston in 1945 found that students had "declined in common courtesies, increased their use of slang, and decreased interest in school life." Most of the pupils questioned wanted to remain in the United States; yet, they were now afraid of the outside. In their confusion about the future, they showed "indifference toward many items which influence character development," the study found.[29]

The more fundamental problems of attitude and achievement, the kinds that such questionnaire surveys could illuminate weakly if at all, were connected with the uses of education in an uncertain future. Because relocation was the dominant theme in the official culture of the camps, suppressing all others by 1945, little was done to measure the vital and fragmentary impressions with which school-children tried to sort out among themselves what was happening to them. Their immigrant parents had been deprived of property and livelihood toward the end of their working lives by the evacuation. Now the children shouldered an exceptional burden of collective responsibility as they set out on their individual quests for educational and material success. "When this present war is over it will be much harder for us to get jobs than it will be for the others," said one commencement speaker at high school graduation in 1945.[30]

The risks on the outside continued to appear lurid enough that some families were still not deterred from finding greater hope in present security than in the immediate possibilities of resettlement. When October 1945 rolled around and the administration showed no sign of opening schools for the many children who remained inside, parents in one camp acted in a way reminiscent of assembly center days. They set up their own school voluntarily. This time, though, it was futile without the college-educated Nisei, who had dispersed widely on the outside. A quixotic battle for coherence, the effort could not resist for long the centrifugal forces brought on by the end of the war. Still, there was a poignant dignity in the gesture. The teachers in this makeshift school had no other job to support them in the camp and worked for nothing. They hoped only to receive a *sha-rei,* an "appreciation gift," for their services.[31]

As this example suggests, the results of tests and surveys tell us little about the complex world of authority, resistance, and aspiration that the children experienced. The educational resource most difficult to fathom is the consciousness of the parents who encouraged their children to excel individually in American schools while also using their family and community authority to preserve the cultural integrity of the group. When the schools were not available, or not acceptable to them, parents raised schools from within the community, meager as it was in exile. The most restricted camp, Tule Lake Segregation Center, produced the greatest number of these renegade schools. In all of the camps educators often saw the parents as the problem the schools were there to solve, an inscrutable opposition to the principles of Americanization. Yet, it is likely that the story of educational achievement would be far less sanguine were it not for the community institutions and family authority mobilized by the parents in support of learning.

Parents continued to build, politically and culturally. They persisted even when their social organization was in direct opposition to the dictates and desires of officialdom. Their claim to be in charge of their own lives and futures, backed by community institutions, the language of the home, the known way of culture and creative arts, was a primary stimulus to literacy for the young. Resistant accommodationists, the old achieved something notable in their darkest hour. They held many of their children and grandchildren back from sudden dispersal after having been uprooted from their homes. By their recalcitrance, they kept their children in camp schools surrounded by a concentrated community that retained the power to organize—to educate—for a future of their own choosing.

Some of the community analysts saw this pattern; most administrators were less patient and saw only foolish reluctance, "Japanization." Remaining in the camps, immovable when the authorities were ready to end the incarceration, the older generation attempted once again to reconstruct something of its own in the place where they had been exiled. "When I left the camp for the last time," recalled an Issei years after leaving Minidoka, "I looked back and saw the entire ground; when we came, it was nothing but wilderness, but now, because of our labor, it had become a beautiful green field. We drew water from one of the tributaries of the Snake River. No matter where Japanese people go, the place becomes green."[32]

As 1945 wore on, many of the older people in camp still did not want to venture forth quite yet. They feared violence and lack of security on the outside. One successful strategy used by the WRA to increase the number of resettling families was to allow families to relocate their children into public schools on the outside. Reinforced by the announcement that there would be no more schooling inside after the spring graduation in 1945, this strategy jolted many families into recognizing that they could not provide for their children by staying within the protected environment. The combination of relaxed restrictions, denial of social services, insistence that the centers would soon close, and an outside structure of relocation offices for at least moving families into place to seek housing and livelihood succeeded in breaking up the camps by the end of the year.[33]

By 1945 even the West Coast was showing some signs of truly

*A family at Topaz,
the camp in Utah,
packing to go
home to California,
January 3, 1945.*

opening. Earl Warren, who before the evacuation had denounced the Japanese Americans in California, where he had been attorney general, spoke again as governor in 1945. He asked the people of the state to be fair and take them back without discrimination. Anticipating opposition, he instructed officers of the law to protect their interests. After Warren's statement, the state superintendent of schools participated widely in meetings and discussions to open the way for children of Japanese descent to return to public schools. He said he would hold local school officials accountable under the compulsory school laws if they did not integrate the children into the program.[34]

The transition back into the nation's normal communities was not without confrontation and sporadic violence. Discriminatory laws were still on the books, and more were added in some places. Organized groups, such as the Native Sons of the Golden West and the California Preservation Committee, continued to engage in symbolic and real battles against the returning Japanese. But there were positive signs of organized action as well. By 1945 the University of California was accepting Japanese American students without charging nonresident fees unless families had officially established residence in other states. The Committee on American Principles and Fair Play and other coalitions of community and church groups were helping to organize campaigns to prepare many local communities for peaceful coexistence with their old neighbors, some of whom were returning to property but many of whom were not. In some places the press finally laid to rest its old grudge against the minority group and began to expose the profiteering, forced sales, and theft that had broken the family economy of Japanese Americans.[35]

In not a few communities of the West, hostility remained intense. Returning to Los Angeles, Estelle Ishigo and her husband were "hustled away to make-shift camps outside the City," she recalled in a memoir of those years, "like tribes of Indians robbed and cast out." The image is deeply resonant when one considers the broader shift in federal Indian policy after the war: from tribalism bolstered by progressive institutions growing out of the New Deal reforms, to termination and forced dispersal in subsequent years. Similarly, the excluded Japanese Americans were carried through a brief span of highly concentrated federal policy history with progressive underpinnings, then suddenly dispersed into uncomprehending and often hostile communities. Dispersal had a tremendous impact on families in both of the excluded groups. "This camp," reported Ishigo of her family's new habitation on the outskirts of Los Angeles, "was behind a fish cannery and it was also surrounded by barbed wire but here the gate was open. We were still the enemy to most of the population in the City."[36]

The pattern of resettlement for the second generation during the war was disproportionately eastward when compared to that of the older generation at the end of the war. The obvious reason was the blanket exclusion of Japanese Americans from the West Coast during the time when many older Nisei relocated. The difference was also related, in a more enduring sense, to levels of education as well as to age, for both translated into places in colleges and jobs where the Nisei remained after the war. The national pattern of migration during the war years was generally westward for the population of the nation as a whole, and more so for those with greater education and in their late twenties through early forties. The pattern for Japanese Americans was exactly the opposite: the educated Nisei of working age tended to migrate east, while the old and the young tended to return to the West Coast in greater numbers. While about 35,000 Japanese Americans relocated away from the western states initially, several million people in the nation migrated from the South to the North, and from the East to the West; total interstate migration from 1940 to 1945 was more than double that of the period from 1935 to 1940. Because of poor conditions of housing and employment on the West Coast for the returning Japanese Americans, the decade after the war was one of continuing hardship for the working population dispersed from the camps into that region. Yet, it was one of relatively normal educational experiences for the schoolchildren, reflected in persistently high levels of education among younger Japanese Americans as a whole in the years after the war.[37]

Attempting to live up to its educational commitments to the children, the WRA transferred extensive academic and personal files on the children of war to the U.S. Office of Education. That office was charged with managing the educational transition and coordinating communication with officials after the WRA disbanded in June 1946. The files, whose existence as an active concern of national government represented continuing wardship, partially holding the children as creatures of the state while they and their families moved freely back into civil society, eventually entered the National Archives, where, along with thousands of cubic feet of records from the years of exile, they remain to this day.

Remembering the Past

"WITH HUMAN beings as they are," wrote Pitirim Sorokin in 1942, "catastrophes are great educators of mankind." Perhaps so, but like other events remembered from the war—Pearl Harbor, the blitzkrieg, the Holocaust, Hiroshima, and Nagasaki—the incarceration of Japanese Americans holds no reservoir of object lessons. Its reality overwhelms moral exegesis, remaining starkly unresolved as history, part of the history of society, a memory that people have decided not to forget. Sorokin's point rings true, if only because to educate is to make sure that the catastrophe continues teaching, that it is recognized and that we as a living society are again recognized in it.[1]

The safekeeping of collective memory is a fragile enterprise. Although social amnesia is one threat to understanding, remembering a catastrophe merely as caricature for later debates is more common. The temptation to appropriate history for sundry purposes is especially great when telling a story of contradictions, like that of the Japanese Americans. Rising from oppression, the "model minority" becomes our modern-day Horatio Alger, the camps an extreme instance of low origins, and the whole ordeal living proof that the downtrodden can make it in the United States if only they try hard enough. Memory is prone to other excesses. The camps become symbols of imperialism, the victims partisans in the struggle of the Third World, their release mere ethnic colonization in a society that continues to exclude them in many ways. Another metamorphosis of social memory is outright denial, as has occurred sporadically with the Holocaust. Alternatively, one keeper of the memory condemns the use of any label other than "concentration camp" for the incarceration of Japanese Americans. But as Richard Polenberg has noted, the only point truly shared between the "final solution" and the wartime treatment of Japanese Americans is the racial criterion applied in both cases by the authorities. It behooves the historian to be cautious with words, especially when they carry such deadly meanings; otherwise, there is no meaning. The first book on Japanese Americans to use the attention-getting phrase in its title was *America's Concentration Camps,* published in 1967. A book with exactly the same title came out eleven years earlier, its subject not the wartime camps but Indian reservations. Genocide was the subject of neither.[2]

This book could lend support to various uses of the memory of the relocation camps. The aim, however, is different and the conclusions are more modest. My inquiry has been confined to exploring educational meanings, the teaching and learning of those years. Thirty thousand children of war attended school in the camps. Educational planners working under the auspices of the federal government claimed that they could make good on the promise of this society to provide educational opportunity for its citizens. The story of what happened is so laden with ambiguity that an open-minded observer must suspend both indictment and approbation, at least long enough to peer into the educational process and grasp the complexity of the experience for those who participated. What began as a story of war hysteria and racial exclusion in 1942 soon became a more complex history of public institutions, embodying conflicting motives and numerous layers of authority and expertise. The result was the establishment of planned communities, the maintenance of an administered democracy of community government under federal authority, the application of progressive methods of education, the creation of channels for dispersal, the segregation of negatively labeled individuals into a separate institution, and the use of social scientists to harmonize public authority with the managed population. Into this structure came a group of people who had their own notions about how to construct their future, and who were aware of coercion behind the purported benevolence.

The camps for Japanese Americans were not military concentration camps, nor did they represent enlightened social engineering to alleviate a "distress migration," like New Deal policies during the Great Depression. They were, in fact, like nothing else that had come before. The camps were products of a historical moment that juxtaposed military authority and civilian social assistance in unprecedented ways. A brief discussion of two other English-speaking nations' policies during the war can offer perspective on the uniqueness of the camps for Japanese Americans as social institutions. The contrasts these countries—Canada and England—provide also suggest how divergent public policies created different wartime experiences for children of war.

In Canada the evacuation of people of Japanese descent in 1942 created a life of exile, as it did in the United States, but under more severe conditions. The government separated a large portion of the fathers from their families and placed them in work crews and road camps. Only a meager effort was made to deliver social services to relocated families, mostly medical care. Primary schools were understaffed; most of the teachers were older siblings of schoolchildren, as in the U.S. assembly centers. The government offered no support for public high schools in the interior settlements where it concentrated the excluded population, and there was no program of planned opportunities for college. Had it not been for the dedication of church groups, a few Caucasian friends, and the Japanese Canadians themselves, the children might have had no schooling during those years. After the war the Canadian government announced a policy of dispersal east of the Rockies. Influential leaders advocated revoking the citizenship of the children and repatriating all families to Japan—a campaign that ultimately failed as the political climate changed in the postwar years. In short, Japanese Canadians did not benefit from government efforts to promote their interests. The children were lucky to receive any education at all during the war.[3]

England's experience was of quite another kind. Beginning in 1939, the government evacuated English children from cities to temporary foster homes and government-sponsored nurseries in the countryside. For these children, the shock of separation from home environments was mitigated by acceptance as equals instead of aliens. Problems did arise because of differences in urban and rural customs, disparities in social class, and conflicting religious preferences; and initially, many children experienced traumatic separation from the security of family relationships, since most children went alone without their parents. But a great many relocated with their entire class in school, so that their teacher became the focal point of social life and discipline. The group that had the most difficulty adjusting to new circumstances was not school-age children but mothers and their younger children; many of these returned to the imperiled cities shortly after the inception of the program. Still, by the time the Battle of Britain commenced in the fall of 1940, the government had evacuated some 1,250,000 children to safe areas. These children stayed long enough in their foster homes and schools to make the program a remarkable achievement during wartime. To the extent that the program was not effective, it suffered from problems vastly different from those of racial exclusion in segregated camps. National policy had allowed those problems to be alleviated by abundant caring and mutual aid among strangers. In the case of England, officials viewed the dispossessed individuals as entitled to all the benefits of an interdependent society, even in the hardest of times.[4]

Against these contrasts, the distinctive features of the Japanese American evacuation stand out more clearly. Military orders and civilian social policy overlapped; while both deprived the incarcerated population of rights, the latter offered services aimed at rehabilitation and eventual reincorporation into normal communities. As social institutions, the camps for Japanese Americans brought together incongruous elements of coercion and idealism; they combined barbed wire and military police with governmental services, a subsidized economy, community councils under administrative control, public education, and conditional opportunities for resettlement into communities on the outside. These incongruities led to conflict in the camps, and the differences of opinion deepened when the government required declarations of loyalty while denying civil liberty. For the children of war, education continued as loyalty demands escalated; education was broader than schooling itself, for the incarcerated population had its own forms of social organization and cultural expression, its own ways of preserving meaning and coping with adversity. The role of the older generation in maintaining cohesion was an important thread in the social history of loyalty in the camps. The politics of education at Tule Lake Segregation Center, the most severe of the camps, provides a memorable example of the attempts of Japanese Americans to control and transmit collective meanings to their children in defiance of public authority.

Despite the coercive features of life behind barbed wire, parents and children continued to use the public school system in the camps. In final education reports from all camps except Tule Lake, educators recorded that the schoolchildren had maintained respectable rates of attendance and regained some of the ground they had lost in academic achievement because of the evacuation. Families persisted in linking their aspirations to conventional achievement, even while resisting public authority in many of its forms. But this pattern does not mean that the children and their parents embraced the legitimacy of the institutions established for them. The more difficult reality to preserve as social memory is how they charted their own course using institutions in which they had been placed against their will. Such a reconstruction of the past does not deny the injustices of the situation but looks further to understand how learning and social action could have proceeded under such circumstances. Maintaining as much resistance as the structure would bear without bringing further repression, Japanese Americans worked with public authority and, at the same time, built up their social and cultural organization within the camps to prepare for a change when the terms might become more favorable. For some, the moment came right away and they regained their freedom within a year after having been evacuated in 1942. For many others, the majority who remained longer in the camps, it seemed more sensible to wait; they used the coercive institution as a barrier, at least for a while, against other uncertainties on the outside.

The educational history of the camps reveals something other than mere adjustment to administrative policies, clearly more than consent given to an authoritarian institution. Parents and children were acting on a plane of experience constructed out of their own cultural meanings, generating plans for the future from their own aspirations, and resisting when necessary to maintain self-determination. Even members of the college vanguard, who dispersed individually to embrace educational opportunities that cut them off from the incarcerated population they left behind, were well aware of the collective meanings being created by their individual achievements.

This inquiry into a difficult moment in the nation's past is intended to deepen understanding of an event whose importance extends beyond those who were touched most directly by it. The wartime history of Japanese Americans is part of the history of our society; it is a standard topic in school textbooks and survey courses, part of the collective memory that we draw upon to understand ourselves as a people. The evacuation has become a watershed in the study of war powers and national security, both controversial issues in the subsequent history of a warring nation. The incarceration of Japanese Americans is also a theme in ethnic studies, offering both an example and a metaphor that helps to interpret the experience of minority groups in the United States. This book places that history squarely in another domain, the history of education.

Many salient features of public education were present in the wartime camps. One was the sense of mission in a moment of social dislocation, typified by educational planners and some of the idealistic teachers. Another was the conflict between the ideal of Americanization and the traditional culture of an immigrant group, a conflict with many precedents in the educational systems of the United States. There was also a familiar gulf between policy and practice, the structural tension between levels of authority that one commonly finds in social institutions attempting to implement centralized mandates for change. Enlarged and intensified by the scope of the camps as a forced relocation, these tensions nonetheless created recognizable forms of conflict and accommodation that shaped the education of the children of war. Teachers, for example, were isolated, inhabiting a difficult middle ground between families and public authorities. They taught students who were also caught in the middle, who were groping between two worlds of cultural authority. As in education generally, competition emerged between official and private forms of learning. Public and community cultures battled to define the social reality and opportunities of the children. Neither can be said to have won this battle, but, again as in education generally, together they helped to shape the consciousness of the schoolchildren in their formative years of mental and moral growth. Meanwhile, the schools went about their business in a spirit of contrived normalcy, teaching ideas of democracy to the children.

This is not to suggest that public institutions were the cause of the evacuation. Rather, their form and values became central to the experience of the children after the camps were in operation. Education, in particular, reveals a great deal about the impact of the camps on Japanese Americans. Idealizing the camps as planned communities, the government brought learning and life closer together, as the educational planners had hoped. Yet, the result was strangely distant from the good intentions of the planners. Teachers and students became embroiled in communal anguish over the further segregation of "disloyals" and selective dispersal of the "loyal" population. The politics of education during this moment of history constitutes a social memory well worth preserving.

Seen through the lives of the children, those years of exile were a crucial time for choosing how to live in the future. And in a larger sense, one that reaches far beyond the camps, it was such a time for the nation. The treatment of Japanese Americans during World War II paralleled a crisis in national security, when greatly expanded official powers had mobilized U.S. society for war against belligerent nations demanding an undemocratic basis of political life. Although World War II brought many changes to the United States, it also preserved the possibility of democratic life for the nation's citizenry. Along the way to that victory the experience of Japanese Americans left an example, not only of some misdirected applications of expanded official powers, but of the reactions of one social group to the policies that resulted. The catastrophe continues to be educational, perhaps most of all because it raises questions about the uses of public authority in a democratic system of government, and because it underscores the central but problematic role of public institutions in teaching a diverse citizenry the ways of democracy.

Notes

Abbreviations

BAN   Bancroft Library, University of California, Berkeley. 67/14 designates the number of the collection containing records of the War Relocation Authority (WRA) and the Japanese Evacuation and Resettlement Study.

HOOV   Hoover Archives, Hoover Institution on War, Revolution, and Peace, Stanford University, Stanford, California.

JARP   Japanese American Research Project Collection, University Research Library, University of California at Los Angeles.

MCA   Mills College Archives, Mills College, Oakland, California.

NARG210   National Archives and Record Service, Washington, D.C., Record Group 210, Records of the WRA.

Prologue

1. *Memoirs 1944: Hunt High School,* Minidoka, Yearbook Collection, NARG210.

2. The WRA recorded a total of 30,132 pupils in its elementary and secondary schools during the war and 27,728 matriculated in 1942–43, according to the WRA Community Management Division, Education Section, "Washington Office Final Report Summary," October 10, 1945, app., p. 1, BAN 67/14 E2.671. For figures on the numbers of incarcerated persons throughout the war, the source is WRA, *The Evacuated People: A Quantitative Description* (Washington, D.C.: U.S. Department of the Interior, 1946), which lists (p. 8) a total figure of 120,313 that includes births in the camps, released seasonal workers, and transferees from institutionalized custody elsewhere. The rough figure of 110,000 evacuees provides a reasonable approximation of the number of Japanese Americans living in the relocation centers in 1942. A few thousand Japanese Americans who resided east of the prohibited zone of the Western Defense Command were not incarcerated during the war.

3. For histories of the evacuation see Morton Grodzins, *Americans Betrayed: Politics and the Japanese Evacuation* (Chicago: University of Chicago Press, 1949); Stetson Conn, "Japanese Evacuation from the West Coast," in Stetson Conn. Rose C. Engelman, and Byron Fairchild, *United States Army in World War II, The Western Hemisphere: Guarding the United States and Its Outposts* (Washington, D.C.: Office of the Chief of Military History, Department of the Army, 1964); Audrie Girdner and Anne Loftis, *The Great Betrayal: The Evacuation of the Japanese-Americans during World War II* (New York: Macmillan, 1969); Jacobus tenBroek, Edward N. Barnhart, and Floyd W. Matson, *Prejudice, War and the Constitution: Causes and Consequences of the Evacuation of the Japanese Americans in World War II* (Berkeley: University of California Press, 1970); and Roger Daniels, *The Decision to Relocate the Japanese Americans* (Philadelphia: Lippincott, 1975). For accounts of events in the camps, see Allan R. Bosworth, *America's Concentration Camps* (New York: Norton, 1967); Dillon S. Myer, *Uprooted Americans: The Japanese Americans and the War Relocation Authority during World War II* (Tucson: University of Arizona Press, 1971), a memoir of the WRA director for most of the war; Edward H. Spicer, Asael T. Hansen, Katharine Luomala, and Marvin K. Opler, *Impounded People: Japanese Americans in Relocation Centers* (Tucson: University of Arizona Press, 1969); Girdner and Loftis, *The Great Betrayal*; tenBroek, Barnhart, and Matson, *Prejudice, War and the Constitution*; Roger Daniels, *Concentration Camps USA: Japanese Americans and World War II* (New York: Holt, Rinehart and Winston, 1972); Michi Weglyn, *Years of Infamy: The Untold Story of America's Concentration Camps* (New York: William Morrow, 1976); and Commission on Wartime Relocation and Internment of Civilians, *Personal Justice Denied* (Washington, D.C.: U.S. Government Printing Office, 1982). Two exemplary studies of individual camps are Leonard J. Arrington, *The Price of Prejudice: The Japanese-American Relocation Center in Utah during World War II* (Logan: Utah State University, 1962), reprinted in Roger Daniels, ed., *Three Short Works on Japanese Americans* (New York: Arno Press, 1978); and Douglas Nelson, *Heart Mountain: The History of an American Concentration Camp* (Madison: State Historical Society of Wisconsin, 1976). For a description of the secondary

literature on the camps, see Howard Sugimoto, "A Bibliographic Essay on the Wartime Evacuation of Japanese from the West Coast Areas," in Hilary Conroy and T. Scott Miyakawa, eds., *East Across the Pacific: Historical and Sociological Studies of Japanese Immigration and Assimilation* (Santa Barbara: American Bibliographic Center–Clio Press, 1972), pp. 140–150; see also Roger Daniels, "American Historians and East Asian Immigrants," *Pacific Historical Review* 43 (1974): 449–473; Daniels, "North American Scholarship and East Asian Immigrants," *Immigration History Newsletter* 11 (1979): 8–11; and the brief bibliographic essay at the end of Daniels, *Concentration Camps*.

4. ACLU quoted in Peter Irons, *Justice at War: The Story of the Japanese American Internment Cases* (New York: Oxford University Press, 1983), p. 349, from a statement prepared for the Commission on Wartime Relocation and Internment of Civilians in 1981. Extensive photographic collections on the evacuation and the camps are in NARG210, BAN 67/14, and JARP; photographs of the evacuation can also be found in the collection of the Farm Security Administration in the U.S. Library of Congress, Washington, D.C. For published examples of the poignant photos taken during the evacuation by Dorothea Lange, see Maisie Conrat and Richard Conrat, *Executive Order 9066: The Internment of 110,000 Japanese Americans* (San Francisco: California Historical Society, Special Publication no. 51, 1972).

5. Eugene V. Rostow, "Our Worst Wartime Mistake," *Harper's* 191 (1945): 193–201. The most comprehensive educational history of the camps to date, primarily an administrative description, is William D. Zeller, *An Educational Drama: The Educational Program Provided the Japanese-Americans during the Relocation Period, 1942–1945* (New York: American Press, 1969). For educational histories of the individual camps, see, for example, Jerome T. Light, "The Development of a Junior-Senior High School Program in a Relocation Center for People of Japanese Ancestry during the War with Japan" (Ph.D. diss., Stanford University, 1947), on the Minidoka Relocation Center; and Carole K. Yumiba, "An Educational History of the War Relocation Centers at Jerome and Rohwer, Arkansas, 1942–1945" (Ph.D. diss., University of Southern California, 1979). See also Charles M. Wollenberg, *All Deliberate Speed: Segregation and Exclusion in California Schools, 1855–1975* (Berkeley: University of California Press, 1976); and Irving G. Hendrick, *The Education of Non-Whites in California, 1849–1970* (San Francisco: R & E Associates, 1977).

6. Quotations from "Disadvantages of Camp Life," student essay by Y. K., and "My Last Day at Home," student essay by M., ninth grade, 1942–43; both essays are among those collected in the Tule Lake Documentary Files, NARG210, box 88. For examples of student aspiration and disappointment after having been taught about U.S. society in public schools, see the case histories collected by the Japanese Evacuation and Resettlement Study under the heading "Case Histories: Abstracts (Education and Schooling)," BAN 67/14; some of the transcripts of interviews also appear in Dorothy Swaine Thomas, *The Salvage* (Berkeley: University of California Press, 1952).

7. Weekly activities report to Don Elberson from Block Manager 51, Tule Lake Relocation Center, September 19, 1942, BAN 67/14 R2.08.

8. Anna Freud and Dorothy T. Burlingham, *War and Children* (New York: Medical War Books, 1943), pp. 18, 22–24.

9. The Evacuation and Resettlement Study at the University of California

calculated the median age of the younger generation as seventeen in 1942; see Thomas, *The Salvage*, p. 19. On the relationship between education and income for Japanese Americans in the postwar era, a useful summary of arguments and research findings can be found in Ki-Taek Chun, "The Myth of Asian American Success and Its Educational Ramifications," *IRCD Bulletin* 15 (Winter/Spring 1980): 1–15 (published by the Institute for Urban and Minority Education, Teachers College, Columbia University). See also Harry H. L. Kitano, *Japanese Americans: The Evolution of a Subculture* (Englewood Cliffs, N.J.: Prentice-Hall, 1976); and Darrell Montero, *Japanese Americans: Changing Patterns of Ethnic Affiliation over Three Generations* (Boulder, Colo.: Westview Press, 1980).

1. Between Past and Future Homes

1. On the dramatic rise in attendance rates in Japanese education, see Japan Ministry of Education, Science and Culture, *Japan's Modern Educational System: A History of the First Hundred Years* (Tokyo: Printing Bureau, Japan Ministry of Finance, 1980), p. 464. The early Japanese population in the United States grew from 2,039 in 1890, to 24,326 in 1900, to 72,157 in 1910, to 111,010 in 1920, as reported in U.S. Congress, House of Representatives, Select Committee Investigating National Defense Migration, *Findings and Recommendations on Evacuation of Enemy Aliens and Others from Prohibited Military Zones,* Fourth Interim Report, May 1942, House Report no. 2124 (Washington, D.C.: U.S. Government Printing Office, 1942), p. 94. The Dillingham Commission quotation is from Immigration Commission, *The Children of Immigrants in Schools,* vol. 5, 61st Congress, 3rd Session, Senate Document no. 749 (Washington, D.C.: U.S. Government Printing Office, 1911), p. 153. Yamato Ichihashi, *Japanese in the United States* (Stanford: Stanford University Press, 1932), pp. 66–67; on the "golden story," see p. 88; and for a description of the first Japanese schoolboy, pp. 19–21. On early educational experiences, also see Issei Oral History Project, *Issei Christians* (Sacramento: Issei Oral History Project, 1977), especially the interviews of Yoshisada Kawai, pp. 3–4, and of Nisuke Mitsumori, p. 126. See also Eileen Sunada Sarasohn, *The Issei: Portrait of a Pioneer: An Oral History* (Palo Alto, Calif.: Pacific Books, 1983), pp. 1–56.

2. On literacy, see Harry A. Millis, *The Japanese Problem in the United States* (New York: Macmillan, 1915), pp. 230–231; figures taken from U.S. Immigration Commission, *Reports,* vol. 23, p. 151. Robert E. Park, *The Immigrant Press and Its Control* (New York: Harper & Brothers, 1922), pp. 150–166, 280–286. On use of immigrant press for social control, see Yuji Ichioka, "*Amerika Nadeshiko*: Japanese Immigrant Women in the United States, 1900–1924," *Pacific Historical Review* 49 (1980): 339–357. On the educational initiatives of religious organizations, see Isao Horinouchi, "Americanized Buddhism: A Sociological Analysis of a Protestantized Japanese Religion" (Ph.D. diss., University of California, Davis, 1973); and Tetsuden Kashima, *Buddhism in America: The Social Organization of an Ethnic Religious Institution* (Westport, Conn.: Greenwood Press, 1977). On the Japanese associations, see Robert E. Park and Herbert A. Miller, *Old World Traits Transplanted* (New York: Harper & Brothers, 1921), pp. 178–179; Kiichi Kanzaki, *California and the Japanese* (San Francisco: R & E Associates, 1971; originally published in 1921), pp. 1–6; Michinari

Fujita, "The Japanese Associations in America," *Sociology and Social Research* 13 (1929): 211–228; and Yuji Ichioka, "Japanese Associations and the Japanese Government: A Special Relationship, 1909–1926," *Pacific Historical Review* 46 (1977): 409–437. For interpretations of other organizations providing economic solidarity, see Ivan H. Light, *Ethnic Enterprise in America: Business and Welfare among Chinese, Japanese, and Blacks* (Berkeley: University of California Press, 1972); and John Modell, *The Economics and Politics of Racial Accommodation: The Japanese of Los Angeles, 1900–1942* (Urbana: University of Illinois Press, 1977).

3. Forrest E. LaViolette, *Americans of Japanese Ancestry: A Study of Assimilation in the American Community* (Toronto: Canadian Institute of International Affairs, 1945), pp. 17–29; quotations on pp. 18 and 19. Another useful study of Japanese family and social organization before World War II is Shotaru Frank Miyamoto, *Social Solidarity among the Japanese in Seattle* (Seattle: University of Washington, 1939). On the evolution of parental authority before World War II, see Sylvia J. Yanagisako, *Transforming the Past: Tradition and Kinship among Japanese Americans* (Stanford: Stanford University Press, 1985), chap. 3, "Nisei Marriage."

4. Census count and percentage figures from Ichihashi, *Japanese in the United States,* p. 72.

5. On the origins of Japanese language schools, see Hilary Conroy, *The Japanese Expansion into Hawaii, 1868–1898* (San Francisco: R & E Associates, 1973), p. 144; LaViolette, *Americans of Japanese Ancestry,* p. 52; and Kashima, *Buddhism in America,* p. 34. Some views of local school history can be found in Kazuo Ito, *Issei: A History of Japanese Immigrants in North America,* trans. Shinichiro Nakamura and Jean S. Gerard (Seattle: Executive Committee for Publication of Issei, Japanese Community Service, 1973), pp. 592–610. The study quoted is Marian Svensrud, "Attitudes of the Japanese towards Their Language Schools," *Sociology and Social Research* 17 (1933): 259–264.

6. The goal of the Japanese Educational Association is quoted in E. Manchester Boddy, *Japanese in America* (Los Angeles: E. M. Boddy, 1921), p. 111. Kiyo Sue Inui, "Japanese Education in America," *Journal of Proceedings and Addresses,* 53rd Annual Meeting, National Education Association (Ann Arbor: National Education Association, 1915), figures from p. 162, quotations, pp. 161, 163. Kanzaki, *California and the Japanese,* p. 5, and pp. 3–6 generally for Americanization activities of the association. See also Yamato Ichihashi, "Americanizing the Japanese: Efforts Being Made by Their Own Leaders," Ichihashi Papers, University Archives, Stanford University, box 2, folder 6.

7. Henry W. Kinney, "Light on the Japanese Question," *Atlantic Monthly* 126 (1920): 836. Marvin L. Darsie, "The Mental Capacity of American-Born Japanese Children," *Comparative Psychology Monographs* 3 (January 1926): 85, 77, 33.

8. Valentine S. McClatchey, "Germany of Asia," in *Four Anti-Japanese Pamphlets* (New York: Arno Press, 1978), p. 44; first appeared in a series published in 1919 by the *Sacramento Bee,* of which McClatchey was editor. Governor William D. Stephens, letter of transmittal for State Board of Control, in *California and the Oriental: Japanese, Chinese, and Hindus* (Sacramento: California State Printing Office, 1922), p. 9.

9. The 1894 case was In Re Saito. On exclusion of Japanese immigrants

from naturalization, see Frank F. Chuman, *The Bamboo People: The Law and Japanese Americans* (Del Mar, Calif.: Publisher's Inc., 1976), pp. 7, 65–71. On the 1922 case, Ozawa v. United States, 260 U.S. 178, and the organized efforts of the immigrants to gain citizenship, see Yuji Ichioka, "Early Japanese Immigrant Quest for Citizenship: The Background of the 1922 Ozawa Case," *Amerasia Journal* 4, no. 2 (1977): 1–22. The 1898 case was U.S. v. Wong Kim Ark, 169 U.S. 649.

10. Ward v. Flood, 48 Calif. 36 (1874). Plessy v. Ferguson, 163 U.S. 537 (1896). School Law of California, article X, section 1662. The case upholding segregated schools for the Chinese was Wong Him v. Callahan, 119 F. 381 (1903). On the history of segregation in California, see Charles M. Wollenberg, *All Deliberate Speed: Segregation and Exclusion in California Schools, 1855–1975* (Berkeley: University of California Press, 1976); and Irving G. Hendrick, *The Education of Non-Whites in California, 1849–1970* (San Francisco: R & E Associates, 1977).

11. On the San Francisco crisis and its international ramifications, see Arthur Butzbach, "The Segregation of Orientals in the San Francisco Schools" (Master's thesis, Stanford University, 1928); Ruth H. Thomson, "Events Leading to the Order to Segregate Japanese Pupils in the San Francisco Public Schools" (Ph.D. diss., Stanford University, 1931); Thomas A. Bailey, *Theodore Roosevelt and the Japanese-American Crises* (Stanford: Stanford University Press, 1934); Roger Daniels, *The Politics of Prejudice: The Anti-Japanese Movement in California and the Struggle for Japanese Exclusion* (Berkeley: University of California Press, 1962); Raymond A. Esthus, *Theodore Roosevelt and Japan* (Seattle: University of Washington Press, 1966); and Charles E. Neu, *An Uncertain Friendship: Theodore Roosevelt and Japan, 1906–1909* (Cambridge, Mass.: Harvard University Press, 1967).

12. Lothrop Stoddard, *The Rising Tide of Color against White World-Supremacy* (New York: Scribner, 1920), p. 49. Valentine S. McClatchey, "Japanese Immigration and Colonization," in *Four Anti-Japanese Pamphlets* (New York: Arno Press, 1978), p. 4. Governor Stephens, letter of transmittal for State Board of Control, in *California and the Oriental*. On the segregated schools around Sacramento, see Reginald Bell, "A Study of Certain Phases of the Education of Japanese in Central California" (Master's thesis, Stanford University, 1928).

13. For a portrait of community life during this era, see Cheryl L. Cole, *A History of the Japanese Community in Sacramento* (San Francisco: R & E Associates, 1974), pp. 23, 31–35.

14. These figures do not include the territory of Hawaii. Ichihashi, *Japanese in the United States,* p. 94. LaViolette, *Americans of Japanese Ancestry,* pp. 37, 41. Edward K. Strong, *Japanese in California* (Stanford: Stanford University Press, 1933), pp. 35, 45, 85. Wollenberg, *All Deliberate Speed,* p. 73.

15. On language schools, see for example Ito, *Issei,* p. 591; LaViolette, *Americans of Japanese Ancestry,* pp. 53–54; and Roderick D. McKenzie, *Oriental Exclusion* (Chicago: University of Chicago Press, 1928), p. 172.

16. William K. Hosokawa, *JACL in Quest of Justice: The History of the Japanese American Citizens League* (New York: William Morrow, 1982). See also Roger Daniels, "The Japanese," in John Higham, ed., *Ethnic Leadership in America* (Baltimore: Johns Hopkins University Press, 1978), pp. 36–63, on the conflicting leadership factions among Issei and Nisei. The 1934 speech competition and resolution are described in Hosokawa, *JACL in Quest of Justice,* pp.

79–81. The JACL credo is published in the *Congressional Record,* May 19, 1941, and quoted in Roger Daniels, *Concentration Camps USA.: Japanese Americans and World War II* (Holt, Rinehart and Winston, 1972), p. 24.

17. Edward K. Strong, *The Second-Generation Japanese Problem* (Stanford: Stanford University Press, 1934), table 23, p. 186; only a small proportion of the second generation was more than twenty years old when the survey was taken, but high levels of educational achievement remained the rule for the group as it came of age. See also Strong, *Vocational Aptitudes of Second-Generation Japanese in the United States* (Stanford: Stanford University Press, 1933); and Reginald Bell, *Public School Education of Second-Generation Japanese in California* (Stanford: Stanford University Press, 1935).

18. For extensive interviews showing the crisis of the Nisei in the 1930s, see the case histories collected by the Evacuation and Resettlement Study, BAN; some of these were published in Dorothy Swaine Thomas, *The Salvage* (Berkeley: University of California Press, 1952). Ichihashi, *Japanese in the United States,* pp. 331, 333.

19. The California bill was SB 231, introduced on January 22, 1935; see Chuman, *Bamboo People,* p. 124. The quotation is from Tsuyoshi Matsumoto, "The Japanese in California: An Account of Their Contributions to the Growth and Development and Their Part in Community Life," unpublished ms., Welfare Committee of the Central Japanese Association of America, 1941, 2010 JARP, 159-15, pp. 45–46.

20. "My Story," by a Nisei, December 14, 1943, NARG210, 61.318, box 22, file 4. For other student reflections on Pearl Harbor and its aftermath for Japanese Americans, see the compositions collected in the McGovern Papers, JARP, box 114, folders 5–9.

21. The evacuation is interpreted in Morton Grodzins, *Americans Betrayed: Politics and the Japanese Evacuation* (Chicago: University of Chicago Press, 1949); Stetson Conn, "Japanese Evacuation from the West Coast," in Stetson Conn, Rose C. Engelman, and Byron Fairchild, *United States Army in World War II, The Western Hemisphere: Guarding the United States and Its Outposts* (Washington, D.C.: Office of the Chief of Military History, Department of the Army, 1964); Audrie Girdner and Anne Loftis, *The Great Betrayal: The Evacuation of the Japanese-Americans during World War II* (New York: Macmillan, 1969); Jacobus tenBroek, Edward N. Barnhart, and Floyd W. Matson, *Prejudice, War and the Constitution: Causes and Consequences of the Evacuation of the Japanese Americans in World War II* (Berkeley: University of California Press, 1970); Roger Daniels, *Concentration Camps USA: Japanese Americans and World War II* (New York: Holt, Rinehart and Winston, 1972) and *The Decision to Relocate the Japanese Americans* (Philadelphia: J. B. Lippincott, 1975); Michi Weglyn, *Years of Infamy: The Untold Story of America's Concentration Camps* (New York: William Morrow, 1976); and U.S. Commission of Wartime Relocation and Internment of Civilians, *Personal Justice Denied* (Washington, D.C.: Government Printing Office, 1982). A detailed account of the role of the JACL during the evacuation period can be found in Paul R. Spickard, "The Nisei Assume Power: The Japanese Citizens League, 1941–1942," *Pacific Historical Review* 52 (1983): 147–174. See also Hosokawa, *JACL in Quest of Justice.*

22. For a legal discussion of the attack on Nisei citizenship by Webb, see tenBroek, Barnhart, and Matson, *Prejudice, War and the Constitution,* pp. 313–

315. The discussion of Tom Stewart's bill in the Senate is reported in the *Congressional Record* 88, pt. 4, 77th Congress, 2nd Session, June 22, 1942, pp. 5427–30; quotation by Senator Orrice Abram Murdock, Jr., of Utah is on p. 5429. The other response, comparing an expanded policy of evacuation with Nazi racial laws, was reported in the *Pacific Cable* 1 (August 12, 1942): 3, a newsletter of the American Friends Service Committee in Seattle, BAN 67/14 B13.00.

23. Leland Ford as quoted in *Congressional Record* 88, pt. 1, 77th Congress, 2nd Session, January 20, 1942, p. 502. For more detailed treatments of the politics surrounding the evacuation, see titles cited in note 21 above, especially Daniels, *The Decision*. Rep. John Rankin in *Congressional Record* 88, pt. 8, February 23, 1942, p. A768. U.S. Department of War, *Final Report: Japanese Evacuation from the West Coast, 1942* (Washington, D.C.: U.S. Government Printing Office, 1943), p.34.

24. "Human vultures" quotation in letter from an evacuee to the National Japanese American Student Relocation Council, February 15, 1943, Thomas R. Bodine papers, HOOV. The words "precautionary detention" and "protective custody" were bandied about as a rationalization for the camps; an account of later attempts by the solicitor of the WRA to justify the usage appears in Peter Irons, *Justice at War: The Japanese Internment Cases* (New York: Oxford University Press, 1983), pp. 256, 359. Hatsuye Egami, "Wartime Diary," *All Aboard*, a Nisei journal of literature and social commentary (Spring 1944): 34–39, Topaz Documentary Files, NARG210, box 4.

25. *The Evacuee Speaks,* Santa Anita Assembly Center, August 1, 1942, Thomas R. Bodine Papers, HOOV; Charles Kikuchi, *The Kikuchi Diary: Chronicle of an American Concentration Camp,* ed. John Modell (Urbana: University of Illinois Press, 1973), p. 57.

26. Janet Cormack, ed., "Portland Assembly Center: Diary of Saku Tomita," *Oregon Historical Quarterly* 81 (1980): 156, 158. Anthony L. Lehman, *Birthright of Barbed Wire: The Santa Anita Assembly Center for the Japanese* (Los Angeles: Westernlore Press, 1970), p. 50. *The Evacuee Speaks,* Santa Anita, August 1, 1942, p.4.

27. Takashi Terami, "Education Department—Merced Assembly Center," in Final Report, Education Section, Granada Relocation Center [Amache], 1945, BAN 67/14 L3.00; see also "Education Report," Merced Assembly Center, McGovern Papers, JARP, box 113, folder 1, p. 2.

28. Henry Tani, "The Tanforan High School," pp. 1–2, BAN 67/14 B8.32.

29. From the interview narrative of Mary Tsukamoto, collected in John Tateishi's *And Justice for All: An Oral History of the Japanese American Detention Camps* (New York: Random House, 1984), p. 14. For an eyewitness account of a similar celebration at Tanforan, see Clara E. Breed, "All But Blind," *Library Journal* 68 (1943): 120–121.

30. Tani, "The Tanforan High School," p. 8. (In the last two sentences of the quotation I have deleted a comma after "teacher" and a hyphen within the word "textbook" as well as changing the final verb "is" to "are.") For program summaries of education at Tanforan, see BAN 67/14 B4.01. This material includes a report of Frank E. Kilpatrick, Jr., Tanforan's director of education under the Wartime Civil Control Administration (the army agency that ran the assembly centers), which acknowledges that evacuees organized the educational system on their own initiative; see especially in this file the memoranda from the eva-

cuee education department to Kilpatrick, outlining school aims and weekly programs for each grade.

31. Yoshiko Uchida, *Desert Exile: The Uprooting of a Japanese American Family* (Seattle: University of Washington Press, 1982), pp. 87–90.

32. On the Mills College connection, see Lovisa C. Wagoner and Evelyn S. Little, "Our Japanese Alumnae in Absentia," *Mills Quarterly* 25 (November 1942): 59–62; "The Mills College Children's School: A Fifty Year History," report dated Spring 1976, in the historical files of the Children's School at Mills College, Oakland, California; "Wartime Activities of the Department of Child Development," Department of Child Development, MCA, file 4; and for suggestions prepared by Lovisa Wagoner and her staff on nursery schools in the camps, file 6, "Correspondence re: WRA educational programs," Department of Child Development, MCA. As an example of the conviction of Wagoner and her associates that preschool education could empower families to build a more democratic future, see the lecture series "Wartime Care of Young Children" from 1942 to 1943, historical files of the Children's School, Mills College. See also Kay Uchida and Grace Fujii, "The Pre-School Program at Tanforan," 1942, BAN 67/14 B8.36, as well as their subsequent report a year later from Topaz, "Educational Report of the Program and Procedures of the Preschool Department." William D. Zeller provides a brief laudatory description of the preschool activities in *An Educational Drama: The Educational Programs Provided the Japanese-Americans during the Relocation Period, 1942–1945* (New York: American Press, 1969). I am grateful to Kristen M. Anderson, a former director of the Children's School at Mills College, for sharing with me her personal files and a paper she wrote for a seminar with David Tyack in 1977 at Stanford University entitled "Nursery School Programs in the Japanese Relocation Camps."

33. A scrapbook of photographs from the preschool at Manzanar is appended to the report by Mary Schauland, "Pre-School Education," n.d., Washington Office Records—Documentary (Manzanar), NARG210, box 66. On ability to speak English, see Final Report, Education Section, Manzanar, NARG210, p. 35. On teaching of language skills, see Schauland, "A Day in the Pre-School," in her Manzanar report on preschools, cited above in this note. "Summary Report: The Educational Program of the Granada Project, Amache, Colorado," 1945, BAN 67/14 L3.01, p. 4. See also *WRA Handbook,* 30.3.10, NARG210.

34. Letter from Ida Shimanouchi to Aurelia Reinhardt, June 24, 1942, Aurelia Reinhardt Papers, MCA, file I 23. Final Report, Education Section, Manzanar; and Project Report no. 20, July 10, 1942, Manzanar Documentary Files, NARG210, box 67. For another example of the activity of sympathetic Caucasians, see Josephine Whitney Duveneck, *Life on Two Levels: An Autobiography of Josephine Whitney Duveneck* (Los Altos, Calif.: W. Kaufmann, 1978). An excellent and not atypical example of educational assistance coming from outside the assembly centers is the letter from the principal of the University Elementary School at UCLA to parents of children in the school, asking for toys and books to send to the Santa Anita Assembly Center; see letter from Corinne A. Seeds to parents, May 26, 1942, BAN Presidents' File, CU 5, box 588.

35. Edith M. Waterman, "Rich Experiences," June 29, 1944, p. 2, Poston Documentary Files, NARG210, box 18.

36. Mine Okubo, *Citizen 13660* (New York: Columbia University Press, 1946), p. 92. On the parental advisory council, see the prehistory of education at Tan-

foran in George Sugihara, "Education in Topaz," Historical Section, Report H419, Topaz Relocation Center, BAN 67/14 H2.12.

37. From Tanforan student papers, ninth and tenth grades, BAN 67/14 B12.60. Letter from a student to Edythe Backus, August 27, 1942, from Santa Anita Assembly Center, Colorado River Relocation Center Collection, box 1, Huntington Library, San Marino, California.

38. Charles Kikuchi, *Diary,* pp. 134, 82, 243. See also Henry Tani, "The Tanforan High School."

39. Final Report, Education Section, Manzanar Relocation Center, 1945, pp. 1–5, and Manzanar Quarterly Report, July–September 1942, NARG210. See also Project Report no. 10, Manzanar Reports Division, June 25, 1942, Manzanar Documentary Files, NARG210, box 67.

40. On the history of the WRA, see Ruth E. McKee, "History of W.R.A., Pearl Harbor to June 30, 1944," unpublished ms., NARG210; *WRA—A Story of Human Conservation* (Washington, D.C.: Government Printing Office, 1946); and Albert B. Turner, "The Origins and Development of the War Relocation Authority" (Ph.D. diss., Duke University, 1967).

41. On congressional opposition and bureaucratic politics, see especially Turner, "Origins and Development."

42. For the personal accounts of these men, see Milton S. Eisenhower, *The President Is Calling* (Garden City, N.Y.: Doubleday, 1974); and Dillon S. Myer, *Uprooted Americans* (Tucson: University of Arizona Press, 1971). When Myer went to the Bureau of Indian Affairs as commissioner in the postwar years, he took with him several former WRA staff members; see Robert M. Kvasnicka and Herman J. Viola, *The Commissioners of Indian Affairs, 1824–1977* (Lincoln: University of Nebraska Press, 1979), pp. 293–299. Note that the name of the Office of Indian Affairs (also widely known as the Indian Service) was officially changed to the Bureau of Indian Affairs in 1947. On the career of Eisenhower, see also Stephen E. Ambrose and Richard H. Immerman, *Milton S. Eisenhower: Educational Statesman* (Baltimore: Johns Hopkins University Press, 1983); and on that of Myer, see Richard Drinnon, *Keeper of Concentration Camps: Dillon S. Myer and American Racism* (Berkeley: University of California Press, 1987). For a suggestive interpretation of the connection between the camps and New Deal policy, see Peter T. Suzuki, "Planned New Communities in War-time America: A Province for the New Urban History," *Societas* (forthcoming). On contemporary CCC administrative and program arrangements, see Educational Policies Commission, *The Civilian Conservation Corps, the National Youth Administration, and the Public Schools* (Washington, D.C.: National Education Association and American Association of School Administrators, 1941).

43. For Milton Eisenhower's own account of the hostility with which his idea of orderly dispersal was met when he spoke with western governors, see *The President Is Calling,* pp. 117–118. The transcript of the meeting with western governors, which took place in Salt Lake City on April 7, 1942, is in BAN 67/14 C1.03.

44. For published examples of contemporary discussions of the notion of planned communities, see Emory E. Bogardus, "Relocation Centers as Planned Communities," *Sociology and Social Research* 28 (1944): 218–234; and John H. Provinse and Solon T. Kimball, "Building New Communities during War Time," *American Sociological Review* 11 (1946): 396–410. Provinse and Kimball, both

trained as social scientists, worked as administrators for the WRA, one directing the Community Management Division and the other overseeing community government in the camps.

45. Eisenhower, *The President is Calling*; WRA Education Section, Summary Report, BAN 67/14 E2.671.

46. On early policy formation in the western regional office see materials in the WRA's San Francisco Regional Office Classified Files, NARG210, box 1. See especially letter from M. S. Eisenhower to Dewey McCormick, April 1, 1942; memo from H. M. Coverley to Leland Barrows, April 4, 1942, outlining the proposed Community Management Division; memo from H . M. Coverley to E. R. Fryer, May 6, 1942, and the attached "Statements of Policy"; and telegram from M. S. Eisenhower to E. R. Fryer, May 18, 1942. On national policy development, see also First Quarterly Report, WRA. On Eisenhower's own role, see his letter to Dillon S. Myer, November 3, 1942, Washington Central Office Files, NARG210, box 131, file 11.312; and also Eisenhower, *The President Is Calling*. For an example of early evidence of schooling policy on the West Coast while top WRA officials in Washington were still discussing dispersal and trying to deal with political opposition to the WRA, see "Planning and Construction of Schools," May 13, 1942, memo from H. M. Coverley to R. B. Cozzens, San Francisco Regional Office Files, BAN 67/14 F1.020A; a staff list of the western regional office can be found in the same file. In December of 1942 the national office revamped its organization chart and created a direct chain of command from Washington to the individual camps.

47. On the policy traditions that Fryer and Adams brought with them from the "Indian New Deal," see Margaret Szasz, *Education and the American Indian: The Road to Self-Determination, 1928–1973* (Albuquerque: University of New Mexico Press, 1974), esp. pp. 50–59; Katherine Iverson, "Progressive Education for Native Americans: Washington Ideology and Navajo Reservation Implementation," *Review Journal of Philosophy and Social Science* 3 (1978): 231–255; Katherine Jensen, "Teachers and Progressives: The Navajo Day-School Experiment, 1935–1945," *Arizona and the West* 25 (1983): 49–62; and Donald L. Parman, *The Navajos and the New Deal* (New Haven: Yale University Press, 1976), esp. pp. 193–216, which describe New Deal educational policies for Indians and the role of Lucy W. Adams in implementing them. See also Kenneth R. Philp, *John Collier's Crusade for Indian Reform, 1920–1954* (Tucson: University of Arizona Press, 1977), including an interesting harbinger for the wartime history of Japanese Americans in the camps: the account of E. R. Fryer's "restructuring" of Navajo community government in the 1930s to implement federal policy aims, pp. 187–193; Graham D. Taylor, *The New Deal and American Indian Tribalism* (Lincoln: University of Nebraska Press, 1980); and Brian W. Dippie, *The Vanishing American: White Attitudes and U.S. Indian Policy* (Middletown, Conn.: Wesleyan University Press, 1982), pp. 322–332. On correspondence between Adams and Beatty, see example in "Organized Education in Poston, 1942–1945," Final Report, Education Section, Poston Documentary Files, NARG210, box 26.

48. "The Educational Program for Evacuees of Japanese American Ancestry at Ten War Relocation Centers," Washington Office Records, NARG210, box 129. See also Lester K. Ade, "War Relocation Centers: Educational Programs for Evacuees of Japanese Ancestry," *Education for Victory* 1 (November 16,

1942): 7–9; and Lucy W. Adams, "Education in the Relocation Centers," *California Journal of Secondary Education* 17 (1942): 477–479.

49. For an example of Nisei educational leaders communicating policy and program ideas to federal officials, see letter from Ernest S. Takahashi to Mr. Throckmorton (attention Lucy Adams), June 17, 1942, "WCCA—Education" (Tanforan), Manzanar Center Records, box 6, University Research Library, University of California, Los Angeles.

50. For the conclusion of the congressional committee, see *Preliminary Report and Recommendations on Problems of Evacuation of Citizens and Aliens from Military Areas,* Report of the Select Committee Investigating National Defense Migration, House of Representatives, 77th Congress, 2nd Session, House Report no. 1911, March 19, 1942, p. 18. Richard A. Pomeroy, Superintendent of Education, Minidoka, "Education for (Future) Victory," Commencement Addresses and Essays, Minidoka Documentary Files, NARG210, box 73.

51. On the greater importance of schools for the children, Richard A. Pomeroy, "Education for (Future) Victory." *WRA Handbook,* 30.3.23.B. "Organized Education in Poston," p. 15.

52. Final Report, Education Section, Manzanar, 1945, NARG210, pp. 7, 14–15. "Proposed Curriculum Procedures for Japanese Relocation Centers," Prepared for WRA by Students in Education 299b, "Curriculum Development," Stanford University, 1942, Paul R. Hanna Papers, HOOV; hereafter cited as "Stanford Curriculum Procedures."

53. Stanford Curriculum Procedures, chart on p. 16, and passim. For examples of how these concepts were applied in the camps, see Final Report, Education Section, Topaz [Central Utah Center] Schools, September 1945, pp. 103–105, BAN 67/14 H2.50; and "Social Studies," Education Exhibit G, Washington Office Records, Manzanar Documentary Files, NARG210, box 66. Cf. *WRA Handbook,* 30.3.2.

54. Wanda Robertson, "Developing World Citizens in a Japanese Relocation Center," *Childhood Education* 20 (1943): 67. Lester K. Ade, "War Relocation Centers," 7–9; "Curriculum Report, Minidoka Project Schools," July 26, 1945, Minidoka Documentary Files, NARG210, box 73, reporting on 1942 conference with Paul Hanna and subsequent developments in the Minidoka schools.

55. *Community School Forum* 1 (November 20, 1942): 2, in Community Analysis Files 64.310, NARG210, box 443. See also "The Place of the School in the Relocation Center," WRA Community Management Division, Washington Office Records, NARG210, box 126. On the comparison with the Eight-Year Study, see Robert C. L. George, "The Granada (Colorado) Relocation Center Secondary School" (Master's thesis, University of Colorado, 1944), pp. 83–84. On the study and its message, see Wilford M. Aiken, *The Story of the Eight-Year Study* (New York: Harper & Brothers, 1942); and Edward A. Krug, *The Shaping of the American High School, Volume 2: 1920–1941* (Madison: University of Wisconsin Press, 1972), pp. 255–267.

56. See Educational Policies Commission, *What the Schools Should Teach in Wartime* (Washington, D.C.: National Education Association and American Association of School Administrators, 1943), p. 6; L. Thomas Hopkins, "War and the Curriculum," *Education* 63 (1942–43): 346–351; Stanford University School of Education Faculty, *Education in Wartime and After* (New York: D. Appleton-Century, 1943); Isaac L. Kandel, *The Impact of the War upon American Edu-*

cation (Chapel Hill: University of North Carolina Press, 1948); and Richard M. Ugland, "Education for Victory: The High School Victory Corps and Curriculum Adaptation during World War II," *History of Education Quarterly* 19 (1979): 435–451.

57. *Community School Forum;* Wanda Robertson, "Developing World Citizens," p. 70. Lucy Adams, "Education in the Relocation Centers," p. 478.

2. The First Year Inside

1. "Life in Poston," school theme, April 1, 1943, NARG210, 61.311, box 8, file 6; "School Term Reports," Washington Office Records, NARG210; see also "Education Summary," Education Section, WRA, n.d., BAN 67/14 E2.671.

2. Eunice Glenn, "Education behind Barbed Wire," *Survey Midmonthly* 80 (1944): 347. Student's comment from A.M., "Life in Tulelake," composition by an eleventh grader at Amache, McGovern Papers, JARP, box 114, folder 7. Final Report, Education Section, Manzanar, 1946, NARG210. "Education—Commencement Addresses and Reports by Students" (Poston), Project Reports, Headquarters File, NARG210, box 18.

3. Poston quotation from Edith M. Waterman, "Rich Experiences," June 29, 1944, p. 3, Poston Documentary Files, NARG210, box 18; "the hearse" recollection is from the same source. See also the narrative reports by teachers in "Education—Commencement Addresses and Reports by Students" (Poston); "Summary of Frustrations Evident during Development of the Manzanar Schools," May 14, 1943, Manzanar Center Records, University Research Library, University of California, Los Angeles; discussion of teacher characteristics in Robert Billigmeier, "School Report," Tule Lake, Spring 1943, pp. 37–41, BAN 67/14 R20.12; and "Interviews with School Teachers," September 1, 1943, Community Analysis Section, Heart Mountain Relocation Center, NARG210, 61.314, box 14, file 3, from which the final remark is taken. Further views of teachers and administrators can be found in personal narratives provided for camp documentarians and, in the case of Topaz, personal "experience reports" appended to the final education report for the center.

4. Bob Sakai, "Experiences, Observations and Attitudes of a Postonian Teacher," c. 1942, BAN 67/14 J7.10. Community Analysis Monthly Report, May 15–June 30, 1943, Heart Mountain, NARG210, 61.314, box 14, file 1; and "Interviews with School Teachers," Heart Mountain.

5. Letter from N. K. to E. S. L., December 8, 1942, Thomas R. Bodine Papers, HOOV. An example of public and political pressure against schools for the camps can be found in "Amache School Controversy," February 9, 1943, Reports Division, Granada Documentary Files, NARG210.

6. Yoshiko Uchida, *Desert Exile: The Uprooting of a Japanese American Family* (Seattle: University of Washington Press, 1982), p. 117. Tule Lake principal quoted in Tule Lake Community Council Minutes, Setpember 2, 1942, p. 4, BAN 67/14 R1.60 ("every day" is spelled "everyday" in the typescript of the minutes). Edith Waterman, "Rich Experiences," p. 4. Student composition by S. T., a high school student at Heart Mountain, October 1942, McGovern Papers, JARP, box 114, folder 5.

7. H. H., "School Life in Poston," student essay, bound together with other essays in "A History of Poston," Ninth Grade Core Class, May 1943, Colorado

River Center Collection, Huntington Library, San Marino, California. Topaz heat and dust decribed by Ida Shimanouchi in a letter to Aurelia Reinhardt, September 28, 1942, Aurelia Reinhardt Papers, MCA, file I 23. Comment on Manzanar from Genevieve W. Carter, "Life in a Relocation Center for Japanese Americans: Democracy behind Barbed Wire," *The Nation's Schools* 31 (June 1943): 18–20.

8. Marshall Field, "Children and Manpower," *Survey Midmonthly* 78 (1942): 324; NEA figures reported therein; national attrition rate reported in NEA Research Division, "To Hastening Ills a Prey," *Journal of the National Education Association* 32 (1943): 94.

9. The best source on recruiting practices is the final education report produced by each camp at the end of the war; on types of teachers, see sources listed in the following note and in note 3.

10. "Teacher Directory, Minidoka Project Schools, Hunt, Idaho," BAN 67/14 P2.76; and faculty descriptions in *Memoirs 1945,* Hunt High School Yearbook, Minidoka, Yearbook Collection, NARG210.

11. "Teacher Directory, Minidoka," and *Memoirs 1945.*

12. "Organized Education in Poston, 1943–1945," Final Report, Education Section, Colorado River Relocation Center, Poston, 1945, p.11, Poston Documentary Files, NARG210, box 26. During the 1930s Carey had been principal of McKinley High School in Honolulu and had known many Japanese American students. His school had acquired a wide reputation in the United States for its progressive curriculum; see Edward A. Krug, *The Shaping of the American High School, Volume 2: 1920–1941* (Madison: University of Wisconsin Press, 1972), pp. 266–267.

13. On local origins of the teaching force, see, for example, the profile of the faculty in *Victoria,* Denson High School Yearbook, Jerome, 1944, Yearbook Collection, NARG210. "A Comparison of Teacher Salaries in WRA Schools and in Cities of Comparable Size in States Where WRA Schools Are Located," Education Section, Community Management Division, WRA, BAN 67/14 E2.63.

14. The Topaz remark was from James F. Hughes, Deputy Director of the Relocation Center, and appears in Russell A. Bankston, "Annual Cabinet Meeting at Topaz," Historical Section, Topaz, Project Report H433, BAN 67/14 H2.07. On the relation of the national teacher shortage to the erosion of local teacher salaries and contemporary efforts to secure federal aid to address the problem, see Gilbert E. Smith, *The Limits of Reform: Politics and Federal Aid to Education, 1937–1950* (New York: Garland Publishing, 1982), pp. 86–89.

15. For the teacher hiring policy, see *WRA Handbook,* 30.3.7, NARG210.

16. First and last quotations from "The First Semester at Amache Elementary and Secondary Schools," February 4, 1943, by Melvin P. McGovern, high school teacher and reports officer, McGovern Papers, JARP, box 113, folder 9. Grace Lewis and Robert Dierban, "School for Japanese Evacuees," *Clearinghouse* 17 (1943): 280. Education reports and personal narratives of educators; see also the letter to new teachers in Amache from the school superintendent, Washington Office Records—Documentary (Granada), in "Teachers' Handbook No. 33," NARG210, box 40.

17. For narratives by teachers who remained, see especially the teacher "experience reports" in Final Report, Education Section, Topaz, pp. 60–98, BAN 67/14 H2.50. On the social backgrounds of teachers in other camps, see Evac-

uation and Resettlement Study, University of California, Berkeley, "Education—1942–43: Biographies of Unit One Teachers," Poston, BAN 67/14 J6.15B; and professional descriptions in the Minidoka Teacher Directory for 1942–43, BAN 67/14 P2.76. Martha Hays's remarks are from her personal narrative in the Poston Documentary Files, NARG210, box 18.

18. Edith Waterman, "Rich Experiences," p. 3. See picture of Thomas Light in *Campus Echoes 1945,* Parker Valley High School Yearbook, Poston, Yearbook Collection, NARG210; his father, Jerome T. Light, had moved from Minidoka to Poston that year as high school principal after disagreements with the administration at Minidoka over his progressive philosophy of education and his liberal attitudes toward the evacuated population. On making adobe for schools, Katharine M. Sheckler, seventh grade teacher, "Young Americans of Japanese Ancestry Practice Democratic Principles in Their Schools at Poston, Arizona," p. 1, unpublished article, fall 1943, Poston Documentary Files, NARG210, box 18.

19. Forrest E. LaViolette, "The Problem of Community Disorganization," May 16, 1943, Community Analysis Section, Amache, NARG210, 61.314, box 14, file 2.

20. On comparison with church workers, ibid. Letter from a teacher at Tule Lake, Sept. 5, 1942, typescript in Margaret Cosgrave Sowers Papers, HOOV, box 2.

21. The teacher comments are from minutes of a meeting of senior core teachers, Poston, c. 1943, BAN 67/14 J7.10. For an example of the progressive programming initiated at Minidoka, see Jerome T. Light, "The Development of a Junior-Senior High School Program in a Relocation Center for People of Japanese Ancestry during the War with Japan" (Ph.D. diss., Stanford University, 1947); also see the personal narrative of Light in the Minidoka Documentary Files, NARG210.

22. "Welcoming of New Teachers," Poston, September 27, 1942, BAN 67/14 J6.25C.

23. On salary for evacuee employees, see *WRA Handbook,* 50.5.6. Figure for Tule Lake from Arthur G. Ramey, "Using Japanese Teachers in Relocation Centers," *California Journal of Secondary Education* 18 (1943): 301. Jerome figure from Final Report, Education Section, Jerome Documentary Files, NARG210, box 63. Topaz figure for residents with college degrees from Final Report, Education Section, Topaz, p. 5. For an example of teacher training activities, see "Report of the Teacher Training Department," December 17, 1942, Minidoka Documentary Files, NARG210, box 74. The issue of limited teaching certificates in Wyoming is recorded in Community Analysis Monthly Report, Heart Mountain, May 15–June 30, 1943, NARG210, 61.314, box 14, file 1; see also Douglas W. Nelson, *Heart Mountain: The History of an American Concentration Camp* (Madison: State Historical Society of Wisconsin, 1976), p. 50.

24. For an example of the detailed profiles available to understand the background of Japanese American teachers in the camps, see the appendix of the final education report from Jerome, cited in the previous note. For an analysis of educational levels as well as sex and age distribution, see Billigmeier, "School Report," pp. 43, 48; see also Melvin P. McGovern, "Evacuee School Teachers," March 24, 1943, Amache, McGovern Papers, JARP, box 113, folder 10.

25. Kate M. Watanabe, "Teachers and Teaching in Wartime: From a Relocation Center," *Progressive Education* 20 (1943): 233. Final Report, Education

Section, Amache, BAN 67/14 L3.00. "Evacuee School Teachers," May 24, 1943, Reports Division, Granada Documentary Files, Amache, NARG210, box 39. Robert Hosokawa, "An Evacuee's Opinion of the Minidoka High School," December 1942, Minidoka Documentary Files, NARG210, box 74. Robert Spencer and Charles Kikuchi, "Evacuee and Administrative Interrelationships in the Gila Relocation Center," March–April 1943, p. 21, BAN 67/14 K8.42. On student attitudes, "The Poston III High School Associated Student Body History, 1942–1943," BAN 67/14 J6.25C. For one of many examples of gratitude toward evacuee teachers from a Caucasian teacher, see Mildred Standing, "Two Years of Teaching in Poston," 1944, p. 3, Poston Documentary Files, NARG210, box 18.

26. N. O., "L.A.—Amache," student essay by an eleventh grader at Amache, McGovern Papers, JARP, box 114, folder 8. Genevieve Carter, "Life in a Relocation Center," p. 19. George Sugihara, "Education in Topaz," Project Report H419, Historical Section, Topaz, BAN 67/14 H2.12.

27. Nisei student quoted in Otis D. Richardson, "Nisei Evacuees—Their Challenge to Education," *Junior College Journal* 13 (1942): 10. Comment from tenth grader in P. M., "The War: How It Affects Me?" student composition, Minidoka Documentary Files, NARG210, box 73.

28. For teachers' views of the childhood experience of the camps, see Wanda Robertson, "Developing World Citizens in a Japanese Relocation Center," *Childhood Education* 20 (1943): 66–71; and Eunice Glenn, "Education behind Barbed Wire," *Survey Midmonthly* 80 (1944): 347–349.

29. "My Story," by a Nisei, December 14, 1943, NARG210, 61.318, box 22, file 4. Hajime Tanaka, "Methods and Techniques Utilized in Promoting Pupil's Opportunity for Self-Expression and Free Discussion on the American Scene," Poston Documentary Files, NARG210, box 18.

30. Caucasian teacher's response is recorded in "Interview with School Teachers," September 1, 1943, Heart Mountain Community Analysis Section, NARG210, 61.314, box 14, file 3. "Junior High School General Education," Grade 8, Amache, December 1–15, 1942, Granada Documentary Files, NARG210, box 39. Student letter to the National Japanese American Student Relocation Council, July 18, 1943, Thomas R. Bodine Papers, HOOV.

31. On the history of the "Problems of Democracy" course in American education, see H. Wells Singleton, "Factors Affecting the Development of the Problems of Democracy Course" (Ph.D. diss., Stanford University, 1975); on the development of progressivism generally in education, see Lawrence A. Cremin, *The Transformation of the School: Progressivism in American Education, 1876–1957* (New York: Vintage Books, 1964).

32. Billigmeier, "School Report," pp. 63, 24. An excellent example of these handmade books, inspired by a progressive curriculum and a caring teacher who emphasized learning-by-doing within the community, is "A History of Poston," which contains student essays bound with artwork and hand-drawn maps of that camp by the students in a ninth-grade core class, May 1943, Colorado River Relocation Center Collection, box 3, Huntington Library, San Marino, California. See also the student essays on camp life at Amache (Granada) and Tule Lake in the McGovern Papers, JARP, box 114.

33. "Education—Commencement Addresses and Reports by Students," Poston, Project Reports, Headquarters Files, NARG210, box 18. "Assembly of Stu-

dents and Teachers, Poston," February 4, 1943, BAN 67/14 J7.10; and for student protest at Amache, see BAN 67/14 L4.60.

34. Minutes of Faculty Meeting, Topaz High School, December 30, 1942, BAN 67/14 H2.70. Memo to L. G. Noble, superintendent of schools, from Ernest Takahashi, executive secretary, Juvenile Board, in George Sugihara, "An Analysis of Delinquent Problems," Historical Section, Topaz, BAN 67/14 H2.02. The remark on Japanese children is from Momo Arita, "The Family and the Children," February 1945, NARG210, 61.300, box 3, file 16. Memo from Henry Tani to G. L. Woolf, principal, April 20, 1943, Topaz, BAN 67/14 H2.70. See description of the "Peacock Gang" in Bob Sakai, "Experiences, Observations, and Attitudes of a Postonian Teacher," n.d., BAN 67/14 J7.10.

35. Retha Breeze, "Youth Organizations," Education Section, Poston, n.d., Washington Office Records—Documentary, NARG210, box 27. Student letter to National Japanese American Student Relocation Council, November 28, 1942, Thomas R. Bodine Papers, HOOV.

36. "Topaz, Utah, Impressions and Observations," December 5, 1942, NARG210, 61.300, box 1, no. 1.

37. Solon T. Kimball, "The History of Community Government," August 1945, BAN 67/14 E2.512.

38. Letter received by F. O., block manager, Manzanar, from Blood Brothers Corps, November 6, 1942, BAN 67/14 03.00. "Preliminary Findings—Surveys on 'Underground' Groups," Project Report no. 74, Manzanar, December 1, 1942; see BAN 67/14 03.00–03.02 on relation of disturbances to failure of self-government. See also Arthur A. Hansen and David A. Hacker, "The Manzanar 'Riot': An Ethnic Perspective," in Hansen and Betty E. Mitson, eds., *Voices Long Silent: An Oral Inquiry into the Japanese American Evacuation* (Fullerton, Calif.: Oral History Program, California State University, Fullerton, 1974), pp. 41–79.

39. Dick Kanaga, "Self-Government at Minidoka Relocation Center," April 1944, Minidoka Community Analysis Section, NARG210, box 20, file 15.

40. "Interviews with School Teachers," Heart Mountain; John Embree, "Notes on Heart Mountain," August 4, 1943, Community Analysis Section, NARG210, 61.300, box 1, file 5; Asael T. Hansen, "Profiles of the Centers—Heart Mountain," September 1944, Community Analysis Section, NARG210, 61.314, box 16, file 9.

41. "Interviews with School Teachers," and Hansen, "Profiles of the Centers—Heart Mountain." See also Douglas Nelson, *Heart Mountain,* for a history of the camp.

42. Plan for "Learning the Ways of Democracy" attached to memo from John H. Provinse to All Project Directors, Superintendents of Education, Chiefs of Community Management, and Directors of Adult Education, August 9, 1943, BAN 67/14 E2.63.

43. Final Report, Education Section, Manzanar, p. 78, NARG210. Transcript of "Special Meeting with Representatives of Community to Discuss and Formulate Policy concerning Leave for Youth under 18 years," April 21, 1943, Minidoka Community Analysis Section, NARG210, 61.317, box 19, file 3.

44. "PTA Massmeeting at Topaz," Project Report H444, Reports Division, Documentary Files, NARG210, box 7. Minutes of Amache Advisory School Board,

November 24, 1942, in Final Report, Education Section, 1945, BAN 67/14 L3.00.

45. Memo from L. K. Ade to J. H. Provinse, "Post-High School Education for Evacuee Students," WRA Washington Office, January 18, 1943, BAN 67/14 E2.673. Letter from J. A. Rademaker to E. H. Spicer, January 31, 1944, Community Analysis Section, NARG210, box 13, file 3. "Conference on Adult Education, Recreation and Leisure Time Activities in War Relocation Centers," October 26–28, 1942, BAN 67/14 E2.61. Allen C. Blaisdell, "Report on Vocational Training and Education above the Secondary School Level," November 1942, Washington Office Records, NARG210, box 126; Blaisdell was president of the International House in Berkeley. Potato incident reported in "Selected Curriculum Procedures and Trends at the Tule Lake Project High School," Education Section, Tule Lake, 1942–43, BAN 67/14 R3.15.

46. Yoshiko Uchida, *Desert Exile: The Uprooting of a Japanese American Family* (Seattle: University of Washington Press, 1982), p. 130.

47. "Survey of Post-Graduate Plans of Seniors," May 5, 1943, Jerome Community Analysis Section, Field Report no. 3, NARG210, 61.315, box 17, file 1. Russell A. Bankston, "Status of Topaz High School Graduates," Topaz Historical Section, Project Report H420, November 1, 1943, BAN 67/14 H2.06. Memo from F. E. LaViolette to M. O. Anderson, June 9, 1943, Community Analysis Section, NARG210, 61.314, box 14, file 1. S. S., "How the War Affected Me," student essay by a tenth grader, Minidoka Documentary Files, NARG210, box 73.

48. George Sugihara, "War, Evacuation, Resettlement, and the Graduating Seniors," Topaz Historical Section, Project Report H441, BAN 67/14 H2.04.

49. "Comments Made by Parents to 'Growth Reports' on the Children by Schoolteachers," April 1943, Minidoka Documentary Files, NARG210, box 73.

50. Junior High School Commencement Address of Y. T., June 25, 1943, in Russell A. Bankston, "First High School Commencement Exercises Held at Topaz," Topaz Reports Division, Project Report H251 (Exhibit H), Documentary Files, NARG210, box 5. Quotation from address of M. O. Note from E. P. Moore to John Embree, attached to the report.

51. High School Commencement Address of M.A., in Bankston, "First High School Commencement."

52. High School Commencement Address of R. N., in ibid.

53. Junior High School Commencement Address of A. F., in ibid.

54. Community Analysis Trend Report no. 49, June 1945, NARG210, 61.310A, box 7, file 5. Commencement speech at Manzanar, June 1943, San Francisco Assistant Director Files, NARG210, box 1, file 005.8.

55. High School Commencement Address of M. K., June 1943, Amache Reports Division E 100–129, NARG210, box 39.

56. John Larison, " 'Jap Crow' Experiment," *Nation* 156 (1943): 517. Norman M. Thomas, *Democracy and Japanese Americans* (New York: Post War World Council, 1942), p. 25.

57. F. S. Cushman, March 30, 1943, WRA Field Office Files, Colorado River (Poston) Schools, NARG210, box 11. The librarian anecdote is recounted by John Embree in "Conditions at Manzanar," September 11–13, 1942, Community Analysis Report, NARG210, 61.300, box 1, no. 1.

3. Loyalty and Its Lessons

1. West Virginia State Board of Education v. Barnette, 319 U.S. 624 (1943). On the history of loyalty controversies in the United States, see Merle Curti, *The Roots of American Loyalty* (New York: Columbia University Press, 1946); and Harold M. Hyman, *To Try Men's Souls: Loyalty Tests in American History* (Berkeley: University of California Press, 1959).

2. Copy of Roosevelt letter in "Army and Leave Clearance Registration at War Relocation Centers," June 1943, p. 32, Community Analysis Section, NARG210, 61.300, box 1; also in BAN 67/14 D2.045.

3. "Army and Leave Clearance Registration at War Relocation Centers," pp. 1, 8. See also Robert K. Thurber, "History of Leave Clearance Operations," WRA Clearance Review Section, April 1945, BAN 67/14 E2.902 and related descriptive reports by WRA administrators. For a concise history of leave clearance procedures, see Jacobus tenBroek, Edward N. Barnhart, and Floyd W. Matson, *Prejudice, War and the Constitution: Causes and Consequences of the Evacuation of the Japanese Americans in World War II* (Berkeley: University of California Press, 1970), pp. 142-154.

4. For narrative histories of the loyalty controversy in the camps, see Dorothy Swaine Thomas and Richard S. Nishimoto, *The Spoilage* (Berkeley: University of California Press, 1946), pp. 53-112; Edward H. Spicer, Asael T. Hansen, Katharine Luomala, and Marvin K. Opler, *Impounded People: Japanese-Americans in Relocation Centers* (Tucson: University of Arizona Press, 1969; originally published under the same title as an official WRA report in 1946), pp. 142-161; Roger Daniels, *Concentration Camps USA* (New York: Holt, Rinehart and Winston, 1972), pp. 104-129; and Michi Weglyn, *Years of Infamy* (New York: William Morrow, 1976), pp. 134-135. For an insightful interpretation of the reasonableness of disloyal responses, see Morton Grodzins *The Loyal and the Disloyal* (Chicago: University of Chicago Press, 1956), pp. 105-131. It is important to note that the original two loyalty questions led to some complications and thus to some refinements. For the women the first of the questions was changed to, "If the opportunity presents itself and you are found qualified, would you be willing to volunteer for the Army Nurse Corps or the W.A.C.?" Through a bureaucratic oversight this question was also given to the older generation, both male and female, who had been defined by law as enemy aliens. At first the older generation was also asked to swear allegiance to the United States, just as their children were. Since these people were legally aliens ineligible for citizenship in the United States, the corollary issue of forswearing all allegiance to Japan was extremely threatening because it could deny them the protection of any government, in effect making them stateless prisoners. During the administration of the loyalty review, the allegiance question was changed to be more fair to the Issei, asking them only to promise "to abide by the laws of the United States and to take no action which would in any way interfere with the war effort of the United States."

5. Robert Billigmeier, "School Report," Tule Lake, Spring 1943, BAN 67/14 R20.12, pp. 19-24, 86. For an analysis of staff attitudes, see Billigmeier, "The Caucasian Staff at Tule Lake," February 3, 1944, BAN 67/14 R20.01. Morris E. Opler, the community analyst at Manzanar Relocation Center, wrote insightfully about Nisei who answered "no" to the loyalty questions in his "Studies of

Segregants at Manzanar," BAN 67/14 03.06; see especially pp. 45, 54, and 121 on past education in public schools and the desire of many Nisei to realize the ideals of democracy that were learned there. On attrition of evacuee teachers, see Monthly Statistical Reports, Education Section, Tule Lake, BAN 67/14 R3.13; Billigmeier, "School Report," p. 45. The data on attrition of Caucasian teachers is taken from Monthly Statistical Reports, February through September, 1943.

6. Spicer et al., *Impounded People,* p. 157, for percentage responding in the negative to loyalty questions; for discussion, see works cited in notes 4 and 5 above; of particular interest is tenBroek, Barnhart, and Matson, for their interpretation of the loyalty procedure in relation to constitutional issues of war powers and individual rights. On the induction of Nisei into the armed forces during World War II, see *Special Groups,* Special Monograph no. 10, vol. 1, Selective Service System (Washington, D.C.: Government Printing Office, 1953), pp. 113–142.

7. Letter from Lucy [Adams] to John [presumably Embree or Provinse, heads of community analysis and community management], February 23, 1943, Manzanar Community Analysis Section, 61.318, NARG210, box 22.

8. U.S. Congress, House of Representatives, Select Committee Investigating National Defense Migration, *Hearings,* 77th Congress, 2nd Session, pt. 29 (Washington, D.C.: U.S. Government Printing Office, 1942), p. 11015. Hirabayashi v. United States 320 U.S. 81 (1943); see also Korematsu v. United States 319 U.S. 432 (1943); on the legal history on the cases affecting Japanese Americans, including the government's suppression of crucial evidence demonstrating that the suspicions of disloyalty before the evacuation were unfounded, see Peter Irons, *Justice at War: The Story of the Japanese American Internment Cases* (New York: Oxford University Press, 1983).

9. Nannie Lee Bauman, "Philosophy of the Elementary Schools," in "Minidoka Project Schools," September 10, 1943, Washington Office Records Documentary, NARG210, box 73. "Educational Program," January 4, 1943, Manzanar Community Management Division, Washington Office Reports, NARG210, box 129. "Interviews with School Teachers," September 1, 1943, p. 19, Heart Mountain Community Analysis Section, NARG210, 61.314, box 14, file 3. On remedial classes for Kibei, see Billigmeier, "School Report," p. 59.

10. *Community School Forum* 1 (July 1943): 9, WRA Community Management Division, Education Section; copy in Washington Office Records, NARG210, box 129. "Do Our Issei Parents Have the Right to Arrange or Approve Our Marriage," survey report, n.d., "A Barracks Becomes a Home" by Beatrice H. White, home economics supervisor at Manzanar, May 1, 1945, and "American Table Manners," a guide for teachers and students; these documents are in the Manzanar Center Records, box 13, University Research Library, University of California, Los Angeles.

11. Frances S. Cushman, director of guidance, "Guidance and Evaluation in the Poston Schools, 1942–43," Poston Documentary Files, NARG210, box 18.

12. A. Glenwood Walker, assistant principal, "Cumulative Record, Tri-State High School," Tule Lake, March 13, 1943, BAN 67/14 R3.25.

13. Erving Goffman, *Asylums: Essays on the Social Situation of Mental Patients and Other Inmates* (New York: Doubleday, 1961), p. 14. Robert A. Mossman, "Japanese American War Relocation Centers as Total Institutions with Emphasis on the Educational Program" (Ed.D. diss., Rutgers University, 1978).

14. John F. Embree, "Community Analysis—An Example of Anthropology in Government," *American Anthropologist* 46 (1944): 279-280.

15. Ibid., p. 281 n. 4.

16. "Dealing with Japanese Americans," WRA Community Analysis Report, Community Analysis Section, NARG210; also published in *Applied Anthropology* 2 (January–March 1943): 37–41. See also Asael T. Hansen, "Community Analysis at Heart Mountain Relocation Center," *Applied Anthropology* 5 (Summer 1946): 15–25; and Spicer et al., *Impounded People*. The best known work to come out of community analysis in the camps is Alexander H. Leighton, *The Governing of Men: General Principles and Recommendations Based on Experience at a Japanese Relocation Camp* (Princeton: Princeton University Press, 1945). John Embree's classic anthropological study published before the war is *Suye Mura: A Japanese Village* (Chicago: University of Chicago Press, 1939).

17. Richard S. Nishimoto, "Firebreak Gang," BAN 67/14 J6.07. The right of the Issei to serve on community councils was granted on April 19, 1943, with a change in WRA Administrative Instruction 34.

18. Edward H. Spicer, "The Use of Social Scientists by the War Relocation Authority," *Applied Anthropology* 5 (Spring 1946): 20. On the battles of the WRA with Congress, see Albert B. Turner, "The Origins and Development of the War Relocation Authority" (Ph.D. diss., Duke University, 1967). A view from inside the camps can be found in Robert F. Spencer, "Notes on the Chandler Committee Hearing at Gila," BAN 67/14 K8.46.

19. Frederick G. Murray, "Japs in Our Yard," *American Legion Magazine* 34 (June 1943): 12–13, 42, 46. For a listing of the half-dozen Japanese Americans killed by guards during the incarceration and the circumstances of their deaths, see Weglyn, *Years of Infamy,* p. 312.

20. On congressional opposition to the WRA, see especially Turner, "The Origins and Development." On larger patterns of opposition to social programs see Roland A. Young, *Congressional Politics in the Second World War* (New York: Columbia University Press, 1946); and Richard N. Chapman, *Contours of Public Policy, 1939–1945* (New York: Garland Publishing, 1981).

21. For a perceptive treatment of these underlying policy assumptions by social scientists, see Robert Redfield, "The Japanese Americans," in William F. Ogburn, ed., *American Society in Wartime* (Chicago: University of Chicago Press, 1943), pp. 143-164; and Morris E. Opler, "Social Science and Democratic Policy," *Applied Anthropology* 4 (Summer 1945): 11–14.

22. U.S. House of Representatives, *Report and Minority Views of the Special Committee on Un-American Activities,* House Report no. 717 (Washington, D.C.: Government Printing Office, 1943); and *Investigation of Un-American Propaganda Activities in the United States,* 78th Congress, 1st Session (Washington, D.C.: Government Printing Office, 1943). See also Turner, "The Origins and Development." On the early years of the House Un-American Activities Committee, see August R. Ogden, *The Dies Committee: A Study of the Special Committee for the Investigation of Un-American Activities, 1938–1943* (Washington, D.C.: Catholic University Press of America, 1943); and William Gellerman, *Martin Dies* (New York: John Day, 1944).

23. Memo from Edward H. Spicer to John H. Provinse, November 11, 1943, NARG210, 61.300, box 1, file 7. "Library Service at Relocation Centers," WRA Policy Memo, June 8, 1943, BAN 67/14 E2.60. On what young people actually

read in the camps, see "Newspaper and Periodical Circulation in Five Relocation Centers," April 17, 1943, Washington Community Analysis Section, NARG210, 61.300, box 1.

24. See Spicer, "The Use of Social Scientists," p. 26. "Excerpt from a letter by Morris Opler," Manzanar Community Analysis Section, NARG210, 61.318, box 22, file 1.

25. "Interviews with School Teachers," September 1, 1943, p. 19, Heart Mountain Community Analysis Section, NARG210, 61.314, box 14, file 3, pp. 7B, 8B.

26. G. S. (a teacher at Amache) in her "Final Monthly Report, English and Social Studies, Rm. 27," June 27, 1945, BAN 67/14 L3.53. Billigmeier, "The Caucasian Staff at Tule Lake," p. 3. Gertrude de Silva, "A School Teacher Observes the Nisei," *California Journal of Secondary Education* 18 (1943): 489.

27. John W. Powell, "The Community and the Management," Poston, April 1944, p. 25, BAN 67/14 J2.111.

28. "Report on School Children," memo from Genevieve W. Carter to Ralph Merritt, August 6, 1943, box 13, Manzanar Center Records, University Research Library, University of California, Los Angeles. Hiro Katayama, "Our Younger Generation," *All Aboard* (Spring 1944): 44, Topaz Documentary Files, NARG210, box 4.

29. On the settling down of the Issei, see especially John W. Powell, "The Community and the Management."

30. John Provinse in "Digest: Washington Conference, WRA Superintendents of Education," March 20–25, 1944, p. 1, BAN 67/14 E2.63.

31. On extra work for evacuee assistants, see Community Analysis Newsletter no. 4, April 22, 1944, NARG210, 61.310A, box 7, file 1. Naomi Wood (a teacher at Poston), "Education," April 24, 1944, NARG210, 61.311, box 8, file 8. On teachers as a forgotten people, see comments in Edward Spicer's notes on a conference of community analysts, September 7–13, 1944, NARG210, 61.300, box 3, file 14.

32. Rachel Sady, "Problems Connected with the Use of the Japanese Language," January 1, 1945, NARG210, 61.300, box 3, file 16, p. 9. Community Analysis Newsletter no. 6, May 20, 1944, NARG210, 61.310A, box 7, file 1.

33. On increase in language study, see Sady, "Problems Connected with the Use of the Japanese Language." On the daily language of evacuees, see, for example, "Vernacular of Evacuees," Minidoka Community Analysis Section, Field Report no. 302, May 2, 1944, NARG210, 61.317, box 21, file 16. See also Peter T. Suzuki, "The Ethnolinguistics of Japanese Americans in the Wartime Camps," *Anthropological Linguistics* 18 (1976): 416–427. The comment from the Japanese language school teacher is from Sady, "Japanese Language," p. 7.

34. Interview of Yoshisada Kawai, in *Issei Christians: Selected Interviews from the Issei Oral History Project* (Sacramento: Issei Oral History Project, 1977), p. 17. Marvin K. Opler and Frank Obayashi, "Senryu Poetry as Folk and Community Expression," *Journal of American Folklore* 58 (1945): 9. (I have changed the initial capital letter of the second and third lines to lower case.) Wakako Yamauchi, "The Poetry of the Issei on the American Relocation Experience," in Ishmael Reed, ed., *Calafia: The California Poetry* (Berkeley: Y'Bird Books, 1979): both the translated poem and Yamauchi's reflections on it appear on p. lxxvi. Constance Hayashi and Keiho Yamanaka, trans., "Footprints: Poetry of the

American Relocation Camp Experience," *Amerasia Journal* 3, no. 2 (1976): 116. (I have added the final period.) See also Peter T. Suzuki, "Wartime *Tanka:* Issei and Kibei Contributions to a Literature East and West," *Literature East and West* 21 (1977): 242–254.

35. These images drawn from traditional arts in the camps reflect the photographed material and descriptive captions in Allen H. Eaton, *Beauty behind Barbed Wire: The Arts of the Japanese in Our War Relocation Camps* (New York: Harper & Brothers, 1952).

36. Ruth Tanaka, "Saga of a People," Poston, 1944–45, used with permission of the author. For a sampling of published student writings from Manzanar, see "Manzanar, By Japanese-American Students in Manzanar High School," *Scholastic* 44 (May 1, 1944): 23.

37. "The Japanese Language Schools and Present Attitudes toward the Teaching of Japanese to Nisei and Sansei," Evacuee Report, Manzanar Community Analysis Section, April 14, 1944, BAN 67/14 03.05. On family control of children, see Anne O. Freed, "Juvenile Delinquency," November 10, 1944, NARG210, 61.300, box 3, file 15. See also Final Report, Education Section, Amache, BAN 67/14 L3.00. The account of the Japanese language school teacher is from Kazuo Ito, *Issei: A History of Japanese Immigrants in North America,* trans. Shinichiro Nakamura and Jean S. Girard (Seattle: Executive Committee for Publication of Issei, Japanese Community Service, 1973), pp. 595–596.

38. "From High School Teachers," Manzanar Community Analysis Section, NARG210, 61.318, box 23, file 9. On renunciation of citizenship and its aftermath, see tenBroek, Barnhart, and Matson, *Prejudice, War and the Constitution,* pp. 175–183.

39. Keynote Address by John Embree, "Topaz Community Youth Conference" Report H446, Topaz Reports Division, Documentary Files, NARG210, box 7.

4. Educating "Projectiles of Democracy"

1. John W. Powell, "Education through Relocation," *Adult Education Journal* 1 (1942): 155. Robert W. O'Brien, "Selective Dispersion as a Factor in the Solution of the Nisei Problem," *Social Forces* 23 (1944): 140–147. A figure of seventeen years for median age of the Nisei in 1942 was computed by the Evacuation and Resettlement Study at the University of California; see Dorothy Swaine Thomas, *The Salvage* (Berkeley: University of California Press, 1952), p. 19.

2. Community Analysis Report of June 1943 cited in Anne O. Freed and Edward H. Spicer, "The Issei and Relocation," May 29, 1944, NARG210, 61.300, box 2, file 11. Speech by Dillon Myer at Poston, March 6, 1945, p. 5, Poston Documentary Files, NARG210, box 20.

3. Margaret Cosgrave, "Relocation of Japanese American Students," *American Association of Collegiate Registrars Journal* 18 (1943): 221–226. John H. Provinse, "Relocation of Japanese-American College Students," *Higher Education* 1 (April 16, 1945): 1–4. Robert W. O'Brien, *The College Nisei* (Palo Alto, Calif.: Pacific Books, 1949), p. 34. WRA, *The Evacuated People: A Quantitative Description* (Washington, D.C.: U.S. Department of the Interior, 1946), pp. 95, 100, 81. For an overview of the work program and compensation, originally published by WRA, see Edward H. Spicer, Asael T. Hansen, Katharine Luomala,

and Marvin K. Opler, *Impounded People: Japanese Americans in the Relocation Centers* (Tucson: University of Arizona Press, 1969), pp. 88–96

4. George Sakata, University of Toledo, as quoted in "Nisei Students Speak for Themselves," *Junior College Journal* 14 (1943–44): 246. Robbins Barstow, "Help for 'Nisei' Students," *Christian Century* 59 (1942): 836.

5. Bulletin no. 2, Student Relocation Committee, May 16, 1942, quoting a written statement by Monroe E. Deutsch, vice president and provost, University of California, Berkeley; in Presidents' File, BAN, CU5 box 588. Also relevant is the testimony provided by Deutsch and other university officials and faculty for the Tolan Committee, *Hearings,* Select Committee Investigating National Defense Migration, 77th Congress, 2nd Session (Washington, D.C.: U.S. Government Printing Office, 1942).

6. Student letter, January 28, 1942, Thomas R. Bodine Papers, HOOV. The organizational files of the National Japanese American Student Relocation Council (NJASRC) at Hoover were augmented in 1982–83 with files of John W. Nason, an NJASRC official and president of Swarthmore College, and the papers of Thomas R. Bodine, a Quaker who served as field director of the council. The Bodine Papers include transcripts of hundreds of letters sent by Nisei students to NJASRC staff. A comparison of these transcripts with the original letters in the NJASRC organizational files, which are also at Hoover, shows the transcripts to be accurate, including grammatical errors. Since only a small percentage of the individual student files of NJASRC were saved in the Hoover collection of the organizational files, the Bodine papers are an invaluable source of Nisei views during the relocation from camp to college.

Throughout this chapter the Bodine papers will be cited as Bodine-HOOV; the NJASRC organizational files in the Hoover archives will be cited as NJASRC-HOOV; and for other NJASRC materials at Hoover but not in the archives I will simply give the Hoover Library as their source. Archival restrictions do not allow use of individual names for the letters written by students, so the letters are identified by their dates for the Bodine-HOOV papers and by student identification number for NJASRC-HOOV Archives.

7. Letter from John J. McCloy to Clarence E. Pickett, May 21, 1942, John W. Nason Collection, HOOV, box 1. Executive Committee Minutes and Staff Reports, NJASRC-HOOV. O'Brien, *College Nisei,* pp. 60–73.

8. Cosgrave, "Relocation of Japanese American Students," *Education for Victory* 1 (September 15, 1942): 2, 24. On funds raised for scholarships at Topaz, see *Newsletter* 6 (August 5, 1943): 2, in NJASRC-HOOV. The newsletter was prepared by NJASRC staff for student counselors in the camps. Letter from Thomas R. Bodine to Joseph S. Daltry, May 24, 1942, Bodine-HOOV.

9. Student application forms, staff reports and memoranda, NJASRC-HOOV and Bodine-HOOV. Cosgrave, "Relocation of Japanese American Students," p. 2. Provinse, "Relocation," pp. 3–4. Also see official list of conditions for leave clearance in letter from John J. McCloy, assistant secretary of war, to Dillon S. Myer, director, WRA, August 5, 1942, BAN 67/14 C1.08.

10. Notes and correspondence of the field director of NJASRC, Bodine-HOOV. Restrictions on movement and communication of NJASRC field staff were gradually relaxed later in the war at most of the camps.

11. Student letter from Smith College, 1942 (undated), Bodine-HOOV. Japanese Evacuation Report no. 5, March 10, 1942, Bodine-HOOV.

12. The notion that Nisei leaders were cultural ambassadors bridging the

gap between East and West had a history going back more than two decades before World War II. For a discussion of this background and the alternate visions of Nisei leadership before the war, see Jere Takahashi, "Japanese American Responses to Race Relations: The Formation of Nisei Perspectives," *Amerasia Journal* 9 (Spring/Summer 1982): 31–32 and passim. "New Pioneers for America," a play presented at commencement services, Amache High School, May 19, 1944, p. 18, Bodine-HOOV. Student letter, January 3, 1943, Bodine-HOOV. *Trek* 1 (February 1943): 34, where the final quotation appeared in an article from a student at Wellesley College, was a literary magazine produced by evacuees at Topaz, Utah. (The word "Nisei" was not capitalized in the article.)

13. Student letter, June 22, 1943, Bodine-HOOV. According to Section 60.4.21.A–C of the *WRA Handbook,* NARG210, return to the camps by those who had been granted indefinite leave was allowed only with the permission of authorities. Evacuees were encouraged not to return, but could reapply for residence if they could convince a relocation officer that they could not keep outside employment. Visitors to the camps were required to give up their indefinite leave permit in order to enter. Although it was returned to them upon leaving, the procedure seemed unpleasantly akin to giving the authorities the power once again to determine the conditions of exit.

14. On the affinity of Japanese Americans for education, see William Caudill and George DeVos, "Achievement, Culture and Personality: The Case of the Japanese Americans," *American Anthropologist* 58 (1956): 1102–26; Isao Horinouchi, "Educational Values and Preadaptation in the Acculturation of Japanese Americans," Sacramento Anthropological Society, paper no. 7, 1967; Audrey J. Schwartz, "The Culturally Advantaged: A Study of Japanese-American Pupils," *Sociology and Social Research* 55 (1971): 341–353; Darrel Montero and Ronald Tsukashima, "Assimilation and Educational Achievement: The Case of the Second Generation Japanese American," *Sociological Quarterly* 18 (1977): 490–503; Bob H. Suzuki, "Education and the Socialization of Asian Americans: A Revisionist Analysis of the 'Model Minority' Thesis," *Amerasia Journal* 4 (Fall 1977): 23–51; and Ki-Taek Chun, "The Myth of Asian American Success and Its Educational Ramifications," *IRCD Bulletin* 15 (Winter/Spring 1980): 1–11, published by the Institute for Urban and Minority Education, Teachers College, Columbia University.

15. Student letters, April 16, February 9, and January 21, 1943, Bodine-HOOV.

16. Gloria Kambara, "Nisei Students Speak for Themselves," *Junior College Journal* 14 (1943–44): 251. *National Legionnaire* quoted in its entirety by Rep. Paul W. Shafer of Michigan in the *Congressional Record,* 78th Congress, 1st Session, vol. 89, pt. 9, app., p. A358.

17. Student quoted in *Newsletter* 6 (September 24, 1943), Bodine-HOOV. Student letters, May 25 and 29, 1944, Bodine-HOOV.

18. Student quoted in letter to NJASRC, December 22, 1943, from a psychologist working for American Friends Service Committee, Bodine-HOOV. Rhetorical question from letter of Nisei girl quoted in Otis D. Richardson, "Nisei Evacuees—Their Challenge to Education," *Junior College Journal* 13 (1942–43): 10. Student letter, November 28, 1942, Bodine-HOOV.

19. Student letters, March 17, and March 31, 1943, Bodine-HOOV. For an example of black opinion toward the situation of Japanese Americans, see Harry Paxton Howard, "Americans in Concentration Camps," *Crisis* 49 (1942): 283–

284, 302. For additional perspectives on the attitudes of blacks amid racist propaganda during World War II, see Delbert C. Miller, "Effect of the War Declaration on the National Morale of American College Students," *American Sociological Review* 7 (1942): 631–644; Wallace Lee, "Should Negroes Discriminate Against Japanese?" *Negro Digest* 2 (September 1944): 66, wherein a national poll of blacks found them strongly opposed to the discrimination taking place against Japanese Americans because "discrimination against the Japanese is based on color, much the same as prejudice against Negroes"; Gunnar Myrdal, *An American Dilemma* (New York: Pantheon Books, 1972, originally published in 1944), pp. 814–815, 1400; and Richard Polenberg, *One Nation Divisible: Class, Race, and Ethnicity in the United States since 1938* (New York: Viking Press, 1980), pp. 71–72.

20. Student letters, April 11–14 and March 12, 1943, Bodine-HOOV.

21. Student letter, October 24, 1943, Bodine-HOOV.

22. Report of the Field Director, September 29, 1943, NJASRC, Hoover Library. Memorandum from Thomas R. Bodine to John W. Nason, November 7, 1943, Bodine-HOOV.

23. Poem entitled "From the Dusk," two of twenty-three stanzas, student letter c. July 1942, Bodine-HOOV.

24. Report of the Field Director, September 29, 1943.

25. Ibid.

26. Notes of NJASRC field director, 1944, Bodine-HOOV. Student letter, January 1, 1943, Bodine-HOOV.

27. Student letter, April 19, 1943, Bodine-HOOV. On the induction of Nisei into the armed forces during World War II, see *Special Groups,* Special Monograph no. 10, vol. 1, Selective Service System (Washington, D.C.: U.S. Government Printing Office, 1953), pp. 113–142; induction figures on pp. 141–142. Student letter, March 14, 1943, Bodine-HOOV.

28. Notes of NJASRC field director, 1944, Bodine-HOOV. Student letters, June 19, 1944, and October 6, 1942, Bodine-HOOV. "Final Composite Report of the Returnee College Leaders, Summer of 1944," NJASRC, Hoover Library.

29. WRA, *The Evacuated People,* p.18; these figures include camp residents who were on short-term and seasonal leave—e.g., as agricultural laborers—but who were still under the control of the WRA.

30. "Final Composite Report," NJASRC, Hoover Library. Also see box 28, "Student Returnee Project" file, NJASRC-HOOV.

31. Nisei son's remark is from file "Education—Commencement Addresses and Reports by Students," Poston Project Reports, Headquarters Files, NARG210, box 18. Student letter, May 19, 1944, NJASRC-HOOV, box 36, file 676.

32. "Administrative Instructions," S-29, in *WRA Handbook,* 130.9. "Student Relocation Counselors," in ibid., 130.46.

33. "Reconditioning Procedures," in ibid., 30.3.22.B. "Essential Information Concerning Movement of Evacuees—Bulletin No. 3," 1944, BAN 67/14 L3.22.

34. Relocation cues for teachers are from individual school reports in the Poston Documentary Files, NARG210, box 18. On the Amache curriculum for relocation, see "W.R.A. Amache Secondary Schools," September 21, 1943, McGovern Papers, JARP, box 114, folder 10. Statement by Jerome administrator in E. B. Whitaker, project director, "A Message," in *Victoria* (1944), Denson High School Yearbook, Jerome, Yearbook Collection, NARG210.

35. "Psychological Blocks to Relocation" in *WRA Handbook,* 30.3.22.A. "Essential Information Concerning Movement of Evacuees—Bulletin No. 4," 1944, BAN 67/14 L3.22.

36. "Emergency Instruction" from Dillon S. Myer to all Project Directors, January 4, 1944, BAN 67/14 L4.48. Responses from camp administrations to "The Contribution of the Education Section to the Relocation Program" are summarized under the several headings listed in this paragraph. For further detail on patterns of instruction under each of the headings, see the *WRA Handbook,* 30.3.20–25; this material was added on April 4, 1944.

37. The poll was taken by the National Opinion Research Center; see Hadley Cantril and Mildred Strunk, *Public Opinion 1935–1946* (Princeton: Princeton University Press, 1951), p. 381, question 11. This attitude softened at the end of the war, according to later polls recorded in this volume; but two-thirds of respondents still thought in May 1946 that the Japanese Americans had done spying for the Japanese government during the war (see question 17 on p. 381). Philip M. Glick, WRA solicitor, "Anti-Japanese Legislation Proposed or Enacted in 1943," November 1, 1943, Washington Central Files, NARG210, 35.000, box 338. On problems with the PTA, letter from M. T. to E. D., October 11, 1944, BAN 67/14 L4.53.

38. *Amache Hi It* 4 (November 13, 1944), BAN 67/14 L4.84. Final Report, Education Section, Amache, 1945, BAN 67/14 L3.00.

39. On goal conflict between teacher and administrators, see Robert C. L. George, "The Granada (Colorado) Relocation Center Secondary School" (Master's thesis, University of Colorado, 1944), p. 61. Further examples of teacher attitudes in other camps can be found in the teachers' reflections, interviews, and reports cited in Chapters 2 and 3.

40. WRA Semi-Annual Report, Education Section, July 1–December 31, 1944, BAN 67/14C E2.60. For a glimpse of the problems faced by Japanese Americans who taught in the camps, see "Interview with Some Resident Teachers," April 1944, Topaz Community Analysis Report, 61.310, NARG210, box 6, file 2.

41. Letter from Solon T. Kimball to John H. Provinse, September 23, 1944, BAN 67/14C E2.60.

42. Students quoted in George Sugihara, "The Relocation Program of the High School," in Education in Topaz, Historical Section, Project Report H419, Topaz, BAN 67/14 H2.12. For an example of the involvement of social scientists in designing relocation strategies, see John Rademaker (community analyst at Amache), "A Syllabus for Social Studies Courses on Relocation," described in "W.R.A. Amache Secondary Schools," September 21, 1943; the syllabus is also cited in an illuminating discussion by Peter T. Suzuki, "Anthropologists in the Wartime Camps for Japanese Americans: A Documentary Study," *Dialectical Anthropology* 6 (August 1981): 26. See also "Teachers' Handbook on Education for Relocation," April 1944, BAN 67/14 E2.64 and E2.68B. The equality of women— an interesting topic in the camps because it reflected wider changes for women generally in the United States during World War II—appears as a curricular emphasis in the Americanization section for teachers in the *WRA Handbook,* 30.3.23.D.

43. John Embree, "Resistance to Freedom—An Administrative Problem," *Applied Anthropology* 2 (September 1943): 10–14. Mildred Standing, "Rich Experiences," June 29, 1945 [shown incorrectly as 1944 on the title page of the

narrative; the internal chronology makes it clear that it must be 1945], pp. 5–6, Poston Documentary Files, NARG210, box 18. On sending high school students out of the camps to attend school, see, for example, Elmer Smith, "Profiles of the Centers—Minidoka," September 1944, Central Files, NARG210, 61.317, box 21, file 20. On parental fears surrounding the quality of education for their children, see Community Analysis Newsletter no. 6, May 20, 1944, NARG210, 61.310A, box 7, file 2.

44. John W. Powell, "Some Comments on a Post-Segregation Community: Poston," January 21, 1944, pp. 5–6, BAN 67/14 J2.111.

45. John W. Powell, "The Community and the Management," April 1944, p. 2, BAN 67/14 J2.111. Also see the memo from Powell to Duncan Mills on employment policies, March 31, 1944, BAN 67/14 J2.111.

5. "The Children Don't Do It That Way"

1. Evacuee mother quoted in James W. Geater, "Observations on Discipline of Children," Poston Community Analysis Section, October 15, 1945, NARG210, 61.311, box 8, file 10. "Preliminary Notes on Effects Center Living Conditions Are Having on Family Life," Minidoka Community Analysis Section, Field Report no. 199, NARG210, 61.317, box 20, file 10.

2. On parental concerns over delinquency, see "Trends in the Relocation Centers: 1," Community Analysis Section, November 15, 1944, NARG210, 61.300, box 5. Interview with a sixteen-year-old, Topaz Community Analysis Section, April 19, 1944, NARG210, 61.310, box 6, file 3.

3. Community Analysis Newsletter no. 3, April 8, 1944, NARG210, 61.310A, box 7, file 1. Community Analysis Weekly Report, Minidoka, September 16–22, 1944, NARG210, 61.371A, box 21, file 1.

4. Korematsu v. United States, 323 U.S. 214 (1944); Ex parte Endo, 323 U.S. 283 (1944). Peter Irons traces the history of the cases in *Justice at War: The Story of the Japanese Internment Cases* (New York: Oxford University Press, 1983).

5. Community Analysis Weekly Report, Minidoka, March 12–18, 1945, NARG210, 61.317, box 21, file 3.

6. Personal Narrative and Final Report of R. R. Best, in "Final Reports of Activities," Tule Lake 1946, p. 23, BAN 67/14 R1.10. The literature on Tule Lake includes S. Frank Miyamoto, "The Career of Intergroup Tensions: A Study of the Collective Adjustments of Evacuees to Crises at the Tule Lake Relocation Center" (Ph.D. diss., University of Chicago, 1950); Dorothy Swaine Thomas and Richard S. Nishimoto, *The Spoilage* (Berkeley: University of California Press, 1946); Rosalie Hankey Wax, "The Development of Authoritarianism: A Comparison of the Japanese-American Relocation Centers and Germany" (Ph.D. diss., University of Chicago, 1951); Wax, "The Destruction of a Democratic Impulse," *Human Organization* 12 (Spring 1953): 11–21; Wax, *Doing Fieldwork: Warnings and Advice* (Chicago: University of Chicago Press, 1971); and Gary Y. Okihiro, "Tule Lake under Martial Law: A Study in Japanese Resistance," *Journal of Ethnic Studies* 5, no. 3 (1977): 71–86; see also Okihiro's earlier article, "Japanese Resistance in America's Concentration Camps: A Re-Evaluation," *Amerasia Journal* 2 (Fall 1973): 20–34. For an early criticism of Thomas and Nishimoto's emphasis on intergroup conflict among evacuees in explaining the

social history of the camp, see Marvin K. Opler's review of *The Spoilage* in the *American Anthropologist* 50 (1948): 307–310, arguing that by the time Tule Lake had become the WRA segregation center in the fall of 1943, the loyalty-disloyalty distinction "had long since lost any objectively significant meaning in the maelstrom of emotionalized reactions to consistently discriminatory treatment" (p.309).

7. Kenneth M. Harkness, "Education Program in Tule Lake Center of the War Relocation Authority," Final Report, Education Section, Tule Lake, 1945, BAN 67/14 R1.10. Personal Narrative of Mary C. Durkin, elementary school teacher, assistant principal, and principal, in "Narrative Reports," Tule Lake, 1946, BAN 67/14 R1.10. On army occupation of the unfinished high school building, see "Attitudes of Segregees," Tule Lake Community Analysis Section, October 7, 1943, 61.319, NARG210, box 24, file 3. Personal Narrative of Kenneth M. Harkness, in "Narrative Reports," Tule Lake, 1946, p. 3, BAN 67/14 R1.10.

8. "Note on Public School Enrollment at Tule Lake," Tule Lake Community Analysis Section, January 27, 1944, NARG210, 61.319, box 24, file 6; Harkness, "Education Program," school statistics summaries; on the cutting back of the high school program, see Donald O. Johnson, "The War Relocation Authority Schools at Tule Lake, California" (Master's thesis, Stanford University, 1947), pp. 69, 48; he describes the entire curriculum in detail on pp. 54–72. On the attitudes of educators generally, see personal narratives of Kenneth M. Harkness, Margaret P. Gunderson, and Mary C. Durkin, BAN 67/14 R1.10. Nisei quoted from Taka Frank Nimura, *"Daruma:* The Indomitable Spirit," unpublished autobiography of the war years, 1973, p. 95, HOOV.

9. Nisei student quoted in Thomas and Nishimoto, *The Spoilage,* p. 111; see also Nimura, *"Daruma,"* chapters entitled "School" and *"Bozu."*

10. "Nisei Report on Their Adjustment to Tule Lake," Community Analysis Notes no. 7, December 20, 1944, NARG210, 61.300, box 5; also relevant are the comments by the social scientist Marvin K. Opler in the Washington Community Analysis Conference Report, September 7–13, 1944, NARG210, 61.300, box 3, file 14; on the jitterbug dance incident, see "From a Letter by Thomas Bodine of the Japanese-American Student Relocation Council," Tule Lake Community Analysis Section, May 9, 1944, NARG210, 61.319, box 25; see also James Sakoda, "Recreation: Dances," BAN 67/14 R20.86.

11. Thomas R. Bodine, as quoted in "From a Letter by Thomas Bodine"; see also his notebooks, reports, and letters in the Thomas Bodine Papers and the materials in the National Japanese American Student Relocation Council Papers, HOOV.

12. Thomas and Nishimoto, *The Spoilage,* pp. 231–232. On the individual hearings and their relation to the legal and procedural aspects of relocation, see Edward N. Barnhart, "The Individual Exclusion of Japanese Americans in World War II," *Pacific Historical Review,* 29 (1960): 111–130; and Jacobus tenBroek, Edward N. Barnhart, and Floyd W. Matson, *Prejudice, War and the Constitution: Causes and Consequences of the Evacuation of the Japanese Americans in World War II* (Berkeley: University of California Press, 1970), pp. 171–181. For a recent interpretation of the legal battle to reinstate the citizenship of the renunciants, see John Christgau, "Collins versus the World: The Fight to Restore Citizenship to Japanese American Renunciants of World War II," *Pacific Historical Review,* 54 (1985): 1–31; Christgau notes that by 1959 the cases stood as follows: 5766

Japanese Americans at Tule Lake had renounced their U.S. citizenship, 5409 had subsequently tried to reinstate it, and 4987 had succeeded by that year. See also Donald E. Collins, *Native American Aliens: Disloyalty and Renunciation of Citizenship by Japanese Americans during World War II* (Westport, Conn.: Greenwood Press, 1985).

13. WRA, Semi-Annual Report, January 1–June 30, 1945, p. 37, BAN 67/14C E2.60; see also Johnson, "War Relocation Schools," 23; Billigmeier, "School Report," Tule Lake, Spring 1943, table 2, p. 31, BAN 67/14 R20.12; and WRA's semiannual report on education for the second half of 1944, BAN 67/14C E2.60. Thomas and Nishimoto, *The Spoilage;* for a critique of this emphasis on intergroup differences among evacuees, see Opler review (note 6 above) and Okihiro, "Tule Lake under Martial Law." Okihiro, pursuing the line of reasoning suggested by Opler, challenges what he calls the "orthodox interpretation" of Thomas and Nishimoto, arguing that positing internal cleavages within the evacuee community obscures the unity of all the evacuees in their "underlying and pervasive struggle for human rights"—p.81. The point is well taken, but Thomas and Nishimoto, as the title of their book, *The Spoilage,* makes clear, do not imply that the administration was benign or that Japanese Americans merely brought the crisis upon themselves. The categories of Thomas and Nishimoto continue to be useful because they permit a close reading of the evidence on competing strategies of cultural cohesion and future-building *within* the incarcerated population, instead of only generalizing the oppression of that population to make the equally important point of a unified ethnic struggle against coercion. On the organization and support of language schools within the barracks blocks, see "Japanese School Situation," Special Report no. 10, Tule Lake Reports Division, March 13, 1944, Tule Lake Documentary Files, NARG210, box 90.

14. "Japanese School Situation"; "School Enrollments as Guides to Local Ward Attitudes," Tule Lake Community Analysis Section, May 10, 1944, NARG210, 61.319, box 25, file 9.

15. From Special Report no. 30, Tule Lake Reports Division, June 22, 1944, Tule Lake Documentary Files, NARG210, box 90.

16. "The Organization of a Tule Lake Language School," written by a Kibei, Tule Lake Community Analysis Section, August 10, 1944, NARG210, 61.319, box 26, file 18; see also "School Enrollments as Guides to Local Ward Attitudes."

17. "The Organization of a Tule Lake Language School"; the anecdote about the Nisei girl is recounted in "Notes on the Trend Toward Japanization," Tule Lake Community Analysis Section, September 1944, NARG210, 61.319, box 25, file 11.

18. Nisei quoted in "A New Slant on Education at Tule Lake," Tule Lake Community Analysis Section, June 7, 1944, 61.319, NARG210, box 25, file 10.

19. Quote on cultural attributes from "A New Slant"; the word "Issei" is not capitalized in the original. The community analyst, Marvin K. Opler, left some moving descriptions of the cultural life at Tule Lake; see, for example, "A 'Sumo' Tournament at Tule Lake Center," *American Anthropologist* 48 (1945): 134–139; and, with Frank Obayashi, "Senryu Poetry as Folk and Community Expression," *Journal of American Folklore* 58 (1945): 1–11. The phrase "mental battlefield" is from Nimura, *"Daruma,"* p. 91.

20. On the induction of Nisei into the armed forces, see *Special Groups,* Special Monograph no. 10, vol. 1, Selective Service System (Washington, D.C.:

Government Printing Office, 1953), pp. 113–142, Nisei induction figure on pp. 141–142. Thomas and Nishimoto, *The Spoilage,* pp. 106, 185; see also Rachel Sady, "Summary of the Social and Administrative History of Tule Lake," September 12, 1945, NARG210, 61.300, box 3, file 18; and Johnson, "War Relocation Schools," p. 18.

21. Nisei quoted in Sady, "Summary," p. 24.

22. N. E. Viles, "Federal-State Cooperation in the WRA School Program," *American School Board Journal* 111 (October 1945): 39, 40.

23. Viles, "Federal-State Cooperation," pp. 40, 38.

24. "Summary Report of the Educational Program of the Granada Project, Amache, Colorado," Washington Office Records—Documentary (Granada), NARG210, box 40; also in BAN 67/14 L3.00; the comment from the Amache school superintendent, Lloyd A. Garrison, comes from his foreword to the report. See WRA semiannual reports for 1944 on teacher shortages and community analysis reports and trend analyses on school isolation. Report on training opportunities from Amache, "Summary Report." "Amache Elementary School Teacher's Handbook," Washington Office Records—Documentary (Granada), NARG210, box 40.

25. WRA Semi-Annual Report, January 1–June 30, 1945, BAN 67/14C E2.60. Final Report, Education Section, Manzanar Relocation Center, p. 75, Manzanar Documentary Files, NARG210, box 69. On the teaching of race relations, "Suggestions for Teaching Supplementary Reading Materials," July 29, 1944, WRA Education Section, BAN 67/14 E2.64.

26. WRA, Community Management Division, Education Section, *Washington Office Final Report Summary,* app., p.24, BAN 67/14 E2.671; see pp. 19–23 for a camp-by-camp summary of test patterns. "A Summary Report of Curricular Offerings of the Manzanar Schools," 1945, Washington Office Records–Documentary (Manzanar), NARG210, box 66. "Summary Report," Amache, pp. 20, 34 and passim.

27. "Summary Report," Amache, pp. 20, 34 and passim. *Washington Office Final Report Summary,* p. 24. See also the final reports from each of the ten camps; and WRA, *Education Program in War Relocation Centers* (Washington, D.C.: Government Printing Office, 1945).

28. "A Report on the Standardized Testing Program of the Poston I Elementary School over the Three-Year Period 1942–45," pp. 39, 46, Project Reports, Headquarters Files, NARG210, box 18.

29. Field notes of Thomas R. Bodine, Bodine Papers, HOOV. Trend Report, Gila Community Analysis Section, February 1, 1945, NARG210, 61.312A, box 12, file 1. The Poston study is reported in Edith W. Derrick, "Effects of Evacuation on Japanese-American Youth," *School Review* 55 (1947): 356–362; quotation from p. 362.

30. Commencement address from Washington Office Records—Documentary (Granada), NARG210, box 40.

31. "Special Report from Rohwer," October 1, 1945, Community Analysis Section, NARG210, 61.316, box 18, file 5.

32. Interview of Yoshisada Kawai at age eighty-one in 1970, in *Issei Christians: Selected Interviews from the Issei Oral History Project* (Sacramento: Issei Oral History Project, 1977), p. 19.

33. WRA, *WRA: A Story of Human Conservation*; War Agency Liquidation

Unit, U.S. Department of the Interior, *People in Motion: The Postwar Adjustment of the Evacuated Japanese Americans* (Washington, D.C.: Government Printing Office, 1947). On use of school closure to pressure parents to leave, see, for example, Final Report, Education Section, Manzanar, p. 92, NARG210.

34. Weekly Trend Report, Amache Community Analysis Section, January 23, 1945, NARG210, 61.313A, box 14, file 1. Executive Committee Minutes, National Japanese American Student Relocation Council, February 27, 1945, HOOV. On the changing posture of Warren toward the Japanese Americans, see G. E. White, "Unacknowledged Lesson: Earl Warren and the Japanese Relocation Controversy," *Virginia Quarterly Review* 55 (Autumn 1979): 613–629.

35. Katharine Luomala, "California Takes Back Its Japanese Evacuees," *Applied Anthropology* 5 (Summer 1946): 27–32. See also WRA, "California Incidents of Terrorism Involving Persons of Japanese Ancestry," 1945, Documents Division, XD81.2908, Main Library, University of California, Berkeley.

36. Estelle Ishigo, "Estelle's Epilogue," *Pacific Citizen* 76 (February 16, 1973): 1; and *Lone Heart Mountain* (Los Angeles: Anderson, Ritchie & Simon, 1972). For a comparison of prewar and postwar status of Japanese Americans, see Leonard Bloom and Ruth Reimer, *Removal and Return: The Socio-Economic Effects of the War on Japanese Americans* (Berkeley: University of California Press, 1949).

37. Jack Goodman, ed., *While You Were Gone: A Report on Wartime Life in the United States* (New York: Simon and Schuster, 1946), p. 99 and passim; Henry S. Shryock, Jr., and Hope T. Eldridge, "Internal Migration in Peace and War," *American Sociological Review* 12 (1947): 27–39; War Agency Liquidation Unit, *People in Motion;* on postwar housing situation, see Harry H. L. Kitano, "Housing of Japanese Americans in the San Francisco Bay Area," in Nathan Glazer and Davis McEntire, eds., *Studies in Housing and Minority Groups* (Berkeley: University of California Press, 1960), pp. 178-197. Kitano notes that by 1950 the adult population of Japanese Americans in California had a substantially higher proportion of high school graduates than the adult population of the state as a whole.

Epilogue

1. Pitirim A. Sorokin, *Man and Society in Calamity* (New York: Dutton, 1942), p. 10.

2. For an example of the model minority literature, see William Petersen, *Japanese Americans: Oppression and Success* (New York: Random House, 1971); for the revisionist perspective see Bob H. Suzuki, "The Japanese-American Experience," in Milton J. Gold, Carl A. Grant, and Harry N. Rivlin, eds., *In Praise of Diversity* (Washington, D.C.: Association of Teacher Educators, 1977), pp. 139–162; see also Suzuki, "Education and the Socialization of Asian Americans: A Revisionist Analysis of the 'Model Minority' Thesis," *Amerasia Journal* 4 (Fall 1977): 23–51. For an example of denial, see Lillian Baker, *The Concentration Camp Conspiracy* (Lawndale, Calif.: AFHA Publications [Americans for Historical Accuracy], 1981). For an insistence of the label "concentration camp," see Raymond Y. Okamura, "The American Concentration Camps: A Cover-Up through Euphemistic Terminology," *Journal of Ethnic Studies* 10 (Fall 1982): 95–109. Richard Polenberg's contrast appears in his *War and Society: The United*

States, 1941–1945 (Philadelphia: Lippincott, 1972), p. 72. Allan R. Bosworth, *America's Concentration Camps* (New York: Norton, 1967); Carlos B. Embry, *America's Concentration Camps* (New York: David McKay, 1956).

3. Robert W. O'Brien, "Evacuation of Japanese from the Pacific Coast: Canadian and American Contrasts," *Research Studies, State College of Washington* 14 (1946): 113–120; Forrest E. LaViolette, *The Canadian Japanese and World War II* (Toronto: University of Toronto Press, 1948); Ken Adachi, *The Enemy That Never Was: A History of Japanese Canadians* (Toronto: University of Toronto Press, 1976); Barry Broadfoot, *Years of Sorrow, Years of Shame: The Story of Japanese Canadians in World War II* (New York: Doubleday, 1977); Ken Adachi, "A History of the Japanese Canadians in British Columbia, 1877–1958," in Roger Daniels, ed., *Two Monographs on Japanese Canadians* (New York: Arno Press, 1978); and Ann Gomer Sunahara, *The Politics of Racism: The Uprooting of Japanese Canadians during the Second World War* (Toronto: James Lorimer, 1981). I am grateful to Patricia E. Roy, Professor of History at the University of Victoria, for an insightful summary of the educational experience of Japanese Canadians during the war. See also Roger Daniels, "The Japanese Experience in North America: An Essay in Comparative Racism," *Canadian Ethnic Studies* 9 (1977): 91–100; and *Concentration Camps, North America: Japanese in the United States and Canada during World War II* (Malabar, Fla.: Kreiger Press, 1981).

4. Carlton Jackson, *Who Will Take Our Children?* (London: Methuen, 1985), number of children evacuated by 1940 on p. 36; see also Susan Isaacs, ed., *The Cambridge Evacuation Survey: A Wartime Study on Social Welfare and Education* (London: Methuen, 1941); Richard Padley and Margaret Cole, *Evacuation Survey: A Report to the Fabian Society* (London: Routledge & Sons, 1940); and St. Loe Strachey, *Borrowed Children: Evacuation Problems and Their Remedies* (New York: Commonwealth Fund, 1940).

Index

Adams, Ansel, 79
Adams, Lucy W., 37, 38, 40, 85
Alien land laws, 17, 134
All Aboard, 103
Amache (Granada Relocation Center), 43, 52, 55, 63, 65, 72, 77, 100, 115, 120, 132, 134–135, 157, 158
Amache Senior High School, 77, 135
Amerasia Journal, 107
American Anthropologist, 93
American Civil Liberties Union, 3
American Friends Service Committee, 23, 116, 119
Americanization, 19, 20, 71, 80, 87, 134, 137, 147, 160, 170
American Legion, 96, 122
American School Board Journal, 156
America's Concentration Camps, 166
Amerman, Helen, 49
Applied Anthropology, 94
Arizona, 22, 33, 36, 37, 43, 51, 63, 68, 156
Arkansas, 43, 50, 51, 59, 73, 132
Armistice Day, 135
Army Corps of Engineers, 34
Assembly centers, 7, 22–33, 37, 59, 81, 96, 103, 116, 160, 167. *See also individual assembly centers*

Backus, Edythe, 31
Barbul, Mary, 63
Beatty, Willard, 37
Berkeley, California, 28, 49
Berkeley Baptist Divinity School, 49
Blacks, 62, 77, 97, 123, 124, 198n19
Blaisdell, Allen C., 72–73
Boatwright, Jewell, 50
Bodine, Thomas R., 147. *See also* National Japanese American Student Relocation Council
Boise Junior High School, 50
Buddhists, 11, 12, 59, 154
Burlingham, Dorothy, 5
Butte High School, 159

California, 12, 14, 18, 22, 23, 25, 30, 33, 38, 40, 43, 51, 63, 68, 84, 86, 123, 138, 139, 158, 163; legislature of, 15, 17, 21
California Joint Immigration Commission, 14
California Preservation Committee, 163

Carey, Miles, 50
Carr, Ralph, 35
Catholics, 124
Census (U.S.), 11, 18
Central Japanese Association of America, 22
Chandler, Albert B., 96
Chicago, 123, 124
Chinese, 11, 15
Christian Century, 114
Christian organizations, 11, 12, 59, 114–117, 163
Citizenship, 3, 14–17, 19, 22, 25, 63, 75, 77, 81–82, 97, 101, 110–111, 118, 121, 122, 124, 130, 143, 148, 156, 167, 168; renunciation of, 111, 147, 148
Civilian Conservation Corps (CCC), 34, 49, 50, 97
Colorado, 35, 43, 51, 135
Committee on American Principles and Fair Play, 163
Committee on Un-American Activities (U.S. House of Representatives), 98
Community analysts. *See* Social scientists
Community Facilities Act of 1940, 29
Community School Forum, 40, 87
"Community schools," 37–42, 56, 64–67, 72–73, 92
Congress, 10, 22–23, 34, 38, 46, 86, 97, 98, 110–111, 148, 154
Connecticut, 49
Conscientious objectors, 49, 83
Constitution, 15, 17, 23, 101
Cultural revival, 106–110, 138–139, 143, 161; and private schools, 145–154, 160–161

Daihyo Sha Kai, 144
Democracy: teaching of, 1, 4, 5, 8, 20–21, 22, 38–41, 52, 63–67, 71, 78–79, 80, 84, 103, 113–114, 135, 138, 152, 170–171; and higher education, 115, 122–123
Democracy and Japanese Americans, 79
Denationalization, 22–23, 122, 149, 151, 154. *See also* Citizenship, renunciation of
Department of Agriculture, 34, 35, 49, 94

Department of Justice, 68, 70, 111, 148
Department of the Interior, 34
Department of War, 23, 33, 34, 117, 143
Desert Exile, 73
de Silva, Gertrude, 101
Detroit, 29, 77, 98
Dewey, John, 56, 63
Dies, Martin, 98
Digger Indians, 127
Dillingham Commission, 10
Draft registration, 71, 81–85, 94, 99, 103, 127

East Texas State Teachers College, 50
Education for Victory, 39
Egami, Hatsuye, 25
Eight-Year Study, 40
Eisenhower, Milton S., 34, 35, 36
Embree, John F., 93–95, 111, 137
Employment Service (U.S.), 49
English language, acquisition of, 10, 12, 13, 19, 21, 27, 30, 37, 62, 72, 84, 87, 89, 91, 95, 105, 106, 118, 124, 127, 134, 146, 158
Evacuation: of Japanese Americans, 3, 23–25, 68, 76, 85, 86, 115, 116, 121, 133, 154, 160, 163, 170; of Japanese Canadians, 167; of English children, 5, 7, 167
Evacuee Speaks, The, 25
Executive Order 9066, 3, 33
Executive Order 9102, 3, 33
Ex parte Endo, 141
Expatriation, 85, 98, 110, 142, 143. *See also* Denationalization

Farm Security Administration (FSA), 29, 41, 97
Federal Bureau of Investigation (FBI), 22, 32, 117
Ficke, Albert, 49
Fleischman, Charles, 50
Ford, Leland M., 23
Fourteenth Amendment, 15
Fresno Assembly Center, 28
Freud, Anna, 5
Fryer, E. R., 36
Fujuii, Grace, 29

Gates Primary Reading Test, 159
Gentlemen's Agreement of 1908, 10, 12
German Americans, 77
German blitzkrieg, 5, 165
Gettysburg Address, 28
Gila (River) Relocation Center, 36, 43, 157, 159
Goffman, Erving, 92
Great Depression, 18, 97, 98, 167
Guadalcanal, 119

Haiku, 106
Hanna, Paul R., 38, 49, 50, 145
Hawaii, 12, 45, 85
Hayashi, Constance, 107
Hays, Martha, 52–53
Hearst papers, 71, 96
Heart Mountain Relocation Center, 43, 47, 59, 60, 62, 70–71, 74, 103, 127
High School Victory Corps, 41
Hirabayashi v. *United States,* 86
Hiroshima, 165
Holocaust, 165, 166; Nuremberg laws, 23
Hosokawa, William, 20
House Un-American Activities Committee. *See* Committee on Un-American Activities
Hunt, Ecco, 49
Hunt, Idaho, 1, 3
Hunt High School, 1

Ichihashi, Yamato, 21
Idaho, 1, 40, 43, 50, 51
Immigration Act of 1924, 17
Indians (Native Americans), 77, 94, 114, 163, 166. *See also* Navajos; Office of Indian Affairs
Indian Service. *See* Office of Indian Affairs
Internment camps (for "enemy aliens"), 68, 70, 95
Inu, 145
Inui, Kiyo S., 13
Ishigo, Estelle, 163
Italian Americans, 124

JACL. *See* Japanese American Citizens League
Japan, 10, 11, 12, 15, 18, 19, 20, 86, 87, 100, 101, 138, 142, 143, 144, 148, 149, 151, 152, 153, 154, 155; as imaginative construct, 154–155
Japan Society of America, 13
Japanese American Citizens League (JACL), 20, 22, 68, 81
Japanese Americans: educational values, 10–13, 25–32, 45–46, 60, 72, 76–77, 104, 119, 161; illiteracy, 11; level of education, 21, 114, 164, 204n37; median age of children, 8, 18, 112; number incarcerated, 3, 25, 128, 131; number in college, 114, 121, 154; number of schoolchildren, 3, 13, 114; soldiers, 81, 85, 110, 122, 127, 131, 135, 154; total number of, 18; total number of children, 12, 13, 18, 20, 25. *See also* Cultural Revival; Resettlement, statistics; Students; Teachers, Nisei
Japanese Canadians, 167–168
Japanese Educational Association, 12
Japanese Emperor, 17, 82
Japanese Evacuation and Resettlement Study, 147
Japanese Hawaiians, 85
Japanese Language School Board, 148–149, 151
Japanese language schools, 12, 17, 20, 21, 32, 37, 86, 95, 106, 110, 149, 160–161; at Tule Lake, 143, 148–154, 160
Jerome Relocation Center, 43, 50, 59, 132
Jews, 10, 23, 79, 124
Journal of American Folklore, 106
Judo, 108
Justice Department. *See* Department of Justice
Juvenile delinquency, 65, 91, 103, 142

Kabuki, 107
Kansas, 123
Kanzaki, Kiichi, 13
Katayama, Hiro, 103
Kentucky, 96
Kibei, 20, 86–87, 106, 146, 147, 151, 152, 153
Kikuchi, Charles, 25, 32
Kobu, 108
Kokumin Gakko, 152

Koreans, 15
Korematsu v. *United States,* 141

LaViolette, Forrest, 11, 74
League of Nations, 10
Leave clearance policies. *See* Loyalty
tests
Light, Jerome T., 50, 53, 187n18
Light, Thomas, 53
Lincoln, Abraham, 28, 47; Emancipa-
tion Proclamation, 77
Literacy, 10–11
Los Angeles (city and county), 18, 27,
30, 49, 65, 71, 77, 163–164
Loyalty tests, 80–86, 94, 99, 101, 103,
117–118, 125, 141, 143, 168, 191n4.
See also "Selective dispersion"

Manzanar Relocation Center, 22, 30,
32, 33, 43, 47, 61, 63, 69, 71, 77, 79,
85, 87, 93, 96, 99, 101, 105, 157, 158
McClatchey, V. S., 14, 17
McCloy, John J., 116
Meiji Japan, 10
Memoirs 1944 (yearbook), 1
Merrill-Palmer School, 29
Michigan State University, 49
Mikado. *See* Japanese Emperor
Mills College, 29, 30
Minidoka Relocation Center, 3, 38, 40,
43, 44, 49, 50, 59, 60, 61, 69, 71, 72,
86, 140, 141, 142, 161
Minorities. *See specific minority groups*
Mississippi, 23
Missouri, 120
Mossman, Robert A., 92
Murdock, Orrice Abram, Jr., 23
Myer, Dillon S., 34, 35, 113, 133–134

Nagasaki, 165
Nation, 79
National Archives, 34, 67, 164
National Education Association, 13,
47
National Japanese American Student
Relocation Council (NJASRC), 116–
119, 126–127, 129, 130, 135, 147,
159
National Legionnaire, 122
National Youth Administration, 41, 49,
97

Native Sons of the Golden West, 14,
163
Navajos, 36–37
Negroes. *See* Blacks
New Deal, 33, 36, 49, 51, 52, 93, 94,
97–98, 113, 163, 167
New York City, 29
Nishimoto, Richard, 148, 154, 200n6,
202n13
North Central Accrediting Association,
146
Northern State Teachers College, 50
Nursery schools, 29–30, 32, 152

Office of Education, 39, 164
Office of Indian Affairs, 34, 36–37, 49,
94
Office of War Information, 35
Ohio, 120
Oklahoma, 123
Okubo, Mine, 31
Oregon, 22
Owens Valley, California, 30

Parent-Teacher Association (PTA), 72,
134
Pearl Harbor, 8, 22, 50, 62, 68, 69, 85,
119, 165
Philadelphia, 116
Pickett, Clarence E., 116
"Picture brides," 12
Planned communities, 35–42, 57, 70,
71, 79, 81, 92–93, 131, 136, 166, 170;
and Tule Lake, 144
Plemmons, Alma, 49
Plessy v. *Ferguson,* 15
Polenberg, Richard, 166
Pomeroy, R. A., 50
Portland Assembly Center, 27
Poston (Colorado River Relocation Cen-
ter), 33, 36, 38, 43, 44, 47, 50, 52, 53,
57, 62, 63, 64, 79, 89, 93, 96, 101,
112, 113, 137, 138, 139, 159
Powell, John W., 139
"Problems of Democracy" course, 63
Progressive Achievement Test, 158
Progressive education, 36–41, 55–56,
63–64, 65, 67, 71, 74, 108, 145,
166
Progressive Education Association, 37,
40

Quakers. *See* American Friends Service Committee

Rankin, John E., 23
Red Cross, 79
Repatriation, 85, 142, 143, 155
Resegregation, 148. *See also* Citizenship, renunciation of
Resettlement, 7, 35, 36, 38, 71, 81, 82, 89, 98, 99, 103, 104, 111–114, 125, 131–139, 142, 144, 155–156, 157, 160–164; and conditions for "release," 92–93, 117–119, 142–143, 160–161; statistics, 99, 113, 128, 164n37
Resistance, 68–69, 83–85, 93, 99, 103, 104, 121, 125, 127, 130, 131, 137–139, 141–155, 160–161, 168–169, 200n6, 202n13. *See also* Citizenship, renunciation of; Cultural revival; Juvenile delinquency
"Resistance to freedom," 137–139
Rising Tide of Color against White World-Supremacy, 17
Rohwer Relocation Center, 43, 50
Roosevelt, Franklin D., 3, 18, 81; administration of, 33, 97–98
Roosevelt, Theodore, 15
Rostow, Eugene, 4

Sacramento, California, 17
Salt Lake City, 121
San Diego, 53
San Francisco Bay area, 15, 28, 36, 37
Santa Anita Assembly Center, 25, 27, 29, 30, 53
Secretary of War, 81
Segregation: in armed forces, 81; of Chinese students, 15; of "disloyals," 82, 99, 100, 101, 110, 142–155, 166, 171; of Mexican Americans, 49; of schools, 15, 17, 21, 61, 145, 159
"Selective dispersion," 112, 117–121, 129–130, 136, 138–139; and Tule Lake, 142, 154–155, 166, 171, 197n13. *See also* Loyalty tests; Resettlement
Senate Military Affairs Subcommittee, 96
Senryu, 106
Sheckler, Katharine, 53

Shibai, 107
Sifton, Iona, 49
Sistermans, Jessie, 49
Slavery, 3, 77, 117
Smith College, 119
Social Forces, 112
Social scientists, 73, 76, 85, 92–96, 98, 101, 112, 113, 114, 130, 131, 132, 137, 140, 142, 151, 153, 159, 161, 166
Soil Conservation Service, 49
Sorokin, Pitirim, 165
South Dakota, 50
Spoilage, The, 148, 200n6, 202n13
Sproul, Robert Gordon, 115
Standing, Mildred, 137
Stanford Achievement Tests, 14, 158
Stanford University, 21, 38, 49, 50, 115, 145
Statue of Liberty, 79, 100, 121
Stephens, William D., 14, 17
Stewart, Tom, 22
Stimson, Henry L., 81
Stoddard, Lothrop, 17
Student files, 89, 91, 148, 157, 164
Student relocation, 116–130
Students, 1, 3, 4, 31, 43, 44, 61–64, 73–77, 101–103, 108, 110, 114, 115, 119–131, 140–142, 146, 147, 148, 152–153, 159, 160, 164, 188n32; commencement addresses, 75–77, 160; compositions, 4, 31, 43, 44, 61, 62, 63, 64, 74, 137, 140–141, 146–148, 152–153, 164, 188n32; letters, 31, 115, 119–131, 196n6; number of, 3, 13, 61, 114, 146, 147, 148, 159; poems, 108–110, 126; published comments, 61, 114, 122; student-teacher ratios, 43. *See also* Japanese Americans; Kikuchi, Charles; Test results
Sugihara, George, 74
Sumo, 108, 146
Supreme Court, 15, 80, 86, 141

Tanaka, Ruth, 108
Tanforan Assembly Center, 25, 27, 28, 29, 30, 31, 32, 59
Tanforan Totalizer, 29
Tani, George, 72
Tani, Henry, 28, 59
Tanka, 106

Teachers: Caucasian, 30–31, 43, 44–45, 49–50, 52–57, 62–64, 83–84, 100–101, 104–105, 126–127, 132–138, 146, 157; language school, 22, 106, 110, 149, 152; Nisei, 19, 21, 27–32, 43, 46, 55, 57–61, 62, 70–71, 84, 105, 136, 160; number of, in camps, 43; recruitment of, 37, 47–52, 156
Tennessee, 22
Terman, Lewis M., 13
Test results (intelligence and academic achievement), 13–14, 74, 158–159
Texas, 50, 77, 98
Thomas, Dorothy Swaine, 148, 154, 200n6, 202n13
Thomas, Norman, 79
Tokyo, 98
Tolan Committee, 85
Topaz (Central Utah Relocation Center), 29, 31, 43, 45, 46, 47, 51, 59, 61, 67, 72, 74, 75, 76, 97, 103, 107, 111, 117, 124, 127, 141, 157
Total institutions, 92
Tri-State High School, 63, 146, 152
Tulare Assembly Center, 25
Tule Lake Relocation Center, 4, 38, 43, 44, 46, 55, 59, 63, 83–84, 87, 91
Tule Lake Segregation Center, 99–101, 103, 105, 110, 111, 131, 142–155, 160, 168

Uchida, Keiko, 29
Uchida, Yoshiko, 28–29, 73
University of California at Berkeley, 28, 115, 163
University of Idaho, 49, 59
University of Texas, 49
University of Wyoming, 59
U.S. Army, 3, 69, 81, 83, 85, 96, 110, 122, 135, 144, 145, 146, 154. See also Western Defense Command
USS Panay, 19
Utah, 23, 29, 43, 45, 51, 124
Utai, 146

Viles, N. E., 156
Vocational education, 37, 41, 72–73, 134, 157. See also National Youth Administration

Wagoner, Lovisa, 29
Wakasa, James Hatsuaki, 97
Walden School, 29
War and Children, 5
War Relocation Authority (WRA), 3, 4, 32–44, 49, 51, 59, 67, 69, 70, 71, 72, 82, 83, 87, 91, 93–106, and passim
Warren, Earl, 86, 163
Wartime Civil Control Administration (WCCA), 33, 36
Washington, D.C., 15, 34, 36, 37, 158
Washington State, 22
Waterman, Edith, 30–31, 47, 49, 53
WCCA. See Wartime Civil Control Administration
Webb, Ulysses S., 22
Wellesley College, 120
West Virginia State Board of Education v. Barnette, 80
Western Defense Command, 22, 23, 33, 36, 86, 99, 117, 121, 141
Wilbur, Ray Lyman, 115
Wiley High School, 135
Wilson, Woodrow, 21
Women's rights, 137, 153, 199n42
Working for Democracy, 63
Works Projects Administration, 29, 49
WRA. See War Relocation Authority
Wyoming, 43, 51, 127

Yamanaka, Keiho, 107
Yamauchi, Wakako, 107
Yearbooks, 1, 3, 4, 73
Young Men's Christian Association (YMCA), 59, 123

Zoot-suit riots, 77

874009

370
JAM   James, Thomas,
           1948-

        Exile within

         10-87

$25.00

DATE			